DEC   2002

CRITICAL LIVES

D0406276

The Life and Work of

Muhammad

Yahiya Emerick

ALPHA

A Pearson Education Company

921
MUHAMMAD

International Standard Book Number: 0-02-864371-2
Library of Congress Catalog Card Number: 2002102220

04 03 02   8 7 6 5 4 3 2 1

Interpretation of the printing code: The rightmost number of the first series of numbers is the year of the book's printing; the rightmost number of the second series of numbers is the number of the book's printing. For example, a printing code of 02-1 shows that the first printing occurred in 2002.

Printed in the United States of America

Publisher:
Marie Butler-Knight
Product Manager:
Phil Kitchel
Managing Editor:
Jennifer Chisholm
Acquisitions Editor:
Randy Ladenheim-Gil
Development Editor:
Phil Kitchel
Production Editor:
Billy Fields

Copy Editor:
Heather Stith
Cover Editor:
Ann Jones
Book Designer:
Sandra Schroeder
Production:
John Etchison
Rebecca Harmon
Stacey Richwine-DeRome

Chapter 2

The Child of Tragedy

Didn't He find you an orphan and care for you? Didn't He find you lost and show you the way? Didn't He find you poor and provide for you? Therefore, be kind to the orphan, gentle to the poor, and declare the mercy and blessings of your Lord.

—*Qur'an 93:6–11*

Within a few years of the death of Qusayy, Mecca had become a major, cosmopolitan trading post on the caravan route that ran along the length of the Hijaz. Prior to its formal establishment, merchants would stop there to fill their depleted water supplies; but now with the building of permanent structures, people from the countryside began to settle in and around the embryonic city. Qusayy was Mecca's first king, and he would also be its last. The difficulty of marshalling support and effectively controlling a highly mobile population in a desert region meant that Qusayy could not maintain a power base. In addition, he had far too many sons who might have contended for power, potentially sapping the resources of the city beyond what it could bear. Qusayy wisely opted to divide his powers among his sons, and they, in turn, began the tradition of ruling Mecca through a relatively egalitarian council of tribal elders.

'Abd Manaf, one of Qusayy's sons, was given the official titles of water-giver to the pilgrims and tithe-taker from the Quraysh, titles that were to be passed down through his family line. 'Abd Manaf's son, Hashim, carried on this office faithfully after his father's death. Hashim was wealthy and esteemed among his peers. Once, while on his way to Syria for business, Hashim stopped in the northern Arabian city of Yathrib and fell in love with a woman named Salma bint 'Amr. He married her, and they lived in Mecca for several years. They were eventually blessed with a son, whom they named Shaybah. Hashim died tragically on a trade expedition to Gaza, so Salma and her son returned to her hometown of Yathrib. Shaybah, now considered an orphan by Arab society, had few prospects for a successful life in Arabia, for customs of inheritance often favored brothers or uncles if the deceased's heirs were minors. Indeed, his life appeared headed nowhere until a generous benefactor appeared.

Hashim's brother, al-Muttalib, took over the two ceremonial jobs his brother had held. The benefits of being in charge of the water enabled him to live prosperously. His large extended family worked together to ensure that pilgrims and visitors enjoyed the now-famous Meccan hospitality. The family was also able to take a tithe from the other members of the very large Quraysh tribe to cover any expenses. After several years passed, al-Muttalib began to wax nostalgic and decided to honor his deceased brother by bringing his nephew, Shaybah, back to Mecca so that he could have a decent chance to succeed in life—with al-Muttalib's support, of course. Al-Muttalib went to Yathrib, and Salma agreed that moving to Mecca would be the best option for her son. When al-Muttalib and Shaybah entered the city a few weeks later, the boy happened to be riding ahead of his uncle on a separate camel. People who saw them come into town thought the unknown child was some new slave al-Muttalib had bought, so they called him *'Abdel Muttalib,* the slave of al-Muttalib. Even though al-Muttalib emphasized to his friends that his traveling companion was his brother's son, people kept using the nickname 'Abdel Muttalib, and the name Shaybah was soon forgotten.

Al-Muttalib was very generous and supportive to 'Abdel Muttalib. He secured his rights of inheritance and established him in Mecca with honor. As the years passed, 'Abdel Muttalib grew wealthy from trade and was even able to marry. After his uncle passed away, 'Abdel Muttalib inherited the two offices of water-giver and tithe-taker.

Fulfilling his duties as water-giver turned out to be a terrible hardship. At the time of his assumption of duty, 'Abdel Muttalib had only one son. Given that the Well of Zamzam had never been rediscovered since it had been buried so many generations before by Mudad when he angrily left Mecca, bringing water from the wells outside the city and filling the numerous vats and cisterns that dotted the city center was an arduous task. Father and son had to work long hours. With the birth of a second child coming soon, 'Abdel Muttalib quickly began to realize that he had to find the Well of Zamzam or his descendants would be doomed to be weary water carriers forever. That night he had a strange dream telling him to dig for something sweet and clear. The next two nights also brought cryptic visions. He began probing all over the city center, making small exploratory digs in and around the courtyard of the Ka'bah, much to the amusement of his neighbors. That the well existed was not in dispute, but few ever thought it, along with the purported treasures of al-Mudad ibn 'Amr, would ever be found.

'Abdel Muttalib had a fourth dream, in which he was told that the lost Well of Zamzam was located between two prominent idols that stood near the Ka'bah. In the morning, he roused his son and went to the spot he saw in his vision. After a few hours of digging, he was overjoyed to see a capstone. When it was removed, water bubbled up through the earth. The Well of Zamzam was recovered! Now water collection would be quite easy for 'Abdel Muttalib's family. What was equally as exciting was that in the bottom of the hole lay two small gazelle statues of made of gold. Some old swords, the weapons of Mudad, were also found. The townspeople rushed to the well when they heard the news, and many of the prominent figures of the Quraysh tribe wanted a share in the treasures. 'Abdel Muttalib, who had only one son to protect him, was forced by his insistent peers to draw lots with them to see who would get the artifacts, though he amazingly won every single draw. He placed the gazelles inside the Ka'bah and ordered the swords to be melted down and incorporated into the existing doors of the shrine, which were in need of repair.

The incident impressed upon 'Abdel Muttalib the true weakness of his position in Meccan society. Besides being considered something of an outsider or foreigner because of where he grew up, he had only one son while his peers in the Quraysh tribe had large families and many strong sons. He made a vow to God as he stood near the Ka'bah that if he were blessed with ten sons who grew to full maturity, he would sacrifice one of them in thanksgiving. In the superstitious climate of seventh-century Arabia, such grave pronouncements about life or death were common.

Why did 'Abdel Muttalib make his promise in the name of God, or Allah? In idolatrous Arabia, belief in Allah was no contradiction. The existence of one supreme God was generally accepted, and Jews and Christians in some locations reinforced this notion among the Arabs, whose own cultural ideology was that they were descended from Ishmael, the son of Abraham. Taking a cue from the God of the Jews, seen as a somewhat remote and stern God, the Arabs went one step further in believing that God made the earth and the heavens and then just forgot about them. In other words, God was too distant, too unapproachable, and little concerned with the daily affairs of men and women. Arabs therefore sought the guidance of idols and demigods in matters of daily life. Safety while traveling, good luck in business, victory over one's enemies, cursing a rival, blessing a house with harmony and fortune—all of these were the province of idols. Every family, clan, and tribe had its own special idols, and many individuals carried small, handheld wooden or stone idols. The name of God was referenced only in truly important, life-or-death issues. Allah was the God of the Ka'bah, but the idols were the lifeblood of Arabian society.

Over the next decade, 'Abdel Muttalib was blessed with ten strong and capable sons. (He had several wives.) When the words of his vow came back to him, in sadness he called his sons together and told them of his dilemma. He asked for their cooperation, and they agreed, realizing that an oath was bound to one's honor and reputation, especially if it were taken in the name of Allah. Each son wrote his name on an arrowhead, which was what the Arabs used for choosing things randomly. Beyond just picking an arrow out of a quiver, however, this process of divination required the participants to stand near a powerful idol. Standing near an idol symbolized the guidance of that deity in influencing which arrow would be selected. 'Abdel Muttalib and his sons decided to gather near the idol of Hubal, located inside one corner of the Ka'bah. Whoever's name was on the arrow drawn would be sacrificed. 'Abdel Muttalib's youngest and favorite son, 'Abdullah, had the unlucky arrow.

'Abdel Muttalib, though filled with sorrow, took 'Abdullah by the hand and dragged him to a spot between two idols, just outside the Ka'bah doors. The crowd that had gathered outside the Ka'bah began to implore the clan chief to spare his son and find some other way to placate Hubal. The clan of Makhzum, in particular, was incensed: 'Abdullah's mother, Fatimah, was one of their own, and they couldn't stand the thought of one of their women's sons being killed. At first 'Abdel Muttalib was unmoved, believing that his religious duty was to fulfill his oath. But so many in the crowd liked 'Abdullah as a person and insisted so strongly that another way be found, 'Abdel Muttalib finally relented and asked what should be done instead. A man suggested that 'Abdullah could be ransomed with money, and all of his family and friends could chip in the money to save him. Because the services of a shaman or soothsayer were needed in this matter, it was suggested that the family consult a famous shamaness known as Shiya, who lived in Yathrib. Relieved, 'Abdel Muttalib let go of his son's hand and allowed him to go home.

'Abdel Muttalib and several of his sons traveled to Yathrib and inquired about Shiya. They learned that she had left for a place named Khybar, about a hundred miles north. When they finally reached her, they found her to be a very old woman, but her frailty belied the fact that she was considered to be knowledgeable in the ways of the gods. People often consulted her on questions of magic, luck, the evil eye, and the jinn, those spirit creatures said to roam the desert at night in search of hapless souls. Shiya refused to see the delegation when they arrived at her dwelling and asked them to return the next day. When the time came to meet her, they explained their dilemma: Was there any way to get out of sacrificing 'Abdullah and still fulfill the requirements of 'Abdel Muttalib's oath?

Shiya promised to consult her spirit guide and bade them return the next day. 'Abdel Muttalib spent the night in prayer, and when they went back to her, Shiya said, "I have the answer. By your customs, how much is a man's life worth if he is killed?" 'Abdel Muttalib answered, "Ten camels," for this amount was how much a family had to pay as a penalty if one of their members killed a member of another clan. She looked gravely at the hopeful old man and instructed him thus: "Go back to your land and draw two arrows near your god, one with the boy's name and the other with the phrase 'ten camels' written on it. If the arrow that is drawn is the boy's, then add ten camels to your tally and then draw again until your god is appeased."

The delegation accepted this answer and returned to Mecca with all haste. Upon arriving, they organized the new drawing under the watchful gaze of many interested spectators. Inside the Ka'bah, in front of Hubal, they drew one of the two arrows. It was 'Abdullah, so they counted ten camels. 'Abdullah's name came up ten times, but on the eleventh draw the camels arrow came up. The tribal leaders who were assembled there congratulated 'Abdel Muttalib on his favorable decision, but the deeply religious man wasn't satisfied. He declared that he wouldn't be truly convinced he could substitute camels for his son unless the arrow draw came up camels three times in a row. The next three draws all came up the same, and 'Abdel Muttalib announced that he was satisfied with the results. When the crowd outside the Ka'bah heard the news, they were overjoyed—especially 'Abdullah!

'Abdullah was soon to be rewarded for the stress of possibly being sacrificed. Perhaps with a twinge of guilt, 'Abdel Muttalib decided to find his youngest and most beloved son a wife. The famously handsome young man was twenty-five years old and already making his own living in the local bazaar. It was time for him to start a family of his own. After a careful search, it was decided that he would be wed to Aminah, the daughter of a local tribal chief. Her father readily agreed to the match. After all, the family of ʻAbdel Muttalib was the most prominent in the city, enjoying the honor of having their houses nearest to the courtyard of the Kaʻbah. In the year 569, the couple was married and spent three days in the house of the bride's father before moving into the groom's new quarters.

> ʻAbdel Muttalib also decided to marry again and took another wife, Halah by name, who was Aminah's cousin. The marriage took place on the same day as his son's wedding. Halah later gave birth to a boy named Hamza, who was Muhammad's uncle, though they would be the same age.

ʻAbdullah had been living with his wife for only about two weeks when his father asked him if he wanted to join a caravan headed for Syria. Trade was the Meccans' lifeblood. Twice every year, in the summer and in the winter, major caravans were organized. The summer trek took the Meccan merchants north to Syria and its environs. Winter saw them heading for the markets of Yemen, whose ports were filled with trading vessels from as far away as China. Being an industrious and eager young man, ʻAbdullah accepted his father's offer and left his wife to join the great summer caravan to Syria, hoping to make his fortune.

Aminah complained to her teenage African servant girl, Barakah, saying, "How can my husband go on a trading journey to Syria while I'm still a new bride and the traces of henna-dye are still on my hands?" Her protestations, however, were to no avail. As the caravan departed some days later, Aminah fainted out of sorrow and became bedridden for several weeks. She would often wake in the night crying and moaning for her absent husband while Barakah would try her best to comfort her and encourage her to be hopeful of ʻAbdullah's eventual return. Barakah and ʻAbdel Muttalib were the only people she would see.

About two months after her husband left, Aminah called her servant in the night and excitedly exclaimed, "Barakah! I've had a strange dream! I saw lights coming from my womb, lighting up the mountains, the hills, and the valleys all around Mecca!" Barakah asked if she felt any signs of pregnancy, and her mistress replied that she did, though she felt no discomfort. Barakah then predicted, "You will give birth to a blessed child who will bring goodness."

Two months of traveling and trading had passed when 'Abdullah decided to return home. On the way back, however, he wanted to visit the city of Yathrib to call on his grandmother's relatives. While there, 'Abdullah contracted a viral infection and fell ill. He was too sick to travel, and the caravan had to leave for Mecca without him. When news of his son's condition finally reached 'Abdel Muttalib, he sent another son to bring him home. Upon his arrival in Yathrib, however, the other son was informed that 'Abdullah had passed away and was already buried. In sadness, he returned to Mecca, telling his father that the one who had escaped being sacrificed had died from an illness no one could protect against.

'Abdel Muttalib hung his head in grief. His dearest son, whom he himself had encouraged to go out on his first trading adventure, was gone. Barakah, who had come to see if 'Abdullah was back yet, cried out in distress upon hearing of the tragedy. She later spoke of what happened:

> "I screamed when I heard the news. I don't know what I
> did after that except that I ran to Aminah's house shouting,
> lamenting for the beloved one who would never return,
> lamenting for the beloved one for whom we waited so
> long, lamenting for the most beautiful young man of
> Mecca, for 'Abdullah, the pride of the Quraysh. When
> Aminah heard the painful news, she fainted, and I stayed
> by her bedside while she hovered between life and death.
> There was no one else but me in her house. I nursed her
> and looked after her during the long days and nights until
> she gave birth to her child, 'Muhammad,' on a night in
> which the heavens were resplendent with the light of God."

Aminah had loved 'Abdullah dearly. Indeed, before they were betrothed, the dark-eyed youth had caught the eye of many unmarried young women around Mecca, both for his beauty and for the intrigue surrounding his near demise and apparent salvation at the hands of the gods. Aminah became more than distraught as she realized the cruel fate that awaited her. In a land where losing a father qualified one as an orphan, both she and her son seemed doomed to a life of poverty or ignominy. Perhaps mindful of his own experience as an orphan, 'Abdel Muttalib told the grieving widow that he would support her financially. He went even further and comforted her by saying that her unborn child "might be a little 'Abdullah for us."

By the year 570, Mecca had developed the reputation in Arabia of being the premiere site for religious pilgrimage. Legends connecting it with the patriarch Abraham and Ishmael were well entrenched, and the Ka'bah's status took on the aura of a house for both the supreme God, Allah, and the lesser gods, which were represented by idols. In addition to the tax revenues generated from the ceaseless tide of caravan traffic passing through the city, Meccan merchants made a fortune catering to the needs of the religious pilgrims who constantly flooded the courtyard of the Ka'bah. Several tall stone idols were placed near the entrance to the shrine, and about three hundred and sixty small to medium idols lined the walls inside the building.

Eyeing the lucrative exploitation of religious sentiments, and mindful of the prestige that comes from controlling an acclaimed religious site, Abrahah al-Ashram, the Abyssinian governor of Yemen, attempted to construct a rival holy shrine of his own. In the capital city of Sana, he built a huge cathedral made with the finest marble, gold work, and ivory that money could buy to divert pilgrim traffic from Mecca to Yemen. But he hadn't counted on the power of tradition. The Arabs took little notice of this magnificent new structure and continued flocking to Mecca. In verse and song, the Arabs ridiculed the rival shrine, and one bold man went so far as to defile the cathedral while on a visit to Sana. Abrahah soon became disenchanted, realizing that the draw of the Ka'bah was too powerful. Out of rage or jealousy, he decided to march an army several hundred miles north to Mecca to destroy the Ka'bah, reasoning that the Arabs would then have no other choice but to visit his magnificent church. The viceroy of Abyssinia assembled an army of several thousand men, including expert javelin throwers, archers, seasoned infantry, and several elephants especially trained for war. These animals were the tanks of their day, and the army that could effectively deploy them had an unmatched advantage.

When news of the impending invasion reached the Arabs of the Hijaz, the rallying cry was passed along from tribe to tribe. Only two tribes in the south tried to stop Abrahah's march, but both were easily defeated, and their leaders were captured. When the word spread that Abrahah was only interested in destroying the Ka'bah, Bedouin resistance melted away. To make matters worse, the leaders of a rival city to Mecca, the hilltop fortress of Ta'if, cooperated with the foreigners and provided a guide to lead the army to Mecca. Ta'if had always bristled with envy at Mecca and felt that its own religious shrine with the prominent goddess al-Lat was underappreciated by the Arabs of the Hijaz. Here would be a chance for the people of Ta'if to reap some of the benefits of a realigned pilgrimage map of Arabia.

After a few weeks, the lumbering army finally came within a few miles of Mecca. The journey through the hot sands had been arduous, and no doubt the elephants were in little mood to cooperate. Abrahah ordered camp to be made and sent out small groups of raiders to capture whatever flocks of animals the Meccans had in the hills all around the city. The men returned with dozens of cows and goats and over a hundred camels that belonged to 'Abdel Muttalib. Clearly the Meccans had been taken unaware. Panic descended upon the city, as people feared the worst from this bold enemy that had come through the desert to attack them. Never before had Mecca been the victim of foreign invasion. Business was disrupted, merchants began fleeing in confusion, and the local residents clamored for guidance from their leaders.

The elders of the Quraysh hastily called a meeting to discuss their options, and the general consensus at first was to defend the city at all costs. 'Abdel Muttalib, who by now had risen to the most prominent position in the council, was more concerned with preserving the people of Mecca than the city itself. He argued that the forces of Abrahah were too powerful and that nothing could be gained by meeting them in battle. Meccan fighters could not withstand the assault of war elephants and seasoned troops.

While the Meccans were beginning to lean towards fleeing, Abrahah sent an envoy to inform 'Abdel Muttalib that his master had come only to destroy the Ka'bah and had no desire to fight against the people who lived around it. If the Meccans stepped aside, he said, then Abrahah would not make war against them. 'Abdel Muttalib quickly told the messenger that Mecca would not fight. The envoy then invited 'Abdel Muttalib to return with him to Abrahah's camp to meet with him directly. Abrahah received 'Abdel Muttalib with great courtesy and even returned his camels to him. He would not, however, listen to 'Abdel Muttalib's entreaties to spare the Ka'bah. Even when the respected elder offered a portion of the harvest of a local orchard district as a yearly tribute, Abrahah dismissed him curtly. 'Abdel Muttalib returned to Mecca with the news that everyone should leave the city and head for the surrounding hills for their own safety. In a mass of confusion the entire population of Mecca, several thousand people, prepared to scatter for their lives into the rocky hills.

'Abdel Muttalib was organizing his own family to go when he asked Aminah, nearing the end of her pregnancy, to pack up as well. She protested that she was in no condition and declared her intentions to stay in the city. Counting on Abrahah's word not to harm civilians, the clan leader reluctantly left the widow of his favorite son in her quarters. On the day of the evacuation, the leaders of the Quraysh tribe assembled in front of the Ka'bah and grasped the door handles and prayed to their gods to save the building. When asked by the frantic crowd how they could just leave the place to its certain destruction, 'Abdel Muttalib answered, "The Ka'bah has God to protect it."

The Ka'bah and the courtyard around it as they appear today.

Meanwhile, as Abrahah was making final preparations to strike camp and march on the city, a curious sickness began to spread among his men. By the end of the day, hundreds of his crack troops lay sick with open sores and pustules that oozed relentlessly. Historians have surmised that smallpox or some other equally devastating viral infection struck the army, possibly as a result of poor sanitary conditions or because the soldiers were city dwellers who may have become susceptible to disease after a long, forced march. The Qur'an describes this incident in Chapter 105 by stating that either birds or winged insects (the Arabic word *tayran* can mean either) carrying a contagion set upon the army and mowed the regiments down as if they had been stoned.

Abrahah's army continued to weaken, and within a few days the men began to die in great numbers. Many more deserted in fear. Even the elephants now refused to move towards Mecca. Abrahah, seeing his army rapidly disintegrating in enemy territory, panicked and ordered a hasty retreat back to his capital in Yemen, but he also contracted the disease and died shortly before he reached home. The Meccans returned to the city and were overjoyed when news of Abrahah's humiliating retreat became known. They held celebrations and ceremonies to their gods and took this good fortune as a sign that the idols that lived inside were truly powerful. The prestige of Mecca increased exponentially among the tribes of the countryside, and the Quraysh took to calling that year "The Year of the Elephant."

As a consequence of this barely averted invasion, the Meccans developed a new municipal spirit. New rules instituted by the council of elders included the creation of a semi-permanent security force and the prohibition of any Christian or Jew from entering the city unless they were a pilgrim, slave, or servant. This last provision was in keeping with their fear that monotheists, as represented by Abrahah, would continually try to destroy the center of idolatry in Arabia. The hundreds of Arab tribes in the surrounding countryside, all of whom kept their most important idols in the Ka'bah, willingly acceded their allegiance to the Quraysh on this matter. Consequently, no Jewish or Christian community ever took root in Mecca.

With the defeat of Abrahah, apparently by supernatural intervention, the Meccan nobility returned to their choice residences encircling the courtyard of the Ka'bah, and the commoners returned to their dwellings on the next circuit out from there. Slaves and servants had their hovels in the furthest outskirts of the city limits under the most spartan living conditions, in keeping with their status as property of their owners. Slaves were treated as harshly or liberally as their masters wished; there was no code of rights or ethics in force.

A few slaves were Christian or Jewish and were not forcibly converted, though they were forbidden to teach or discuss their beliefs. Such restrictions did not really matter, because religious knowledge among these slaves was scanty. Generally, slaves were required to follow the faith of their masters or mistresses.

In other parts of the Hijaz, one could subscribe to Judaism or Christianity more freely, though reliable religious knowledge was always hard to come by. Arabia had no permanent churches, schools, libraries, traveling evangelists, or seminaries, so whatever religious notions a slave might have came from light contact with a decrepit monastery or from a hermit wandering the roads. (There were no Bibles in Arabic either—not that many people in Arabia could read anyway.) Religious options in Mecca, therefore, were limited strictly to idolatry. Yet idolatrous slaves did not know much about their religions either. They were not formally instructed in the beliefs of idolatry; they were merely told to bow and worship the idols of their owners.

A third current at work in Arabia subscribed neither to idolatry nor to the Judeo-Christian model. This was a path that was suspiciously similar to agnosticism, or an informal acceptance of religious values without attempting to define the divine. Certain individuals known as *hanifs*, or pure monotheists, lived among the tribes and made no secret of their disdain for idol worship, even in Christianized forms. They believed in the one God and spent their religious devotions in individualized prayer to Allah. The name *Allah* itself literally means "the one and only God," and the hanifs, though not organized at all, aired their views when the opportunity arose. One thing agreed upon by the hanifs and the Christian monks who occasionally passed through Arabia was that a prophet would soon arise among the Arabs. The Quraysh dismissed such notions out of hand, insisting that their idols were sufficient for them. 'Abdel Muttalib, in particular, epitomized the depth of the Meccans' belief in their religious traditions. With his leadership position reconfirmed after the aborted invasion of Abrahah, his fortunes soared. He was around seventy years of age and therefore widely respected. His experience coupled with his large family and positions as water-giver and tithe-taker caused the council of elders to defer to his judgment. For 'Abdel Muttalib and the great majority of Arabs, the idols were real.

Aminah, who enjoyed the support of 'Abdel Muttalib and the status it brought, awaited the arrival of her baby eagerly. While the Meccans were still celebrating the victory over Abrahah, a voice in a dream told her, "You carry in your womb the lord of this nation. When he is born say, 'I place him under the protection of the One, from the evil of every envier,' then give him the name Highly Praised." On April 20 in the year 570, on a crisp evening under a stunning sky, Aminah gave birth to a beautiful baby boy. Barakah was the first to hold him, and then she reverently handed him to his grateful mother.

'Abdel Muttalib, who had been waiting by the Ka'bah in anticipation of the birth, was called in. He took his grandson eagerly and bounded off back in the direction of the Ka'bah, rousing his neighbors along the way. As a joyful crowd gathered, clapping and singing, the old man walked seven times around the Ka'bah, rejoicing and smiling. He held the baby up to his own toddling son 'Abbas and told him to kiss him. On his last circuit, in keeping with Aminah's wish, he announced, "Blessed child, I shall call you Highly Praised. The birth of this child coincided with the glory and triumph of the Ancient House, blessed be he!" Highly Praised is the translation of the Arabic name *Muhammad*, which was an unusual name in Arabia at that time. Seven days later, following Arab custom, a great feast was held in honor of the baby Muhammad.

Aminah, frail from her depression and weakened by the arduous childbirth, engaged a wet nurse in the city, the slave of one of Muhammad's uncles. Every day the wet nurse would come and care for her baby while she attempted to recover. A custom loomed over her, though, one that would rekindle the sense of loss she suffered with the death of her husband. The Arab nobility of Mecca routinely sent their babies off to be raised by foster mothers in the countryside. Meccans believed that city air was bad for babies, especially in this city enclosed by high valley walls. In addition, many of the tribes and clans in the city were only a few generations removed from the Bedouin lifestyle and thus felt a certain nostalgia for the open air of the desert. A baby raised in the pristine wilderness would be strong, eloquent, well mannered, and brave, so the belief went. This practice of raising city children in the country developed over time into a profitable business enterprise for the poor Arab tribes populating the empty tracts of the Hijaz. Only the more well-to-do citizens of Mecca could afford this private school of sorts. Every year wet nurses would come to Mecca and offer their services to households with newborns. They would keep the babies and return them anywhere from five to ten years later.

When the wet nurses arrived from the renowned tribe of Banu Sa'd and made the rounds, none of them went to Aminah's house because they heard she had no husband. Widows couldn't afford the service, and the women of the Banu Sa'd expected bonuses for their hard work. As they made ready to return to their tribe's camp with their new charges, a woman by the name of Halimah asked her party to wait. She wasn't able to find a family who would let her take their baby; because of her slender build, people just didn't think she could adequately feed their babies. She told her husband that she didn't want to return empty-handed and thought about taking the orphaned son of Aminah. He agreed, and the deal was made: Muhammad would be raised by a foster mother in the countryside.

Muhammad grew up in a Bedouin tent in the open desert. Halimah was more than able to keep him fed, and she exclaimed in later years that her goats gave steadier milk, her chickens grew fatter, and her donkey moved faster while the young Muhammad was with her. When Muhammad was two years old, Halimah had to bring him back to Aminah in Mecca, according to the contract. Aminah was overjoyed, but she was also fearful for his safety. An epidemic was going around the city, and a few people had fallen ill. Mindful of the dangers of disease, especially to small children, Aminah reluctantly agreed to Halimah's request to take him back to the desert for a few more years. Muhammad thus went back to the tents of the Banu Sa'd tribe. From Halimah the baby learned the language of the Bedouins, a form of pure Arabic greatly distinguished from its city counterpart, with its slang and vulgarisms. She taught him manners and how to perform different chores. Her daughter, Shayma, also played a role in Muhammad's upbringing, carrying him, taking him for walks, and teaching him the songs and rhymes of the nomads.

One day when Muhammad was about three years old, Halimah's own son came running to her crying, "Mother! Two men in white are holding my Qurayshi brother!" Halimah and her husband ran to the open field and found Muhammad standing alone and looking pale. He told them, "Two men in white came and laid me on my back. They took something from my chest and then left." A search of the area revealed nothing and the incident was soon forgotten. In later years, Muhammad would describe the two men as angels who had come to remove the taint of any sin from his heart.

Two years later, Halimah returned with Muhammad to Mecca again. The epidemic was long over, and Aminah was anxious to regain permanent custody of her son. Just inside the city, however, Muhammad wandered away from Halimah's watchful gaze. 'Abdel Muttalib sent his men to search for the boy, and he soon turned up in the care of Waraqah ibn Nawfal, a prominent hanif, or unaffiliated monotheist who also had some knowledge of Christianity. When the boy was presented to Aminah, she was overjoyed and proud of the strong boy who stood before her. Having to part with him at birth and then again when he was two had been a great strain on her. Now there would be no more separations. 'Abdel Muttalib generously rewarded Halimah, who returned to her tribe wistfully, missing the little boy she had raised for five years.

Beyond the lavish love of Aminah for her recently returned child, it was 'Abdel Muttalib who showed the greatest public affection toward Muhammad. The Meccan leaders used to sit and discuss current events in a makeshift pavilion in the shade of the Ka'bah. 'Abdel Muttalib had a special cushion there that no one could sit on but he. His children used to arrange themselves around it in respect but would never usurp it. Whenever the little Muhammad would wander into the gathering, however, 'Abdel Muttalib would beckon the boy to sit right next to him on the cushion, holding him close and making no secret of his special bond with the child. None of his uncles ever interfered.

Muhammad's principal playmates were Hamza and Safiyyah, 'Abdel Muttalib's children from his last wife, whom he had married on the same day Muhammad's parents were married. The three children spent long hours playing together, and a strong bond was forged between them.

When Muhammad was about six years old, Amina decided to take a trip to the city of Yathrib so that her distant relatives could see her son. She traveled with Barakah, taking only two camels and enough provisions for the week-long journey. After she arrived in the famed city of date palms and tall houses, she immediately asked to see the grave of her beloved 'Abdullah. Leaving her son in the care of his distant cousins and uncles, Aminah went to the gravesite every day to cry and weep. After a month spent in sorrow and melancholy, she packed up her son and, accompanied by Barakah, headed south towards home. A few days of traveling passed uneventfully, but then Aminah, who was already in poor health due to depression and stress, began to feel ill. On the outskirts of a small village named al-Abwa, she instructed Barakah to make camp. During the evening an intense fever engulfed her, and she asked her servant to send Muhammad outside the tent for a few minutes. Aminah then whispered into the young woman's ear, "Barakah, I shall leave this world shortly. I give my son, Muhammad, to your care. He lost his father while he was in my womb. Here he is now, losing his mother under his very own eyes. Be a mother to him, Barakah, and don't ever leave him." Barakah began to weep, and the little Muhammad rushed in, threw himself into his mother's arms, and held on tightly. A few moments passed, and the lady Aminah breathed her last. Barakah and Muhammad cried long into the night.

In the morning, Barakah sorrowfully dug a grave with her own hands in the hard, sun-baked earth and laid the noble woman to rest. Then she took the sad, small boy and journeyed the rest of the way to Mecca. His grandfather received Muhammad with tears in his eyes and promised to care for him completely. Barakah moved into 'Abdel Muttalib's sprawling house to be Muhammad's caretaker and keep her promise to Aminah. 'Abdel Muttalib showed

Muhammad a great amount of tender affection, even more than he had shown his own sons, who were now all grown. But the sorrow of losing both of his parents was relieved only slightly by the love of Barakah and his grandfather. Unfortunately, Muhammad's sense of loss was about to increase.

'Abdel Muttalib was now approaching eighty years old and knew he could not be in Muhammad's life much longer. He held a meeting with his son, Abu Talib, and made him promise to care for Muhammad in the event that something happened to him. Although Abu Talib was the poorest and least influential of 'Abdel Muttalib's sons, he was the kindest, so he readily agreed to his father's request. This agreement was made none too soon, for 'Abdel Muttalib passed away at the age of eighty. Eight-year-old Muhammad was inconsolable and followed his grandfather's funeral bier, sobbing uncontrollably. The last family member who truly loved him was gone.

Abu Talib took Muhammad in and treated him with great affection. Although Abu Talib was poor, he and his wife did their best to take the place of Muhammad's lost parents. Abu Talib was surprised at the boy's good manners compared to his own children's. When mealtime came, Abu Talib's own progeny would push and shove and grab at the communal food dishes, as was the common table etiquette of the day, whereas Muhammad would wait to the side and eat whatever was given to him. He was also respectful and spoke the clear and direct language of the Bedouin, not the coarse slang of the city.

Abu Talib had more than his new charge to occupy his mind, however, for with 'Abdel Muttalib's passing, the extended family experienced a shocking reversal of their fortunes. None of 'Abdel Muttalib's sons was wealthy or influential enough to assume his mantle as the de facto leader of the clan council of Mecca. To make matters worse, the more numerous Qurayshi clan of Banu Ummayah took over many of the functions of leadership. Although 'Abdel Muttalib's son 'Abbas retained his father's official duties, his influence was weak. The clan of Banu Hashim, so named after its common ancestor, retreated from prominence and suffered economically.

As a result of his diminished resources, Abu Talib could not support his family very well. Money was tight from then on, with no luxuries. Muhammad had to pitch in and was given many small jobs, chief among them taking care of his uncle's flocks and camels. The heavy work kept Muhammad from playing with other children his age, but it enabled him to avoid the kinds of trouble that young men usually get into. Muhammad soon gained a reputation for being sensitive, caring, honest, and courteous. In time he even garnered the nickname of *al-Ameen*, or the trustworthy one.

Around the year 582, Abu Talib decided to join the great caravan going to Syria in order to boost his finances. As preparations got under way, Muhammad, who was twelve years old at the time, begged and pleaded with his uncle to let him go along. At first reluctant, for children were rarely allowed on such long and dangerous journeys, Abu Talib eventually gave in and assigned Muhammad several symbolic tasks to keep him busy. Soon, the great caravan, made up of hundreds of fully loaded camels laden with silk, spices, ironware, and other goods, lumbered out of the staging area outside Mecca in a ritual thousands of years old. The rhythmic calls of the camel drivers, the swaying of the loads, the decorative ribbons and flags, the merchants bundled in their desert attire and turbans, and the call of certain adventure all made the caravan an exciting draw for the young men of the time.

After a couple weeks of long, hard travel, the caravan and its attendants decided to make camp in a region called Bostra, just short of Syria. Just ahead on the road was a small Christian monastery where a solitary monk by the name of Bahira lived. That morning, Bahira had watched the caravan coming down the road and was startled to notice a cloud that seemed to follow over them, shielding them from the sun. He had read in one of his old religious books that clouds only make constant shade over prophets, so he felt sure someone special had come. He sent an invitation to the men of the caravan to come to the monastery for a banquet, asking that everyone attend. When the merchants arrived, the priest looked them over and found nothing special about any of them. He asked if everyone from the caravan was present and was told that everyone was there except a small boy who was left behind to watch the animals. Bahira requested that he also be invited, so someone went to fetch young Muhammad.

After Muhammad joined the gathering, Bahira watched the boy carefully and noted his physical features and behavior. He seemed to have an otherworldly look in his eyes, a strength in his bearing. After a little while, as the merchants feasted and talked, Bahira took Abu Talib aside and asked him if he was the father of the boy. Feeling protective, Abu Talib answered that he was. The monk protested that it couldn't be so, so Abu Talib relented and admitted that Muhammad's real father had passed away.

Bahira then called Muhammad over and began asking all sorts of questions about his life, his dreams. At first the monk asked Muhammad to speak in the name of the idols of his people, but Muhammad boldly told the monk that he hated the idols. This statement impressed the aged Christian further. Then he asked for the boy to lift his shirt, and the monk found a birthmark on his back, just between the shoulder blades. Bahira looked at the spot, which was about the size of a small egg, and declared, "Now I am most certain that this is the last prophet for whom the Jews and Christians await ...." He then instructed the baffled Abu Talib to take special care of Muhammad and to keep him safe. Abu Talib, perhaps feeling the old monk was a little eccentric, continued his journey to Syria in the morning. After he finished his business, he returned home with his caravan. This strange incident with Bahira caused Abu Talib to keep a closer eye on his nephew, however.

Excitement came into Muhammad's life when he was about fifteen. A war broke out between the Quraysh tribe and the Hawazin tribe of Ta'if over a petty revenge issue that spiraled out of control. It was called the al-Fijar War. A few battles broke out, with both sides raining down arrows on the other. Muhammad didn't participate in any of the fighting, but as a teenage boy, it was his job to gather all the arrows that he could find on the battlefield for reuse by his own side's archers. (He may have shot a few arrows as well during a later battle.) It was a dangerous job, and doubtless a few boys were struck by arrows or captured by the enemy. But Muhammad came through each battle unscathed and thus saw his first taste of martial action.

Muhammad also had an early experience with civil action. The issues that led to the al-Fijar War emphasized the need for a fairer code of honor and justice among the tribes of the desert. With no police or courts, revenge was the only recourse. One man who was cheated out of his goods by swindlers in Mecca complained openly to the Quraysh leaders, invoking their custodianship of the holy shrine, so they attempted to bring more reason to intertribal disputes. One of 'Abdel Muttalib's sons, Zubayr, gathered the leaders of several clans in Mecca, and this group took a pledge to "help the poor and the needy, assist the oppressed, protect the weak and secure their rights from tyrants, and to establish peace and harmony among the people." Muhammad, who was still in his teens, participated in this meeting and took the oath along with a slightly younger boy by the name of Abu Bakr, with whom he would soon establish a close friendship. In later years, Muhammad said, "I would not trade that oath that I took in 'Abdullah ibn Jud'an's house for a herd of red camels. Even today I would not hesitate to be a member of such an institution."

In his early twenties, Muhammad displayed his good upbringing. Other young men his age spent their time dancing, drinking wine, and hanging out with prostitutes. Muhammad had no desire to participate in such wanton activities. Although he asked a friend to watch his uncle's flocks a few times so he could go and see what there was to do in town, he always seemed to get sidetracked on the way. On his first trip into town at night he stopped to watch a wedding, and it got so late he had to return home. Another time he paused to listen to a song being sung inside a house on the edge of town and fell asleep. In short, he never had the chance to become a part of the popular crowd. Instead, he continued to spend most of his time working for his uncle in the hardscrabble pastures outside Mecca. It was a quiet job that gave him a lot of time to think.

In the afternoons, he wandered in the bazaars and listened to the poets grandstand and recite epic stories of heroes past and glories gained. The oral poetic tradition was so entrenched in Arabia that many cities held annual contests. Winners in Mecca were sometimes honored by having their poems being written on leather and displayed inside the Ka'bah, where the Quraysh hung all their important documents and treaties.

> *Poetry was the vehicle for oral history in Arabia. Arab poets recited historical events, repeated propaganda in times of war, rallied tribes to take pride in the glorious histories of their ancestors, taunted and teased those who were despised, and entertained in a land where the mobile lifestyle of most people precluded the acquisition of musical instruments or books. In this regard, Arabian poets played the same role as the famed bards of Europe during the Middle Ages. The Qur'an even has one chapter titled "The Poets," in which a clear distinction is made between noble poetry and slanderous verse. Although Muhammad allowed poetry and often listened to it after he was commissioned as a prophet, he forbade it as a vehicle for libel.*

Muhammad had no schooling or education. There were no academies in Mecca, nor could Abu Talib afford to send his nephew to a tutor for writing lessons. But this lack of education did not stop Muhammad from observing. He liked to join the meetings of the leaders of Mecca and watch the proceedings. He also saw the yearly pilgrimage during the so-called holy months when the Arab tribes called a truce to allow for the free travel of religious pilgrims. Muhammad never liked idol worshipping and never bowed to any statues during or outside the annual ritual. When he was a boy at the Banu Sa'd, he lived the Bedouin lifestyle, which had little time for formal rituals or idols, so from an early age he never believed in gods of wood or stone. His years as a shepherd also taught him that the world was a wide and mysterious place that could never have been created by an idol. An idol was only a thing made by a man's hands. Many evenings Muhammad must have looked out over the endless horizon and watched as the sunset disappeared in a haze of brilliant reds, yellows, and oranges to be replaced by a dark blue curtain of night dotted with stars and the bright face of the moon. No, idols were not real, Muhammad knew.

Occasionally, Muhammad's uncle would give him a few goods that he could take into the marketplace and trade to try his hand at business. He was always fair and honest in his dealings with others and employed only the best manners. Although he never made much money, people soon gave him another nickname, *al-Sadiq*, or the truthful. His excellent reputation soon paid off, however; for although he was a penniless orphan working for his uncle, his honesty and character would become his principal assets in a series of events that would change his fortunes forever.

Chapter 3

Muhammad: Merchant of Mecca

*In the creation of the heavens and the Earth, and in the
alternation of night and day, and in the sailing of ships
through the sea for trade, and in the rain allowed to fall
for the parched land to live, and in the diversity of living
creatures, and in the changing patterns of the clouds and
winds, in all of these things are signs for the wise.*
—Qur'an 2:164

Muhammad, the son of 'Abdullah, grew into the prime of
manhood in the clear air of the open desert outside the valley of Mecca. His light tan complexion contrasted with his thick
black hair, which tended to curl slightly. A broad, smooth forehead
gave way to a finely chiseled nose set over a friendly smile. He was
tall, as young men went, but not overly so. His hands and feet were
broad and large. He walked purposefully and stood straight. He carried himself with confidence but was not overbearing or conceited.
The painful childhood losses of his father, mother, and grandfather
taught him to cherish relationships and not to be haughty.

He was friendly towards all, but especially loved the compan-
ionship of his uncle Abu Talib's children, his sons Talib, 'Aqil, and
Ja'far in particular. Muhammad even asked his uncle if he could
marry his cousin Fakhitah, who was of age. Though Abu Talib
loved his nephew, he had other plans for his daughter and married

her to Hubayrah of the Makhzum clan. She would later have a son named Hani and thus become known as *Umm Hani*, or the mother of Hani. Muhammad's chance to marry came, however, and it was quite unexpected.

Muhammad's humble occupation as a shepherd impressed upon him the value of hard, honest work. His sense of responsibility earned him a solid reputation in town. Though his clan, the Banu Hashim, was poor and unable to provide any economic uplift to its members, it was nonetheless full of nurturing and supportive individuals. Muhammad, now in his early twenties, began to consider how he would assume his rightful place in Meccan society. This task was made all the more uncertain given all the changes that had taken place since the days of his grandfather, 'Abdel Muttalib.

Ever since the Year of the Elephant, Mecca had been a different town. In addition to the regular activities connected with business and religious pilgrimage, the virtually autonomous elders of the clan of Quraysh tended to act more in unison on matters of security and municipal need. Given that the city no longer had a central figurehead, greater cooperation was essential, though that fact did not always maintain unity among the various clans of the Quraysh. Still, many Meccans compared their new spirit to the earliest days of the city when Jurhum and Mudad walked the land. Muhammad became interested in the affairs of the clan leaders and used to sit with other spectators and observe their important meetings, perhaps remembering when he would sit on his grandfather's cushion among the Meccan leaders of the time. Being practically a commoner, he was rarely allowed to participate in a meaningful way, but he nevertheless reflected the new citizen of Mecca: someone who felt a sense of civic duty.

Other changes also had taken place in Arabia following the days of Abrahah's defeat. Yemen, in the south, was no longer ruled by the Christian Abyssinians from across the Red Sea in Africa. Bristling under successive corrupt governors, one Yemeni dissident by the name of Sayf bin Dhi Yazan appealed to the Byzantine emperor to oust the ineffectual Abyssinians. After being politely declined, Sayf approached the Sasanid Persian emperor who, though he balked at first, eventually sent a contingent of 800 condemned convicts under the command of Sayf to try and wrest control of the city of Sana from the hated foreigners. After a relatively short campaign, these Persian mercenaries succeeded and set up a colony for their master, who ruled in far-off Iran. They settled down to live with the local Yemenis, and their descendants would come to be called the *abna*, or children of the Persians.

With all the changes in the central and southern Arabian Peninsula, however, several constants remained. Caravan traffic continued to be the single most important revenue source in the entire desert. Many traders plied the trails continuously; others hired people to do this dangerous work for them. In Mecca there lived just such a profit-minded person, a woman by the name of Khadijah bint Khuwaylid. She was a member of the Banu Asad tribe who married not once but twice into the Meccan clan of Banu Makhzum. Each husband died in turn, leaving her with a huge personal fortune. Although it was rare for a woman to inherit anything in Arabian society, due to unique circumstances in her husbands' families, their property fell into her hands. She had one daughter from her first marriage and a son and a daughter from her second.

Khadijah was an ambitious woman. She could have retired and lived a very comfortable life: she was almost forty years old and had no financial worries. Moreover, with the beauty she retained and her large fortune, many Meccan nobles asked for her hand in marriage, a status that would have benefited her. She refused every time, however, perhaps feeling that her suitors wanted her money more than her happiness. In Mecca, a woman's property could be seized by her husband for his own benefit. So instead of marrying or remaining idle, she established herself as a successful businesswoman by building a very profitable trading enterprise that sent large caravans north and south and reaped huge gains. She never went on the expeditions herself; she hired caravan bosses and porters to do her work for her.

The economic system of Arabia was founded on both currency and barter. The imperial dinar of the Byzantine Empire was the most common form of coinage, with the dirham being of a lesser denomination. Coins were generally made of gold, silver, or copper and were the preferred method of exchange for traveling merchants. For the settled and nomadic Arabs, wealth was more often based on livestock: camels, horses, sheep, and goats in particular. A wealthy family would own hundreds or even thousands of animals and would use them for payment and trade as easily as coins. Not surprisingly, young men in search of easy wealth would often raid another tribe's flocks.

In about the year 595, Khadijah announced that she would hire a local man to lead a particularly important caravan to go to Syria. He would be paid two young camels in compensation. Abu Talib, always on the lookout for opportunities for his own or any family member's advancement, suggested to his nephew Muhammad that he try to get a job with Khadijah's caravan. Muhammad, who was twenty-five years old and still living with his uncle, saw this caravan as an excellent opportunity to earn money and see the world. After the one foreign trip he had taken when he was twelve, he had never been out of the Hijaz. Muhammad didn't know Khadijah personally, but he knew of her and her lucrative business, so he agreed to let his uncle speak to her. Abu Talib confidently told his nephew that he could get him double the salary of the man already hired.

Abu Talib walked along the dusty streets past rows of houses made of baked clay and mud bricks until he reached Khadijah's spacious home, where he asked permission to enter. One of the servants led the venerable elder into a waiting room. When Khadijah appeared and inquired as to the nature of Abu Talib's visit, he said, "Khadijah, would you like to hire Muhammad? We heard that you hired a man for two camels, but we won't accept less than four." Khadijah smiled at the son of the legendary 'Abdel Muttalib and answered, "If *you* would have asked this for a foreigner or an unfit man, I still would have granted your request. So how can I refuse when your request is for a close relative?" Khadijah decided to send along with the caravan one of her slaves, Maysara, to secretly keep an eye on Muhammad and assist him in managing the caravan workers and animals. Abu Talib knew of Maysara's good character and encouraged his presence on the journey.

Abu Talib returned quickly to his nephew to give him the good news. This job would be Muhammad's first big break. Leading a caravan of dozens of fully loaded camels on a journey of several months to the trading capital of the Middle East, Syria, and being responsible for thousands of dinars' worth of merchandise must have been exhilarating for young Muhammad. As his caravan wound its way up through the Hijaz and into southern Syria, Muhammad had the opportunity to see ancient ruins from past civilizations, as well as different customs and religious sites from the people of his own time. He saw Roman and Syrian Christians (mostly of the Nestorian sect), Jews, and even a few Magians, who were prominent worshippers of fire. He must have been impressed and was certainly curious, for in his native Mecca he never picked up the habit of idolatry and was something of a hanif himself. Though he had little time to stop and chat with those he met, he must have absorbed much in these first encounters with the diversity of the world and its people.

While in the markets of Syria, known as *Ash-Shaam* to the Arabs, he peddled his goods and always struck an honest bargain. He was never rude to customers nor did he treat his workers harshly. Maysara soon became very impressed with Muhammad. When the time came for the return journey to Mecca, the camels were loaded with the new merchandise, and the lumbering train of animals headed south into the Arabian desert. After a few weeks, the party neared the outskirts of Mecca. Maysara urged Muhammad to ride ahead and tell Khadijah about the trip. Maysara said he would bring the caravan into the city in due time and unload the wares. Muhammad rushed his camel forward and entered Mecca. He went straight to Khadijah's house and gave her a full report on the success of the expedition. She was extremely pleased with his management skills and later sold the new goods for double what Muhammad had paid for them. Khadijah then paid Muhammad and dismissed him. After he left her house, however, she couldn't get his face out of her mind. He was young and handsome, but his soft-spoken personality, his lovely eyes, and his gentleness in her presence were what attracted her. Later, when Maysara gave his report, he had lavish praise for Muhammad's manners and honesty in business.

As the days passed, Khadijah's interest in Muhammad grew into a longing to be near him. She already knew of his reputation about town as a fine young man, but her own contact with him made her wish to marry and be close to him. But how could she express her desire to marry him without putting herself in danger of embarrassment? An older woman (she was about forty) marrying a man fifteen years younger was unheard of in Arab society, where a man was usually decades older than his wife or wives. What of the boldness of a woman proposing to a man which was quite unheard of for the time? What if he rejected her, what if he spurned her? Beyond a broken heart—for she was falling deeper and deeper in love with him—the humiliation and damage to her reputation would be an even greater wound to bear. She spoke to her best friend, Nafisa. After some discussion, the two women decided that Nafisa would go to Muhammad and find out his thoughts about Khadijah to avoid an embarrassing situation.

Nafisa went to see Muhammad and asked him why he hadn't gotten married yet. The shy young man with the long, dark eyelashes replied, "Because I don't have the money to support a wife."

Nafisa then asked, "What if you had the money, would you turn down a woman with beauty, skill, wealth, and honor?"

"Who could that be?" Muhammad asked.

"Khadijah," Nafisa answered.

Muhammad was surprised. He hesitated for a few moments. It had never occurred to him that he could marry a woman of such high status. After all, she was known for rejecting all suitors, no matter how noble or influential they were. He asked how such a match could be possible. Nafisa replied that she could arrange it. Muhammad already respected Khadijah and must have felt an attraction towards her as well, for he quickly told Nafisa that he would be honored to marry his recent employer. Nafisa returned joyously to Khadijah with the news.

Khadijah's uncle performed the marriage ceremony in her family's ancestral home. Muhammad, flanked by his own uncles, must have felt the whole situation a bit surreal. Not only was he suddenly getting married, his fortunes were also taking a dramatic turn for the better. Khadijah was wealthy, with her own house and business, and he would probably never have to work hard again. This change was certainly an unusual break for an orphan with no income of his own. The newlyweds were given a modest, joyous banquet, and they settled into their home. In the months that followed, Muhammad's nature delighted his new bride. Although Khadijah was neither young nor a virgin, which were essential traits in a wife in pre-Islamic Arabia, Muhammad treated her as his loving life-partner from the start. He did not take her wealth as his own, nor did he attempt to limit her activities. He also helped in the upkeep of the household.

Muhammad and Khadijah would have six children together, two boys and four girls. Tragically, both of their sons, Qasim and 'Abdullah, died as infants. Undoubtedly the grief any parents would feel at such unthinkable losses was a strain on their marriage, but the strength of their love carried them through, and their four daughters, Zaynab, Ruqqayah, Umm Kulthum, and the littlest, Fatimah, brought much joy and pleasure into their home. The three older girls were eventually married and moved in with their husbands' families. Zaynab married a cousin named Abu al-'As, and Ruqqayah and Umm Kulthum were wed to two sons of Muhammad's uncle, Abu Lahab. (Khadijah's three children from her previous marriages were already married off long before.)

Muhammad remained faithful to Khadijah and never married another wife, as would have been common in those days, for as long as his beloved lived. In later years, after Khadijah passed away, he would speak of her so fondly and lovingly to his new wives that one day one of them complained, saying that he dwelled too much on an old woman while she was young and present in his life right now. Muhammad became slightly angry and declared that no woman could ever compare to Khadijah.

Muhammad could have lived a very comfortable life. He was the father of many children and the husband of a successful businesswoman. However, remembering the days of his own deprivation—being an orphan, the poverty of his uncle's house, and the now-defunct pledge of social justice he made as a youth—he felt a great sense of responsibility for the plight of the poor in Mecca. Despite the amount of money made in the merchant trade, many people slipped through the cracks. Some were victims of crime or had lost everything because of the heavy interest on their debts, and others were economic refugees from the poverty-stricken countryside. Muhammad, who had little money of his own, often gave to the destitute and lame and expressed his frustration to Khadijah that he wished he could do more. One day, Khadijah invited several of the prominent leaders of the Quraysh tribe to her home and announced that she was giving full control of her wealth to her husband to do with as he pleased. The elders, who already had a high opinion of the young man, approved the decision heartily. That Khadijah took such a generous action proved the depth of her love and trust in Muhammad, who took over his wife's business affairs and donated the profits he made to those less fortunate.

> *Generosity was a highly regarded virtue in Arabia. Guests in someone's tent or home were treated as members of the family for as long as they stayed, and strangers were often taken in and sheltered for no other reason than camaraderie. Of course, this virtue contrasts starkly with the vices of Arab society, where blood revenge, raiding, slavery, infanticide, and drunkenness were also normal, but societies often consist of paradoxical values. One legendary figure in the Hijaz was Hatim Tai, a renowned tribal leader who gave his own horse to feed his neighbor's hungry children, even though his own circumstances were also dire.*

Muhammad's role in the rebuilding of the Ka'bah illustrates his reputation in Meccan society. An unusual flash flood had damaged several buildings in Mecca, including the Ka'bah, which was left with cracked walls and a caved-in roof. Everyone agreed that repairs were necessary, but the superstitions and taboos connected with the structure raised many concerns. As the house of God and the resting place for the idols, any alteration of it for better or worse might bring supernatural retribution. Debate among the Quraysh about what to do might have dragged on for months had not one brave elder taken action. Al-Walid ibn al-Mughirah took a pickaxe and, in front of a large crowd, struck one corner of the Ka'bah, pulling down a section of one wall. Everyone waited to see if some harm might befall him. The next day, al-Mughirah was unharmed, so the leaders of the Quraysh decided to put each major clan to work on a rotating schedule removing one part of the structure.

Stone by stone, the entire Ka'bah was carted away. Muhammad also participated in this backbreaking work. When the workers reached ground level, they found that the underlying foundation of the Ka'bah was made up of large green stone slabs. Try as they might, they couldn't lift them, so they decided it was God's will that the foundation first laid by Abraham should stay. Blue-toned granite stones from a nearby quarry were used to reconstruct the walls. Wood purchased from a shipwreck on the coast provided the needed timber.

A photograph of the Ka'bah as it appeared at the turn of the twentieth century.

When the rebuilding was halfway complete, it was decided that it was time to return the fabled Black Stone to its traditional position on the eastern wall. Legend had it that a white meteorite had fallen to earth in ancient times and became black because of the sins of man. Abraham used this meteorite in his original construction of the shrine, and it was the Meccans' one physical reminder of their noble ancestry. Which clan would have the honor of returning the Black Stone to its proper place? The issue quickly assumed great significance as the leaders of each clan claimed the honor for themselves and began squaring off right on the construction site! Men from every faction swore they would kill if they weren't given the honor. The members of one group dipped their hands in a bowl of blood and swore that there would be war if they were denied. Abu Umayyah of the Banu Makhzum clan stepped forward and narrowly averted a civil war, telling the crowd to wait for the next person to come through a nearby gate into the courtyard of the Ka'bah. That person, he explained, would then decide the matter. After a few minutes, Muhammad came walking in. Everyone shouted that they would abide by his decision because he was al-Ameen, the trustworthy. The elders explained the problem to Muhammad and asked for his verdict.

One can imagine Muhammad's nervousness at suddenly being placed in the middle of such a tense situation. He saw the inflamed passions on the men's faces and knew he had to adjudicate in such a way as to please everyone. No one could be seen to lose face. After considering the problem for a minute or two, he asked that a large sheet be brought to him. He spread it on the ground and placed the Black Stone in the middle. Then he said, "Let the elders of each clan take hold of the edges of the sheet." They came forward and lifted the sheet in unison. Muhammad led them to the eastern wall of the Ka'bah as they carried the Black Stone together. He placed a ladder on the wall and mounted it. Then, with the clan leaders holding the sheet high enough for him to reach the stone, he lifted it up and into place with his own hands. Nobody felt slighted, and every clan had participated. The elders agreed that it was the wisest decision they could have hoped for, and

Muhammad was further established as a strong moral and judicious personality in Mecca.

Arabia did not exist in a vacuum. The great empires of the north, Byzantium, heir to the Romans, and Persia, the ancient cultural jewel, both exerted influence on the periphery of the peninsula. Their frequent wars and constant machinations against each other ensured that neither side could leave border territories untouched. Within Arabia itself were both Christian communities and Zoroastrian colonies. The Zoroastrians, followers of the Persian prophet Zoroaster, worshipped a god of light represented by fire. Judaism also had a presence in Arabia. Arab idolatry was well entrenched in the Hijaz, but the great transnational faiths were starting to make inroads into Arab life. One result of this trend was the emergence of the hanifs, Arabs who didn't necessarily want to convert to an outside faith but who also no longer believed in idolatry. They believed in one God, without having a religion that could give full expression to their ideals, and they presented the first challenge to Arabs' belief in gods of their own making.

The political climate that made such challenges possible in Mecca was brought to light during the rebuilding of the Ka'bah. The fact that civil war almost broke out between the clans demonstrated a serious lack of leadership in the city. No single Meccan held the status, reputation, or natural qualities to unify the city and guide its affairs. 'Abdel Muttalib had been the last to hold such a position, and he was long gone. With no leader in charge, every clan felt emboldened to press its interests. Old customs and laws came into question, and even the restrictions on Jews and Christians within the city fell into disuse. Some of the clan elders saw that even idolatry itself, the foundation of Meccan society, was in jeopardy. If people began converting to other religions or waning in their commitment to the idols, they reasoned, then the lucrative religious business would suffer. The caravans might begin to take an easier alternate route to their destinations. To maintain a sense of cohesion in the city and preserve its unique character and economic status, the clan elders loosely agreed to emphasize the benefits of idol worship and to suppress dissent as much as possible.

It soon became apparent that their concerns were well founded when four prominent Meccans refused to take part in the annual festival to the goddess al-'Uzza. Waraqah ibn Nawfal, with whom the young Muhammad had been found when he became lost upon his return to Mecca from the Banu Sa'd, was one of four men who protested that idolatry was without foundation and that the Ka'bah should be cleansed of all such nonsense. Their fervent insistence on the existence of only one true God got them into trouble, however, and they were quickly ostracized. Two left Arabia altogether; a third became an agnostic. Waraqah refused to be driven out and defiantly announced that he was going to become a Christian, but he was advanced in age and could do little more against idolatry. He settled into a quiet life as a retired, though disgruntled, merchant, said by some to have translated into Arabic a few scattered passages from the Gospels. (In those days it was difficult to obtain a complete Bible, so merchants would sometimes offer individual pages for sale.) Nevertheless, he kept his beliefs to himself and did not proselytize.

Muhammad didn't join any rebellion against idolatry, even though he didn't participate in the veneration of the idols himself. He was a family man with many responsibilities and duties. He managed the property turned over to him by his wife and spent his free time listening to the poets in the bazaar, walking the streets of Mecca, and building friendships with people such as Abu Bakr. He knew something of Judaism and Christianity, as most people did, but he never had the opportunity to look at these religions in depth. His geographic location and lifestyle didn't permit it. In addition, he never learned to read or write, which was not uncommon in a land without schools.

As he entered his thirties, Muhammad became more introspective. He was dissatisfied with idol worship and began to ask himself the questions of a spiritual nomad. He wanted to know why he was alive, what the purpose of life was, and how the truth could be known. He was not alone: These were precisely the questions that drove the scattered hanifs to renounce idolatry. After the deaths of his two baby sons, his wife, Khadijah, had sacrificed animals to the gods of the Ka'bah. Muhammad, while not participating himself in these devotions to Hubal, al-Lat, al-'Uzza, and Manat, must have had very intense emotions and conflicting thoughts. Was the intercession of these deities necessary? How did people in other religions handle grief? Which way was right, if any at all?

Muhammad began to withdraw from business and the affairs of the city and returned often to the solitude and stillness of the pastures outside Mecca. As the years passed, Muhammad would often be seen heading out into the hills with a few supplies to spend a full day or more in retreat. This practice was not unusual; religious-minded people had been doing it in Arabia for centuries. Even idolaters were known to wander off in the desert to think and ponder on questions of spiritual importance. There was even a name for this practice: *tahannuf*.

During one of his frequent forays, Muhammad was lucky enough to discover a cave hidden in the cleft of Mount Hira', a small mountain about two miles from the city. The cave provided the perfect sanctuary for his lengthy meditations. Every year he would spend the month of Ramadan there, being resupplied by one of Khadijah's servants. He often forgot to eat and grew slightly thinner, much to the chagrin of his wife, but he found his time alone to be tranquil and refreshing. He would reflect on nature and the enormity of the cosmos, and attempt to find reasons for all that had happened to him. The loss of his parents, his grandfather, and his own beloved sons weighed heavily on his heart. At the same time, the strange twists of fate that allowed him to grow up among the Bedouins, enter into his uncle's house as an equal, and eventually to marry into a comfortable lifestyle confused him. Perhaps his inner quest was not unlike that of Gautama Buddha, who saw suffering amidst the luxuries of wealth and wondered at the meaning of it all.

> *The ancient Arabs followed a twelve-month calendar based on a lunar cycle. The names of the months predate Islam by centuries and, according to custom, four of the months were designated truce months in which all Arab tribes agreed to a general cease-fire to allow religious pilgrimage and trade. The month of Ramadan had no special significance to the Arabs before Islam; only after Muhammad began preaching was the tradition of the annual dawn-to-dusk fast instituted.*

By about the year 610, three of his daughters were grown and married. The youngest, Fatimah, remained very attached to her father. Khadijah, who was fifteen years Muhammad's senior, was still quite robust and healthy, though she could bear no more children. Muhammad, ever the eager paternal figure, wanted to add to his household, though he wouldn't consider marrying a younger second wife. Passing by the main market in Mecca he saw a slave boy offered for sale. (Slavery was common in most of the world at that time, and people were routinely kidnapped and sold into bondage throughout the Middle East.) He liked the slave's demeanor and asked Khadijah to buy him. When they brought the boy home, Muhammad freed him and adopted him as a son. Zayd ibn Harith, as he was called, soon became known as Zayd ibn Muhammad, or Zayd, the son of Muhammad. Years later, Zayd's real father, who had searched ceaselessly for his son, eventually tracked him down in Mecca. When the father showed up at Muhammad's door and asked for his son back, Muhammad allowed Zayd, now a teenager, to either go with his real father or stay with his adopted one. The boy had grown to love Muhammad very much and explained to his biological father that he wanted to remain with Muhammad. Although Zayd's real father was saddened, he was nevertheless relieved that his son was alive and in good hands. Another addition to Muhammad's eclectic family was his nephew, 'Ali, who was one of the last of Abu Talib's children. 'Ali began staying regularly in his Uncle Muhammad's home to reduce Abu Talib's financial burden. Despite the expanding circle of family members in his house, Muhammad still felt the same occasional restlessness that directed him to go out and ponder the stars and the endless plains.

Part Two

The Coming of Prophethood

Chapter 4

From Citizen to Prophet

*And when Jesus, the son of Mary said, "O Children of
Israel, I am God's messenger to you, bringing affirmation
of the Torah before me and giving the good news of a
prophet who will come after me who shall be called the
Praised One."*

—Qur'an 61:6

The causes that lead a person to radically alter his path in life
are never easy to enumerate. Explaining the rise of important
religious figures merely by relating a few prominent incidents
would also be far too simplistic. Whether it's Moses' encounter
with the burning bush or Buddha's first tour of a town filled with
suffering, without a look into the previous life and experiences of
the individual we can never understand how and why these events
were so influential. More than a single revelatory moment, everything we know of Muhammad's upbringing and the course of his
life tells us what compelled him to seek a unique religious ideology.
Before becoming a prophet, Muhammad already possessed many of
the qualities that would serve him.

In order to understand just how different Muhammad's teachings were from traditional Arabian customs and how they were
received in Mecca, one must review the prevailing social conditions in Arabian society, which stood in clear contrast to

Muhammad's message. Human life was continually debased by such common practices as female infanticide, the torture and murder of one's enemies, slavery, the lack of women's rights, tribal warfare and rivalries, drunkenness and gambling, and a cult of idolatry with often contradictory beliefs. Muhammad's reputation as an exceptionally upright soul and the fact that this characteristic was pointed out by many of his contemporaries as setting him apart from many others shows the region's endemic lack of morals. It is no stretch of the imagination to assume that many in Arabia felt that the situation was unacceptable. The rise of the hanifs and the slow but steady conversion to Christianity of a few scattered outlying tribes (and hence its link to organized Byzantium) was a response to the barbarity found in the desert. But the heartland of Arabia, the Hijaz, remained locked in a downward spiral of selfishness and savagery.

Jews in the northern Hijaz and the Christian monks found throughout northern Arabia had long foretold that a prophet would one day rise from among the Arabs and reform them. The majority of idolatrous Arabs dismissed these predictions, but those who desired a more civilized society were a ready audience. The Jewish tribes who inhabited the northern towns of Yathrib and Khaybar were keenly interested in spreading this belief because they often had uneasy relations with the Arabs, whom they considered quite uncivilized. In addition, Judaism taught a monotheistic view of the supreme deity, which was diametrically opposed to idolatry. Small wars with neighboring Arab tribes, most notably the Khaybari's struggles with the powerful Ghatafan tribe, made the Jews hope for some sort of reformation in the peninsula.

A fair amount of literature exists on the portents and signs prior to the rise of Muhammad as a religious leader. These writings may be based more on retrospective idealism than proven facts. One can logically assume that Muhammad had no knowledge of his future significance and that premonitions and recognition of his greatness by his contemporaries were greatly exaggerated. Beyond the episode with the monk Bahira when he was twelve, which was related not only by Abu Talib but also by several of his associates and thus gains more credibility, little except the predictions of a man named Waraqah seem historically tenable. The abruptness and unexpectedness of Muhammad's rise may be simply inexplicable.

Early in the seventh century, Muhammad continued to live his quiet existence, engaging in intense meditation in his mountain redoubt. He rarely frequented the markets of Mecca, nor is he reported to have honed his poetic skills in the public forums where bards from far and wide used to entertain travelers for tips. Historians assume that by the time he neared his fortieth birthday he had all but given up his business activities and spent the lion's share of his time in solitude or with his family.

One night Muhammad's life, and human history along with it, changed forever. He had reported to his wife that he had been having strange dreams. Visions, voices, and images he couldn't quite make out plagued his sleep and troubled his mind. Khadijah reassured her husband that those dreams would bring him no harm on account of his being a moral and honest man. God would never let a just person come to peril, she noted. In time, Muhammad found that his dreams took on the form of events that had not yet occurred, small incidents and happenings that soon would come true in his waking hours. This new development influenced him to spend even more time in solitude. His cave overlooking the vast desert plain increasingly became his place of retreat.

One night in the year 610, near the end of the month of Ramadan, an intense supernatural experience happened to him. He was sitting alone, resting and dozing off, when a presence seemed to enter the cave. Muhammad awoke and was startled to see a vision of light in the form of a man standing before him, holding a scroll. "Read," the strange apparition commanded him. Muhammad, his lips trembling, honestly replied, "I can't read." The being spread his arms around Muhammad, who could not resist, and squeezed him in a numbing embrace that took the breath out of him. "Read," the being repeated. Muhammad, reeling from the embrace, protested, "But I can't read!" Again the being embraced him, tightening his hold until Muhammad's lungs felt like they were about to burst. "Read," the voice of the strange one ordered gravely. Muhammad, not wanting to undergo another crushing embrace, snapped, "What should I read?" The otherworldly being recited, in melodious

Arabic verse, "Read in the name of your lord who created humans from a clinging substance. Read for your lord is most generous. He taught people through the use of the pen that which they did not know before." (Qur'an 96:1–5)

Muhammad repeated these cryptic words several times until he had them memorized. Then, as suddenly as the being had appeared, he disappeared, leaving Muhammad in the darkness and stillness of the cave. Muhammad's mind raced in a panic, wondering what he had just witnessed. The words were real enough, and he still felt the effects of the intense pressing. Had he gone mad? He didn't know.

A view of the cave of Hira' where Muhammad received his first communication from the angel Gabriel. It is now sealed and closed to tourists.

In fear, he ran out of the cave and toward Mecca at full speed. A servant of Khadijah who was on his way to check on Muhammad just missed him. Muhammad, meanwhile, was running as fast as he could in the darkness over the rubble-strewn paths leading down from the small mountain. When he looked up, he saw the same ghostly figure, now a giant filling the cool night sky and looking down on him. The being said to him, "I am the angel Gabriel and you, Muhammad, are the messenger of God."

Khadijah, who was anxiously awaiting word from her servant about her husband's welfare, was startled abruptly when Muhammad burst in through the door and cried out, "Cover me! Cover me!" He was shivering and panic-stricken. She ushered him into bed and covered him with blankets, trying her best to console him. When he calmed down he explained to his wife what he had seen and wondered aloud if something bad was about to befall him. Khadijah comforted him by saying, "Be happy, dear cousin, for by the One who owns my soul, I hope you are the prophet of this nation. God would never humiliate you because you're good to your relatives, are honest, you aid the needy, support the weak and respond to the call of the distressed."

The mountain where Muhammad received his revelation. Today it is known as Jabal an-Nur, *or the Mountain of Light.*

Muhammad began to relax and soon fell fast asleep. As the morning rose over Mecca, Khadijah left her husband to his slumber and paid a visit to her aged cousin, Waraqah ibn Nawfal. As mentioned in Chapter 3, "Muhammad: Merchant of Mecca," Waraqah had joined a mini-rebellion years before against the idolatry of the Quraysh. He and his three fellow hanifs were all but silenced, however, so he declared himself a Christian and settled down to a quiet life of contemplation. He was forbidden to proselytize, so he used to engage in reading, writing, and some translation work. Now advanced in years and stricken with blindness, he spent much of his time in his home, venturing out only to the Ka'bah occasionally to pray with the assistance of relatives who led him there.

Khadijah told her cousin of what had happened to Muhammad. He listened intently and then exclaimed,

"Holy! Holy! Holy! By the one who has power over my soul, if you would believe me, Khadijah, the one who came to him is the Holy Spirit who used to go to Moses. He is going to be the prophet of this nation, so tell him to hold on steadfastly. He will be called a liar. He will be persecuted. He will have to fight, and if I'm alive then, God will see that I'll give a good account of myself."

Khadijah returned home with a lot on her mind and found her husband still asleep. Muhammad was sweating and shivering slightly. Suddenly he woke up and said the following words:

"You who are wrapped up in a blanket, arise and warn. Glorify your Lord and purify your clothes. Shun what is bad. Do not give with the expectation to get. For your Lord's sake persevere." (Qur'an 74:1–7)

Khadijah tried her best to convince Muhammad to lay back down, but he was adamant. He said, "No, Khadijah, the time for sleeping is over. Gabriel has ordered me to warn people and to call them to God. But whom shall I call? Who will listen to me?" Khadijah told him of her meeting with Waraqah and conveyed his advice. Then she confidently told her husband that she believed in him and accepted his message. Thus, the first convert to this new way of life that Muhammad was asked to teach was his wife, Khadijah, who trusted in him completely.

For the next several days no further revelations came, though Muhammad reported seeing the angel a few times. Khadijah began to ask her husband if he was seeing the angel at any given moment. She wanted to be told every time it came. When Muhammad said he saw the angel, Khadijah would take hold of him and sit him down and ask if he still saw it. He would reply in the affirmative. She wanted to be sure that it was an angel from God, because she couldn't see it, so she devised a unique test. One day, when Muhammad announced he was seeing the angel looking at him, Khadijah threw off her clothes and asked him if he still saw it. He answered that the angel had abruptly left. She surmised that a demon would not have cared if a person was disrobed and concluded that only a true angel from God would be disturbed by the immodesty. She had no doubts about the veracity of her husband's message thereafter.

Muhammad told no one else of what happened to him. A few days later, he happened to be walking near the Ka'bah when he saw the venerable old Waraqah sitting near it. He went to talk to him and was quickly asked about what had happened. Muhammad recounted everything, and Waraqah repeated what he had said to Khadijah. He told Muhammad that he was a prophet and that his people would oppose him. Then Waraqah drew Muhammad's forehead close and kissed it. Then he went away. (He died of natural causes a few months later.)

Muhammad pondered the old man's words. The Quraysh, given their history, were quite attached to their idols. They believed that the idols brought both wealth and protection to their city. Although Muhammad had received only two revelations thus far of a book that would soon be called the Qur'an, or the Reading, he knew that this message from the one God would have no room for idolatry. His ruminations were confirmed when he awoke in a hot sweat one morning with the following words (Qur'an 73:1–9) he saw in a dream rolling off his tongue with forceful elegance:

You who are covered in a cloak! Stand in prayer by night,
but not all of it, half of it or a little less or more. Recite
the Qur'an in slow and measured tones. Soon We will
send you an important Message. Indeed rising by night is

*the most powerful for controlling the soul, and the best for
forming words of praise. You are certainly too busy in the
day with ordinary duties, but remember the name of your
Lord and devote yourself to Him completely. He is the
Lord of the East and the West. There is no god but Him.
Take Him, then, as the One to manage your affairs.*

Muhammad excitedly told Khadijah of his new revelation, and
a feeling descended upon them both that something major would
soon happen. Each day the pair anxiously awaited their next message from the supernatural. But no more messages came, and
Muhammad had no more strange experiences. As the weeks
passed, Muhammad began to despair. He thought that perhaps
God was angry with him. He longed to feel the power of those messages flowing through his heart and mind, and he began to lose
interest in the world. He withdrew to his lonely cave on Mount
Hira' and prayed to God for some kind of sign. Once he stood on
a nearby mountain and almost threw himself off in his desperation
to come near that divine power again. Doubts crept into his mind,
and he wondered if all that had happened to him had been a
dream. Then, after six months, Muhammad saw the same angel he
had seen before, who gave him this revelation (Qur'an 93:1–11):

*By the brilliance of daybreak and the still of the night,
your Lord is with you, and is not displeased. Indeed, your
future is brighter than your past, because your Lord will
grant you [what you wish], and you will be well pleased.
Didn't He find you an orphan and care for you? Didn't
He find you lost and show you the way? And didn't He
find you poor and provide for you? Therefore, be kind to
the orphan, gentle to the poor, and declare the [mercy]
and blessings of your Lord.*

Gabriel began to appear to Muhammad more regularly after that.
He taught him how to wash ceremoniously and to pray. (The highly
ritualized form of Muslim prayer is known as *salah*, a name that literally means to make a hot connection.) There was no set number of
times to pray or specific points throughout the day to be mindful of as
of yet. A title was given to his belief system also: *Islam*, which was an
Arabic word that meant to surrender and to be contented. He taught

these things to his wife, who would join him in prayer. Muhammad also learned the most important chapter of the Qur'an, which is known as the Opening (Qur'an 1:1–7) and is found at the beginning of every copy of the Muslim holy book today. It is the Islamic equivalent of the Lord's Prayer for Christians and goes as follows:

In the Name of God, the Compassionate Source of All Mercy. Praise be to God, the Lord of the worlds; the Compassionate Source of all Mercy, and Master of the Day of Judgment. You alone do we serve and to You alone do we turn for help. Guide us in the straight way, the way of those who have earned Your favor, not the way of those who have earned Your anger, nor of those who have gone astray.

Muhammad began to make more converts, though he limited his conversations about Islam to those closest to him. Zayd, his adopted son, became a Muslim, or follower of Islam. Muhammad's four daughters, three of whom were already married and living with their husbands, believed in their father's words and joined the faith, though they kept it to themselves. Barakah accepted the message as well. Islam was almost a year old, and it had less than ten converts. The Qur'an, such as it was, consisted of less than fifty verses in the form of rhymed couplets whose contents spoke of dedication, sincerity, and one's duty to God. Nothing in the form of laws, stories, or regulations was revealed as of yet. In the beginning, the Prophet would recite them orally and his followers would memorize them. After five or six years in Mecca, he began to employ secretaries who wrote the words as he dictated them.

Muslims consider the Qur'an to be the literal word of God, transmitted to Muhammad by the angel Gabriel. It was revealed over a period of twenty-three years between the years of 610 and 632. It has 114 chapters, called surahs, *and over six thousand verses, called* ayahs. *It is not in chronological order, and it uses references to historical events, past prophets, nature, and philosophical ideas to prove its arguments. Muhammad received several hundred verses a year, usually in response to conditions that he or the Muslim community faced. The Qur'an has the feel of a collection of impassioned speeches and essays rather than a record of one man's mission.*

Two converts in this early period played a pivotal role in the Muslim community both during and after the passing of the Prophet. These converts were Abu Bakr, Muhammad's friend, and 'Ali, his nephew who was living with him at the time due to hardship in his own family's finances. 'Ali, the son of Abu Talib, had an interesting conversion experience, all the more so because he was only about ten years old when it happened. One day 'Ali happened to come home and find his Uncle Muhammad and Aunt Khadijah bowing and chanting some verses. He watched quietly and then afterwards asked them to whom they had been praying, because the family kept no idols in the home.

Muhammad answered, "We were bowing to God, who has made me a prophet and who commanded me to call people to Him." Then he invited 'Ali to join him in the new way of life and to give up the religion of the Quraysh. He then recited some verses of the Qur'an, and 'Ali was overwhelmed with their poetic beauty. He asked to have time to ask his father's permission to accept the new teachings, and rushed out. 'Ali spent the night in bed, tossing and turning, but he never spoke to his father. Instead, he went straight to Khadijah and Muhammad in the morning and said, "God created me without asking my father, Abu Talib. So why should I ask my father now to serve God?"

Muhammad's acquaintance from his teenage years, Abu Bakr, had by now become a successful businessman. He was thirty-eight years old, the head of his clan, the Banu Taym, and quite wealthy. He kept aloof from the nighttime reveries and drinking binges that took place around the Ka'bah at night and avoided the sacrificing of animals to the gods that happened frequently in town. When Muhammad approached him with the teachings of Islam, he listened carefully to them. Idols were false, Muhammad proclaimed, and God was one. Muhammad said that goodness was the way to live life and the time of the last revelation to the world had come. Abu Bakr, who had known Muhammad for years and trusted him completely, accepted Islam without hesitation. Soon he was talking to his own close associates and succeeded in making a few converts himself.

Whenever someone new wanted to become a Muslim, that person would seek out Muhammad and declare his or her profession of faith. The conversion was done fairly discreetly. Muhammad did not go public with his message for several years. During that time, dozens of small chapters of the Qur'an were revealed to him. He did not know what final shape the oral book would take, nor did he know that more than twenty years of hardship and pain lay ahead before his mission would be complete. For now he devoted his time to instructing the new Muslims in the basic teachings of the faith: monotheism, daily prayer, and moral living. This first phase of Islam was purely spiritual in nature and affected less than thirty people. Thus it went virtually unnoticed by the Meccan leadership, which was already accustomed to waves of esoteric spirituality in a city that was the focal point of religion in Arabia.

In time, people began to see that Muhammad and others associated with him were doing something new and different. A visitor to Mecca was near the Ka'bah one day talking to 'Abbas, the son of 'Abdel Muttalib, when he noticed an unusual rite being performed. It was an established tradition to circle the Ka'bah slowly and to chant to the idols in and around it, but there were no set ways to go about it. The newcomer noticed a man walking with a boy and a woman who wore a flowing robe. They walked seven times around the shrine and then stopped and started bowing and prostrating in unison. The visitor asked 'Abbas if this was some old ritual that was being resurrected, or a new fad. He replied, "That is my nephew, Muhammad, beside him is my other nephew, 'Ali, and the woman is Khadijah, the daughter of Khuwaylid and the wife of Muhammad. They are the only people on earth who worship in this odd new way."

Muhammad also developed the habit of sitting near the Ka'bah with a few people who had accepted his message and teaching them the principles of the faith. He would also help them commit to memory the ever-growing number of Qur'anic verses he was receiving all the time from Gabriel. Most of the earliest converts were from the lower classes in the city; a few were even slaves who stopped on their errands to listen.

The Meccan nobles and wealthier citizens paid little attention to Muhammad's teaching at first, for it was common for bards, poets, and wandering religious men to attract small audiences for a time and then leave. A few occasionally listened on the edge of the meeting and laughed in amusement before going on their way into the hustling crowds of merchants and religious pilgrims. It would be beneath the dignity of an upper-class citizen to sit with slaves and common folk. The Meccans assumed that Muhammad's message, whatever it was, would soon fade away like all those before it had and that he and his followers would eventually revert back to idolatry. After several months of seeing these impromptu classes, however, some of the Meccan clan leaders wanted to get a clearer picture of what Muhammad was preaching. One day they came in a group and approached Muhammad's study circle. They asked him to send the commoners and slaves away so they could sit and listen to him. He was about to comply, given that separation of the social classes was a part of Meccan custom (a culture he had grown up in), but suddenly he sat up straight and began sweating on his forehead. A moment later he recited the following verses (Qur'an 6:52–53):

> And don't drive away those who call upon their Lord morning and evening, seeking His face. You are not responsible for them and they are not for you, that you should drive them away and become wrong. Likewise we test some of them through others, so they will ask, "Has Allah favored these poor people among us?" Doesn't God know best who are thankful?

The Meccan leaders were shocked at the insult. They could not believe that commoners were being given preference over themselves. They left and told others about this perceived affront to their dignity. Soon rank-and-file tribal members began to harass Muhammad and try to break up his prayer and instructional meetings wherever they found them. The situation escalated dramatically as people began to consider Muhammad fair game for abuse. One woman soon made it her mission to throw thorns on Muhammad's doorstep and to tease him in the streets when she saw him.

After several weeks of being harassed in and around the Ka'bah, Muhammad decided to hold his meetings and group prayers in the mountains outside of town. The Muslims would undergo this hardship for three years until a man named Arqam converted and offered his spacious house as a meeting hall.

Meanwhile, Abu Bakr, who had the high status of a clan leader, began to pray openly in a small enclosure he built in his yard for that purpose. Women and children used to stop as they passed by and watch in curiosity. This behavior alarmed some Meccans, who complained that they didn't want their families to be influenced by what he was doing. He refused to alter his habit, so men who passed by were encouraged to shoo the onlookers away whenever they found them there. The underground appeal of Islam was gaining ground as Abu Bakr succeeded in converting even some of his wealthy friends. Muhammad, for his part, purposely limited his contacts, but he soon sought a wider audience.

Exactly three years after the first revelation was transmitted through the angel Gabriel, Muhammad was given the Divine command to preach to his entire clan, the Banu Hashim. So, one evening, he invited his uncles and cousins and their families to a large and sumptuous banquet. The crowd was enjoying itself and was about halfway through the meal when Muhammad stood up and began talking about God and his new teachings. One of his uncles, a man named Abu Lahab (flame father) on account of his bad temper, interrupted him and angrily told everyone to leave. Muhammad invited the clan to return the next day for lunch, saying,

> I don't know of any man among the Arabs who has
> brought you people better than what I have brought to
> you. I bring you the best in this world and the best in the
> next, so who will support me in this mission?

The guests all began shaking their heads and leaving when 'Ali stood up and declared that he would help in the mission and that he would fight anyone who opposed him. The clan members left, laughing at the boldness of the boy.

Meccans in general took issue with many points regarding Islam. Besides espousing monotheism and rejecting idolatry, which was reason enough for traditional-minded people to be uneasy, the expanding Qur'an began to present an entire array of beliefs that were foreign and unthinkable to the Arabs. One was that men and women were equal in the sight of God. For the idolatrous Arabs, females were chattel to be bought and sold, traded and used, divorced on a whim with no support, or even killed if they were infants and unwanted. Another controversial teaching was the concept of a heaven, a hell, and a judgment day. Arabs believed there was no afterlife. Equally disturbing was the notion that status was not to be determined by lineage, wealth, or accomplishments, but rather by personal piety. The following verse (Qur'an 49:13), which seems uncontroversial today, was regarded as scandalous by the Meccans:

> O Humanity, We have created you from a single male
> and a single female and made you into tribes and nations
> so you can get acquainted. In Allah's sight, the highest
> status among you is determined by the one who is the
> most devout.

Muhammad represented a threat to Mecca and its way of life that it had never encountered before, which caused otherwise upstanding citizens to behave in intolerant ways. To combat the religious chauvinism that the Muslims were feeling, new Qur'anic verses began to recount the stories of ancient prophets and their struggles with their recalcitrant communities. These verses heartened the Muslims, but the verses couldn't stem the tide of anger that was rising against them. The conflict was also a generational one: Most of the early converts were younger men and women who were easily motivated to join a new concept and idea that upset their parents. In the same way, Jesus is quoted in the Bible as saying his message would set a son against his father.

Abu Jahl, a prominent member of the Quraysh tribe, began to publicly slander and abuse Muhammad. One day he was particularly abusive, pushing, shoving, and taunting Muhammad in the street. Muhammad did not fight back but simply retreated home. When his rugged and strong Uncle Hamza returned from a hunting trip and was told about what happened, he went straight to Abu Jahl, struck him with his bow, and forced him to apologize.

Afterwards Hamza went to Muhammad and declared that he was now a Muslim as well. The fledgling Muslim association, for it was not a community yet, was overjoyed to add such an able and feared man to their ranks.

Muhammad tried again to present his message in a public forum. He ascended a small hillock that legend said was trod upon by Hagar in her search for water for her son, Ishmael, so many centuries before. He called loudly into the nearby town square, addressing each major Qurayshi clan by name. When word came that they were being called, multitudes of people came rushing to see what was happening. Muhammad called for silence and asked them if they trusted him. Many people loudly expressed their assent, for his reputation as an honest man was well known. Then he asked them if they would believe him if he told them an army was behind the hill. Some of the gathered people began shifting nervously as they agreed they would. Then he announced that his message was true and that they should listen to him for their own salvation. Abu Lahab, who was standing nearby, angrily cursed Muhammad and told him he should die. Muhammad held his tongue, because the ancient code of respect for elders was ingrained in him. Soon thereafter, a small couplet of verses was revealed to him in which Abu Lahab was told that he would be the one who was doomed.

In the court of public opinion, Muhammad and his followers seemed to be getting the best of things for a time. The Meccans defended their beliefs, but they offered little that was new to the discussion. As a result, the Muslims had a certain advantage, especially when they would approach the city's frequent visitors with their message. The Meccan leaders feared that this new religion might spread more quickly if outsiders began accepting it, so they held several meetings to decide what to do. The Meccans soon realized that they had a secret weapon. Abu Lahab, joined by the prominent Abu Sufyan, hatched a plan to take back the initiative from Muhammad. They encouraged the eloquent poets of the city to begin a propaganda war. Soon poets from every clan were coining choice phrases and reciting well-crafted verses to ridicule

Muhammad and call into doubt the veracity of his beliefs. However, Muslim converts who had skill in poetry began to construct rebuttals, and soon there were dueling poets all over the city.

Encouraged by the counterattack, Meccans began approaching Muhammad in the streets and daring him to perform miracles like the prophets of old were said to have done. He was asked to predict market prices, turn mountains into gold, make angels appear, or bring a book from heaven that could be touched. Muhammad endured these taunts, and frequent verses of the Qur'an were revealed to him as a way to rebut the many challenges. A large number of early Qur'anic verses answer specific issues brought up by people who called into doubt its authenticity. Muhammad was also quick to explain that he was only a mortal man and that the Qur'an was his miracle. This last affirmation was not without merit, because the lines Muhammad recited were difficult for people to explain. One of the features of these verses was that they were genuinely nice to listen to. The rhyme schemes were well metered, the content was impassioned and appealing, and the utter newness of the concepts seemed geared towards firing people's imaginations. Another puzzling factor for the Quraysh to consider was that Muhammad had not been a poet before, and his sudden eloquence and verbosity was inexplicable. (Some clan leaders even began sitting outside Muhammad's window at night to hear him reciting his verses, until they shamed each other into stopping.) Some Meccans postulated that Muhammad had been possessed by a jinn, an evil spirit. Others accused him of learning his new beliefs from a teenage Byzantine slave working as a blacksmith. The two had been seen talking occasionally, but the Qur'an noted that the boy couldn't even speak fluent Arabic and the verses of the Qur'an were highly sophisticated.

The Qur'an then laid out the challenge to the poets of the Quraysh to try and duplicate the style and content of just one chapter of the Qur'an. After repeated attempts, no poet succeeded, coming up instead with poor copies patterned after their traditional modes of poetry, which centered on glorifying heroes or insulting other tribes. These frustrated poets did resort to another tactic, however. Whenever a new caravan came into town,

Muhammad's habit was to go out and greet it and ask permission to speak to its attendants about Islam. Now groups of rabble-rousers would follow behind Muhammad shouting at the top of their lungs that the man was mad and that no one should listen to him. Passions ran high in these encounters, and the weary merchants entering Mecca's precincts undoubtedly wanted nothing to do with anyone in this tiresome procession. The poets could not be everywhere, however, and news of Muhammad's teachings eventually began to filter into the countryside and from there into the rest of the Hijaz.

Muhammad continued to declare that the idols were false, but few of his followers were so publicly brave. By now, to speak against idolatry near the Ka'bah was to invite an assault. One bold newcomer who had specifically come to Mecca to accept Islam was Abu Dharr from the outlying Ghifar tribe. After he met with Muhammad and declared his belief by saying, "I declare that there is no god but God and that Muhammad is the messenger of God," he decided to go to the Ka'bah in midday and announce his faith to all gathered there. Muhammad counseled against it, fearing that an outsider with no local connections might get himself killed, but Abu Dharr insisted. He walked right up to a large group of Meccans and exclaimed that he was a Muslim. One of the men shouted, "Go get the one who left his religion!" and they set upon him, beating him. They would have killed him had not one of the elder clan leaders warned them that the Ghifar tribe might harass their caravans. When asked later why he was so adamant about his seemingly reckless course of action, Abu Dharr simply replied, "It was a need I felt in my soul, and I fulfilled it." Apparently he wanted to test his resolve in the face of determined opposition.

Muhammad himself, although the victim of verbal assaults, slander, and the occasional shove in the street, was at the same time protected to a certain degree by his family ties with Abu Talib. Although his uncle did not convert, he continued to extend to his nephew the immunity traditionally due to a member of a large clan. A member of a tribe was protected by every other member, and the same held true for clans. If one member was attacked or killed, the rest were duty bound to avenge their fallen comrade.

Chapter 5

The Unwelcome Prophet

*Perhaps you will kill yourself from grief, following after
them pleading because they aren't believing in these words.*
—*Qur'an 18:6*

The clan elders of the Quraysh now thought of Muhammad,
who had once been considered merely a religious oddity, as a
serious threat. Where once he would have been mentioned with
simple derision in their collective meetings around the Ka'bah or
in their great hall, *Darul Nadwah*, open hostility was now heaped
upon him and his cause. Suggestions for dealing with the problem,
however, were always limited by longstanding tribal customs.
Outright murder or banishment were out of the question. The last
thing the fractious Quraysh needed was an intertribal war.

The energetic Prophet, for his part, was actively engaged in
preaching his message to anyone who would listen. Given the city
leadership's opposition, however, he made few converts. The clan
elders issued orders to their compatriots forbidding them to join
Muhammad's religion. The Quraysh threatened that anyone who
converted to Islam would find their future dark and their lives mis-
erable. Muhammad was finding more rejection than acceptance.
No longer could he walk the streets and enjoy the hustle and bus-
tle of his hometown. Gone was the respect he engendered when
people spoke of him and the easy life of a settled merchant. He had

become a religious rebel, and he and his followers bore the brunt of the public's anger.

The name Islam comes from the Qur'an itself. This word has a dual meaning: surrender and peace. The religious implication is that when people surrender their will to Allah and adopt a godly lifestyle, they no longer have a reason to fear life or death and thus achieve a state of peacefulness in their soul. Mohammadanism is not a proper name for this religion; it implies that Muslims worship Muhammad, and they don't. The term Muslim means a follower of Islam.

Muhammad sometimes became frustrated and depressed, and numerous Qur'anic verses addressed to him tell him to persevere, that things would get better. Other passages mention specific incidents or policies of the Quraysh that hurt Muslim morale and provide reassurance that God is on the Muslims' side. Some days no Muslim could get his message across to another as evidenced by the following highlight on Meccan behavior: "The concealers [of God's truth] say, 'Don't listen to the Qur'an, but talk loudly when it's being recited so you can gain the upper hand.'" (Qur'an 41:26)

This battle of wills caused Muhammad a great deal of mental stress. Imagine being ostracized by so many once-friendly peers and even close relatives. The stress began to take a toll on Muhammad's health, and he often complained to his wife of an aching weight that he seemed to feel on his shoulders. The pressure to form a religious identity from scratch among his followers also added to his sense of weariness. Islam was beginning to touch on many areas of life: religious devotion, neighborly conduct, morals, manners, and even personal hygiene. While Muhammad labored to change the habits of others, though, the Qur'an was also seeking to change him.

This facet of the development of Islam, the alteration of Muhammad's adherence to cultural habits and customs, is best illustrated by an episode when a prominent clan leader agreed to listen to what Muhammad had to say. The Prophet eagerly began to explain the tenets of Islam, and the noble listened casually. Just then, an old blind man, who had previously converted, heard Muhammad speaking and shuffled over in his direction. When he reached Muhammad's side, he began interrupting and asking for more information about his new way of life. He was insistent, and this annoyed the Prophet, who felt he was on the brink of making a breakthrough with a very important person. In addition, Arab tribal custom dictated a certain deference toward influential nobles over mere commoners. Muhammad frowned and turned his back on the blind man and continued to address the noble, who soon lost interest and left. On the way home, he felt ashamed at how he treated the old man and a new revelation came to him (Qur'an 80:1–12):

> [Muhammad] frowned and turned away when the blind
> man came. Who would have thought? Maybe he might
> have become a better man or remembered something that
> would have helped him. As for the one who was indiffer-
> ent, to him you gave your full attention, even though you
> weren't responsible for his salvation; as for the one who
> came rushing to you eagerly, you ignored him. But no, this
> book is a reminder, so remind whoever really wants it.

This episode provides an excellent example of how the revelation of the Qur'an was often in lockstep with issues that affected Muhammad or his fledgling cadre of followers. In general, the shortest chapters of the Qur'an were those revealed during what is called the Meccan Period, which lasted from the years 610 to 622, the first thirteen years of Muhammad's mission. These verses provide a snapshot into the daily life and struggles of the first Muslim collective. Many charges that the idolaters made are repeated in the Qur'an almost verbatim before a rebuttal is given. References to specific individuals and their situations as well as suggested solutions abound. Muslims believe this interactive nature of the Qur'an provides guidance for their lives right up to this day.

The first Muslims intrepreted the fact that Muhammad was receiving such guidance as a sign of God's favor. The Quraysh, on the other hand, felt that the Qur'an was talking as much against them as for the new belief system. Although the charge that Muhammad was insane or possessed was made less frequently, the Quraysh still found it more and more difficult to come up with an alternative to Muhammad's logic. One particularly difficult aspect of the Qur'an's challenge came when the Quraysh were dared to ask their idols for help even though the idols could not see, hear, speak, or even protect themselves. The argument contained in the following passage (Qur'an 7:194–198) is typical:

> Truly, those whom you call upon besides God are created servants like you. Call upon them and let them hear your prayer if what you claim is true. Do the idols have feet to walk with, or eyes to see with, or ears to hear with? Declare to them, "Call your god-partners. Scheme your worst against me and don't give me any chance. Because my Protector is God, Who revealed the Book and He will choose and help the righteous. But those you call upon besides Him can't help you, nor can they help themselves. If you call on them for guidance, they don't hear. You will see them looking at you, but they don't see anything."

The ever-growing Muslim underground, which now included more than forty members, was also reciting the fabled story of Abraham and how he smashed the helpless idols of his people when they were away. Idol worship was made to look foolish in Mecca. After repeated provocation, the clan leaders went to Abu Talib, now head of the Banu Hashim clan, to ask him to intervene. One of them said, "Abu Talib, your nephew is blaspheming our gods, attacking our religion, ridiculing our ideas, and condemning our ancestors for disbelief. You must either stop him or at least relinquish your protection of him. Our religion, which he attacks, is your religion also. Why don't you let us take care of him?" Abu Talib knew what the clan leaders meant by that last request. They wanted to kill his nephew. Perhaps mindful of his promise to his own father to care for Muhammad, Abu Talib politely explained that he would continue to extend his clan's protection to him.

Muhammad was safe from those outside his clan for the moment, but those within the clan were another matter. Muhammad's uncle, Abu Lahab, continued to abuse him and vandalize his house. At one point the Prophet arranged for a guard to stand outside his door, though he later canceled this service after a verse from the Qur'an told him that God would protect him. Most of his followers, however, were poor and had few tribal protections. The ones who suffered the worst violence were the slaves who converted without their master's permission. (In Arabia, a slave often followed the religion of his master.) One Meccan slave owner had a black slave named Bilal. When he found out that his slave had converted to Islam, he angrily had him whipped and ordered him to recant. Bilal stubbornly refused. Thereafter, the enraged owner turned his slave over to a gang of youths who took him out into the desert and beat him mercilessly. On more than one occasion they forced him to wear metal armor plates and tied him down under the sun. The worst of it, however, was when his owner ordered him to be crushed under heavy stones. Abu Bakr, who happened to be passing by one day, saw the broken man being tortured, all the while whispering, "He is One. He is One." Abu Bakr immediately sought out Bilal's owner and offered to buy his slave. At first hesitant, the cruel master finally agreed. Abu Bakr granted Bilal his freedom and soon began to buy the freedom of other persecuted slaves, both men and women.

> *Islam, like Christianity and Judaism, accepted the existence of slavery. It also tried to regulate the practice and make it humane. Before Islam, slavery in Arabia was practiced similarly to slavery in America: slaves were property to be used at will. Islam created many regulations that make slavery something of a burden on the owners. Only captured enemies can be enslaved, as punishment. Muslims must feed, shelter, and clothe a slave as they do themselves. They cannot overwork them, prevent them from marrying, or stop them from having outside work in their off time. A slave has the right to demand a contract of manumission whereby the slave may buy his or her freedom. If an owner slaps or hits a slave, Islamic law says the slave is automatically to be freed. Finally, the Qur'an declares that freeing a slave is a meritorious act that will earn the favor of God. Is it any wonder so many slaves in Mecca began converting to Islam?*

The leaders of the Quraysh, alarmed at the appeal of Islam among their slaves and others, especially because Muhammad was preaching that slaves were equal to their masters, decided to try again to reason with Abu Talib. This time they went to his house with an able-bodied young man named 'Umarah and offered to give him to the old man to be his adopted son in exchange for Muhammad. Abu Talib refused the request sharply.

Undaunted, the elders tried a third and final time. This time they issued an ultimatum: Stop Muhammad, or we will fight him and you. Abu Talib, not wanting to bring turmoil on his clan, called Muhammad into a private meeting and said, "Save me as well as yourself. Don't give me a burden that is too much for me to bear." Muhammad, who was fond of his uncle but resolute in his mission, politely answered, "Uncle, by God, if they put the sun in my right hand and the moon in my left and ordered me to give up this cause, I would never do it until either God has vindicated me or I perish in the attempt." When the answer was conveyed to the clan leaders, they ordered their fellow tribesmen to redouble their efforts persecuting the Muslims. Abu Talib, for his part, told Muhammad that he would protect him no matter what Muhammad preached. He then called the clans of Banu Hashim and Banu 'Abdel Muttalib together and made them swear an oath to protect Muhammad.

Islam had now gone far beyond what any hanif ever called for. Although Arabian society more or less accommodated every religious persuasion, this new faith taught that truth was absolute and that there was no validity to beliefs that contradicted it—which is not an uncommon sentiment in most world religions. Not that Islam was asking for forced conversion, as evidenced by verses such as this one, which said, "To you your way of life and to me mine." On the contrary, the Qur'an charged that the Quraysh were denying the Muslims freedom of religion, which in itself was proof of their unfitness to rule.

Muhammad had been preaching for almost ten years, and still people could not freely convert without harassment from their clans and families, nor were Muslims able to meet or pray openly. Moving among different secret locations or meeting in the dead of night was the only way Muhammad and his followers could hold classes and discuss the events of the day. During this difficult time, the Prophet relied heavily on Khadijah for her moral support and strength. In addition, Muhammad's youngest daughter, Fatimah, played an increasingly important role in her father's life. Muhammad still ventured out to the Ka'bah to pray publicly, and sometimes he took his daughter with him. Once Abu Lahab threw the entrails of a recently sacrificed goat on his back, and Fatimah cleaned the mess off, weeping. She became his constant companion. Barakah, too, played a part; she had left for Yathrib several years before at Muhammad's urging to get married, but she returned to Mecca after her husband's death. She bravely carried secret messages back and forth between Khadijah and Muhammad.

Being a Muslim in Mecca at this time was clearly dangerous, but throughout all of the persecution, Muhammad never allowed his followers to fight back. Patience and perseverance were common Qur'anic themes during the late Meccan Period. Chapter 18 of the Qur'an, in particular, contains the Islamic version of the famous story of the Sleepers of the Cave, Christian youths who escaped execution at the hands of a Roman emperor by going into deep hibernation in a cave until the policies of Rome were more favorable to their religion. The message to the Muslims was that things would eventually get better.

A conciliatory Arab leader named 'Utbah approached Muhammad with a stunning offer from the Quraysh. If he would stop preaching his religion, or at the very least make an accommodation for idolatry, then the Meccans would give him whatever compensation he wished: money, the title of king of Mecca, or the medical attentions of a shaman or spirit medium to cure him of his visions. In response, Muhammad recited Chapter 32 of the Qur'an, which is an impassioned essay outlining the truth of monotheism, God's purpose for making creation, and the methodology whereby he chooses prophets to convey his message of salvation. 'Utbah was spellbound by the eloquence and, satisfied that Muhammad wasn't crazy at all, returned to the Meccan leaders and told them they should leave Muhammad alone.

Not surprisingly, the elders didn't appreciate 'Utbah's change of heart. Their policy of fomenting the persecution of Muslims took on a decidedly deadlier tone. Clan members were encouraged to beat any member of their tribe who converted to Islam. Muslims were tortured, starved, left to die on the hot desert sands, and murdered. One family that converted, two parents and a son, was set upon by their tribe, and the mother was beaten to death. A young slave who worked in a smithy was burnt with a hot poker by his mistress. One man continually beat a slave girl who had converted until his arm became weary. Muhammad was powerless to stop the abuse that his followers suffered and used to pray for deliverance and the salvation of those who underwent persecution for their belief in the one God.

The answer came from across the Red Sea in the land of Abyssinia, where a Christian king with the title of Negus ruled with a fair and just hand. Muhammad counseled the more vulnerable members of his flock to secretly emigrate and reside in that kingdom for a time until the situation improved in Mecca. In about the year 616, fifteen men and women slipped quietly out of Mecca and went to the western coast of Arabia. From there they sailed to Abyssinia, that ancient bastion of Christianity in Africa whose religious traditions could be traced back to the time of the apostles. Upon their arrival, the Muslims petitioned the Negus, and he graciously agreed to allow them to remain as guests in his realm. They lived peacefully there for three months, until word came from Mecca through travelling merchants that the conversion of a high-ranking noble had improved the Muslims' situation. Overjoyed, the small group headed home, but they found that things were not at all as they had expected. Conditions for Muslims had deteriorated dangerously. Murders of converts to Islam were on the rise, and public harassment and humiliation of Muslims had increased as well. Muhammad then decided to send an even larger contingent of refugees back to Abyssinia under the leadership of his Uncle Ja'far. In a well-coordinated operation, eighty men and their families crept secretly out of Mecca after dark and headed for the coast. The Quraysh noticed their absence too late to stop them, and the Quraysh became even more concerned when they found out where the Muslims had gone. The last thing the Quraysh wanted was to have Muslims living out of their reach and possibly tampering with their foreign alliances. However, the Quraysh had always enjoyed good relations with the Negus and considered him a facilitator of trade in Africa. Consequently, they felt sure that they could do something about the situation if they acted quickly enough.

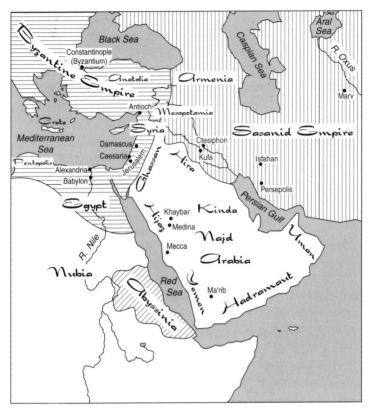

A map of Arabia showing the nearby political arena.

Some weeks later two of the more eloquent members of the Meccan nobility, 'Amr ibn al-'As and 'Abdullah ibn Abu Rabi'ah, were sent to Abyssinia. When they arrived, they offered expensive gifts to some of the Negus's government officials and were able to secure the right to arrest and forcefully return the Muslims to Mecca. After the Negus heard about the situation, however, he refused to allow it. He had a policy of giving people a fair hearing and thus asked to hear the Muslims' argument. On the day of the meeting, the Meccan ambassadors told the Negus,

> *Great King, some rabble from our land has come to your*
> *country. They have left the religion of their ancestors and*

yet have not entered into your religion either. They follow
a new religion unknown to both us and you, which they
made up themselves. We have been sent by their peers,
their uncles and their fathers and their leaders who know
them best, to ask for their return. Their elders at home
are better judges of the differences between them. We beg
that they be handed over to our custody.

Representatives of the Muslim refugees were brought forward.
The Negus asked them, "What is this new religion which has
caused you to separate yourselves from your people, a religion that
is different from mine as well as from any other known religion?"
The Muslim spokesman, Ja'far, the son of Abu Talib, rose to his
feet and answered,

Great King, we were in a state of ignorance and immoral-
ity, worshipping idols, eating dead animals we found, and
engaging in all sorts of wickedness. We didn't honor our
relatives nor did we assist our neighbors, and the strong
among us exploited the weak. Then God sent us a prophet, one of our own people, whose lineage, honesty, and
loyalty are well known. He called us to worship God
alone and to reject the idols and sacred stones our fathers
had worshipped. He commanded us to be true to our
word, to return a trust to its owner, to be kind to our relatives and neighbors, and to stop sin and bloodshed. He
forbids us to engage in fornication, lying, and false witness. He ordered us not to rob orphans or to falsely
accuse a married woman of infidelity. He ordered us to
serve only God and to never hold another equal with him,
to establish prayer, to fast, and to give in charity. We
believed in him and what he brought us from God and followed him in what he told us to do and in what he told us
not to do.

Perhaps the representatives of the Quraysh felt a little uneasy
when Ja'far turned his attention to how Mecca treated this new,
seemingly reasonable religion. He continued,

Our people have tried to sway us from our religion and
persecuted us. They have inflicted on us terrible suffering

*in an effort to get us to return to the evil ways of our
ancestors. Because they crushed and assailed us unjustly
and made life unbearable for us in Mecca, we have chosen your country and came here to live hoping that in
your land we would not be wronged.*

The Negus listened thoughtfully and then curiously asked to
hear some of what the new prophet in Arabia was receiving from
God. J'afar recited verses 29 through 33 from Chapter 19 of the
Qur'an, ostensibly titled the Chapter of Mary:

*So she pointed to him and they asked, "How can we
speak to a baby that belongs in a cradle?" The infant
Jesus spoke miraculously and said, "I am the servant of
God. He gave me the Book and made me a prophet. He
blessed me wherever I will be and made prayer and charity my way of life so long as I live. He has made me kind
to my mother and not overbearing. Peace will be on me
the day that I was born, the day that I die, and the day I
am raised again to life."*

The Negus and his advisors, all deeply religious men, exclaimed
in astonishment that the message they heard sounded pleasantly
close to what they believed. The chief patriarch said, "These words
must have sprung from the same fountainhead from which the
words of our Lord Jesus Christ have sprung." The Negus went even
further in proclaiming, "What you have recited and the revelation
of Moses must have come from the same source. Go out into my
kingdom. I will not have you extradited."

Seeing the Quraysh case crumble, the quick-thinking 'Amr
sought to draw a wedge between the Muslims and their newfound
sympathizers. "Great King, there is another side to the Muslim
belief about Jesus by which they judge the Son of Mary in different
and disrespectful ways." The Negus asked the Muslims to clarify
this issue, because faith in Jesus was the cornerstone of the kingdom. Ja'far answered again, "Our judgment about Jesus is what has
been revealed to our prophet. Jesus is a servant of God, his prophet,
a spirit sent from him and his word upon Mary, the innocent virgin." The Negus arose from his throne, stepped forward and traced
a line with his staff on the floor in front of him. "Between us and

you," he said, "the difference is no more than the thickness of this line." The Negus was convinced that Christianity had more in common with Islam than idolatry and sent the Quraysh ambassadors back empty-handed. In time, the Negus converted to Islam at the direct invitation of a letter from Muhammad.

Islam teaches that Jesus was a prophet of God, even labeling him a word from God—not a word in the Christian sense but a command for him to come into existence. His virgin birth is affirmed in the Qur'an, and his message to call the lost children of Israel back to God is highlighted. Islam diverges from Christianity, however, over the nature of Jesus and his ultimate disappearance from this world. Jesus, according to Muhammad, was not a god, nor a son of God, nor a part of a trinity with God. In addition, Muslims believe that Jesus did not die on the cross, lie dead for three days, or rise from the grave. Nor, according to Islam, did Jesus' death atone for the sin of Adam inherent in all people. Muhammad taught that Jesus escaped from his captors and that God took him supernaturally into heaven to await a triumphant return in the End Times. He will announce then that he is a follower of Islam before going on to defeat the anti-Christ. He will live for forty more years on earth and then will die a natural death and go back to heaven.

'Umar ibn al-Khattab, a strong, willful Meccan who had made life especially intolerable for Muslims through abuse and torture, decided to kill Muhammad outright after another inconclusive meeting with Quraysh leaders on confronting the new religion. He marched angrily through the streets of Mecca with his sword drawn and would have made it to Muhammad's door had he not been diverted by a friend who pointed out that 'Umar's own sister and her husband had converted.

'Umar stalked off in the direction of his sister's house and burst through the door. He found his sister and her husband reading a written copy of one chapter of the Qur'an and began to beat his brother-in-law. He swung his fists so wildly that he accidentally struck his sister when she tried to intervene, bloodying her face. He froze for a moment and suddenly felt guilty. Calmer now, he asked to see the paper they had been reading. His sister made him wash his hands first. After perusing the lines from Chapter *Ta Ha* of the Qur'an and letting his guard fall enough to consider the import of the words, 'Umar exclaimed that this must be the word of God. He asked to be taken to Muhammad and converted to Islam by him—just an hour after wanting to go to his house and kill him.

Losing one of their stronger members to the other side didn't sit well with the Meccan nobles, whose power was dissolving with each conversion. 'Umar, whose martial prowess was well known, boldly led a group of Muslims out of their secret prayer hall and proceeded to offer congregational prayers with them right next to the Ka'bah. (It was this news that reached the immigrants in Abyssinia and gave them a false sense of the safety of returning.) Even more alarming than their internal weakness was the fact that the season for the annual pilgrimage to Mecca was fast approaching, and Muhammad had made no secret of his plan this year to address the throngs of visiting pilgrims and to call them to his religion. The Muslims had been contained locally, but with the rising tide of conversions (a small but steady trickle of people from every clan and tribe were joining the new faith), the Meccans' options were dwindling.

Indeed, additions to the Muslim bloc were still common, despite the Meccan persecution. The message of the Qur'an was captivating to a people steeped in the rhythms of emotive verse. At the same time, the Qur'an's logical arguments against idol-worship, and its promise of salvation in an afterlife were appealing in a land where deprivation made most people desire something more ethereal. The Qur'an presented its message in captivating Arabic eloquence.

People of Faith, give (in charity) out of what We've given to you, before the day comes when no bargaining will be accepted, when no friendship nor intercession will matter, when the rejecters (of truth) will finally realize that their corruption was great.

God! There is no god but He, the Living, Who needs no other but whom all others need. He is never drowsy nor does He rest. To Him belongs space and the Earth; who can intercede without His consent? He knows everything people have done and will do, and no one can grasp

*the least of His knowledge, without His review. His
throne extends over space and the Earth and He doesn't
tire in their safekeeping. He alone is the Most High, the
Lord Sovereign Supreme. There is no forcing anyone into
this lifestyle. The truth stands clear from falsehood.
Anyone who rejects wrongdoing and believes in God has
grasped a firm handhold that never breaks, because God
hears and knows everything. To those who believe, God is
a friend who will lead them out of darkness into radiant
light. To those who cover up (the truth), Satan is a (false)
friend who will lead them out of light into murky darkness.
They will be the Companions of Hell, and that's where
they'll stay.*

(Qur'an 2:254–257)

Fearful that Muhammad would gain outside support and mindful of their inability to murder most Muslims outright due to their
tribal ties, the Quraysh renewed their propaganda war. Walid al-
Mughira suggested that they should say that Muhammad was a sorcerer whose words bewitched people and made them abandon the
religion of their forefathers and that his message caused division
within families because sons and daughters rebelled against the
ways of their parents. Any visitor from the countryside could readily note the divisions within the once-united Meccan polity and
would take fair warning that Islam would only bring trouble. The
Quraysh would suggest that by clinging more tightly to tradition,
visitors could better preserve their wealth and safety. If visitors
harkened to Muhammad, he would bewitch them, divide them,
and bring ruin to their reputations.

How effective was this propaganda campaign at keeping visitors
away from Muhammad? At-Tufayl al-Dawsi was a tribal chieftain
from a distant territory as well as an accomplished poet who came
to Mecca for business. After being told by a Meccan on the road to
beware of the sorcerer named Muhammad, At-Tufayl was guarded
when he saw the Prophet sitting by a small hill a block away from
the Ka'bah with a crowd gathered around him. At-Tufayl would
have avoided him altogether, yet he felt ashamed at his cowardli-
ness. He resolved to go and listen, and after standing on the edge

of the crowd, he found that he liked what he heard. He followed Muhammad to his house and converted after exclaiming that the Qur'an was better than any poetry he had ever encountered.

Christians began to disregard the Quraysh's frantic fear-mongering as well. A delegation of twenty men from the Christian territory of Najran was sent by their people to investigate Muhammad. The men sat with him and listened to what he had to say. After several hours of dialogue, each and every man converted to Islam. The tribesmen of the Quraysh were furious. They scolded the men as they left, saying, "May God humiliate you, you shameful delegation. Your people sent you to get news of this man, but no sooner did you sit with him than you abandoned your religion and believed him!"

The Quraysh then sent messengers to the Jewish settlement of Khaybar, a fortress town far to the north renowned for its orchards and commitment to Judaism. They wanted to know how to combat a religion that taught that idolatry and superstition were wrong, and they figured who better to ask than people who believed similarly. They asked that a Jewish delegation be sent to Mecca to ask Muhammad religious questions that no Arab would have the answer to, given that most Arabs had never studied any Jewish religious writings. When the Jews arrived in Mecca and questioned the Prophet, they found that he had the uncanny ability to give straight answers to complicated questions on ancient prophets, the nature of God, and righteousness.

Realizing that their propaganda war was ineffective, the Quraysh angrily chose a new and unprecedented course of action. In the year 617, they decided to gather their warriors and forcibly eject the two clans of Banu Hashim and Banu 'Abdel Muttalib, from which most converts came, and drive them into a barren, enclosed valley just outside the city. The scene was chaotic as roving bands of armed men descended on every house belonging to these clans, rousted its inhabitants into the street, and herded them past crowds of shouting and jeering mobs. With barely the clothes on their backs and few supplies, several hundred men, women, and children were cast into the harsh desert, Muhammad among them. Abu Lahab even forced his two sons to divorce their wives, Muhammad's daughters, as a way to humiliate him.

This event became known as the Boycott and was the greatest trial the Muslims faced. Its purpose was to starve the two clans into lifting their protection of Muhammad so the rest of the Quraysh's clans could murder him without blame. Not all of the members of the two exiled clans had become Muslims, so the collective punishment was designed to cause division in the clans as well. The Boycott was a total economic, social, and political blow. During the day the sun would bake the outcasts, and the chill at night would freeze them. Sympathetic Meccans who disagreed with this drastic action began to smuggle food and supplies to the exiled clans so that they could at least establish a makeshift tent city. The situation was still desperate, however, because the Meccans forbade anyone from trading with the exiles, intermarrying with them, sheltering them, or supplying them. The Quraysh wrote their proclamation on vellum and hung it inside the Ka'bah as a sign of their resolve. With the blessings of the gods, no man could ever question the policy again.

As the weeks turned into months and the months into years, the pitiable state of the people in the valley deteriorated exponentially. The children were malnourished, the elderly grew sick and frail, and the rest went hungry almost daily. Muhammad showed his organizational abilities, however, by setting up a system of food distribution and religious instruction. Without outside interference, his message was reaching more people from his clans, and more people were converting.

For a few days each year, Muhammad quietly left the valley and entered Mecca during the annual religious pilgrimage that brought idolaters from all over Arabia to worship and trade. These were truce months when every tribe was expected, by custom, to suspend blood feuds and banditry to allow for the free passage of travelers. Muhammad would address the crowds and call their attention to his message and to what the Quraysh were doing to his clan and followers. Within a short time the cruelty of the Quraysh was known far and wide, and even some members of Meccan society were disgusted at the inhumane Boycott. One man used to load camels with food and take them to the entrance of the valley at night and whip them into running into the valley. The Quraysh themselves soon became divided about their course of action.

One man named Hisham ibn 'Amr couldn't hold his tongue any longer. He went to his friend Zuhayr and told him, "Are you content to eat and marry while your uncles are starving in the mountains? If they were my uncles, I wouldn't let this injustice stand." The two men then agreed to work against the hard-hearted leadership of the Quraysh. Soon the small group grew to five members and hatched a plan to publicly confront the Quraysh.

One day Zuhayr stood near the Ka'bah and challenged the crowds to consider what they were doing to their relatives. When Abu Jahl heard the call, he rushed towards the center of the throng and shouted, "Never will it be broken!" On cue, Zuhayr's four compatriots angrily began calling for the lifting of the Boycott, and soon the masses in the courtyard of the Ka'bah began echoing the call. Abu Jahl, realizing that the matter was decided for him, said no more. When the men opened the doors of the Ka'bah and went inside to tear up the proclamation, they found that white ants had eaten away at the vellum. All that remained was the top portion that said, "In Your Name, God."

After three years, the Boycott was over. The clans of Banu Hashim and Banu 'Abdel Muttalib left the barren valley and returned to their homes inside the city. They were pitiful to behold, with gaunt faces and ragged clothes. Abu Talib, an old man in his eighties, was so frail that he quickly began to deteriorate. The Quraysh wanted the issue resolved between them and Muhammad before the venerable elder died and called a meeting in Abu Talib's house. The clan leaders addressed Abu Talib, who lay on his deathbed:

> *Abu Talib, we hold you in great respect and appreciate your counsel and wisdom. Now that you are about to leave us, and knowing the discord that has ensued between us and your nephew, please call him and ask him to ... leave us alone and we will leave him alone, that he will leave us to practice our religion and we shall leave him to practice his.*

Muhammad arrived shortly afterwards with a few followers, who became known as *sahaba*, or companions, and answered the elders by stating, "Truly, all I ask is one word, one word that you will give me. With it you will dominate the Arabs and have ascendance over all foreign nations." Abu Jahl sarcastically chided, "Ten words, not just one. Ask all you want." Muhammad ignored the remark and went on, "Say, 'God is One,' and then stop worshipping idols." One of the elders asked, "Do you want us to make all the gods into one?" Then the clan leaders decided against further reasoning with Muhammad and left.

As the days passed, Abu Talib's condition worsened. As he lay near death, Muhammad desired to visit his beloved protector and try one last time to convince him to convert to Islam. Unfortunately he found some of the prominent men of the Quraysh already there. He ignored them and begged his uncle to say, "God is One," so that he could ask God to forgive him. Abu Talib, a man of tradition and too accustomed to the old ways, politely refused his nephew, whom he had protected from the Quraysh for ten hard years. He explained, "If I wasn't afraid that the women of the Quraysh would say I said it out of fear of death, I would say it to please you."

Abu Jahl suddenly said, "No, no, the religion of 'Abdel Muttalib." Upon hearing the name of his father mentioned, Abu Talib stiffened in his resolve to remain true to his traditional beliefs. Muhammad continued to plead desperately, for he wanted salvation for his uncle, but every time it seemed his uncle would acquiesce, Abu Jahl and his friends would remind Abu Talib of his father's name. Finally Abu Talib said, "I never want it to be said that Abu Talib abandoned the ways of his ancestors." Muhammad left in sorrow, though a new revelation (Qur'an 28:56) came to him that stated: "You cannot guide all of those whom you love. God guides whom he wills and he knows best those who are guided."

Abu Talib, Muhammad's gallant protector, passed away a few days later, and his death would have a profound effect on Muhammad's next move. With no one standing in the way of the Quraysh, Muhammad's very life was at stake.

Chapter 6

Finding a Home for Islam

This is indeed the word of an honored Messenger. It's not the versifying of a poet—how little you believe! Nor is this the word of a fortune-teller—how few warnings you take!
—Qur'an 69:38–40

Muhammad had now lost his clan protector and beloved uncle, Abu Talib, who had taken him in as a child and shielded him from the full wrath of the tribe of Quraysh. This loss did not bode well for his personal safety, because he was much more than merely a reviled religious figure in the minds of the Meccan leadership. His beliefs about monotheism and personal accountability for one's actions in an afterlife were diametrically opposed to the city's foundation as the center of Arab idolatry. The very lifeblood of the city, as its elders understood it, was predicated on their status as the guardians of the holy shrine and its attendant idols representing every tribe. Anyone who would undermine such an arrangement and, further, still seek to impose rigid moral regulations on an otherwise unrestrained culture had to be stopped. Abu Talib had kept him safe from real harm until now. Ironically, even though Muhammad had frequently derided such tribal solidarity, preferring religious brotherhood, he had always depended on the system of mutual clan protection to allow him to preach in the face of determined opposition. With that protection gone, he soon would share the fate of many in his fledgling community as a constant victim of hate crimes.

Muhammad had always been able to count on his stable home as a source of comfort and sanctuary. In addition to his wife, Khadijah, and his youngest daughter, Fatimah, he had also taken in two of his older daughters who had been cruelly divorced by their husbands just before the Boycott. His house was full of the kind of life and love that surrounds families who pull together in times of crisis. Khadijah remained Muhammad's biggest source of solace. She had given him a job in his youth when he had none, had married him though he was poor and without status, had turned over all her money to him so he could engage in philanthropy, and was the first who affirmed him as a prophet and convinced him he wasn't mad. Although she was fifteen years his senior, she bore him six children as well. However, the years of acute deprivation during the Boycott had taken its toll on her health, and she began to suffer from illness just a few months after Abu Talib died. Muhammad was distraught and often lingered by her bed, comforting and caring for her. She did not recover, however, and the day she died was forever after known to Muhammad as the beginning of his year of sorrow.

As a small child, Muhammad had lost the three people who were closest to him: his father, whom he never met; his mother; and his grandfather, only a few years later. Now he had lost his supportive uncle and his loving wife in the same year! Although his mission and the encouragement and sympathy of his followers helped him manage the pain, sadness tinged his speech for a long while. He was barely able to comfort his grieving daughters by saying that Gabriel had told him Khadijah would be in paradise. His youngest child, Fatimah, began to care for and dote on her father, and in time she earned the nickname "the Mother of her Father." Their closeness is legendary among Muslims to this day.

Meanwhile, the Quraysh were sizing up the new reality in Mecca and were preparing for an even more concerted campaign against Muhammad and his religion. They became much more aggressive and cruelly taunted Muhammad about his recent losses. Even well-connected Muslim men and women became fair game for jeering mobs and callous vandalism if their conversion became known. Members of a rival clan once set upon Abu Bakr and a close associate, beating them and leaving them tied up by the side of a road. No one from his own clan intervened to help him, suggesting that they had all but disowned him, reviled as he was for making many converts to Islam. The ancient system of clan loyalty began to loosen as the clans tacitly let their Muslim members be attacked with no calls for revenge.

The major teachings of Islam, as it existed in the Meccan Period (610– 622 C.E.), consisted of three main areas: theological, ritual, and moral. The theological beliefs included an unwavering faith in monotheism, angels, a line of prophets from Adam to Muhammad, revealed scriptures, a modified form of destiny, and a rejection of idolatry and common cultural superstitions. Rituals included daily prayers, fasting, voluntary charity, and making supplications. Islamic rituals such as the pilgrimage began much later, after Muhammad was established in the city of Yathrib. In the Islamic moral code, lying, gossiping, theft, disrespect, fraud, foul language, infanticide, and racism were forbidden. Prohibitions on vices such as interest money, drinking alcohol, and gambling were also revealed later in Yathrib. Virtues included freeing slaves, feeding orphans and the poor, giving kind counsel, and respecting elders and relatives.

Abu Bakr was being harassed by Bilal's former owner, Umayyah, the chief of the Bani Jumah, and feared that he could be killed at any moment. Considering the loss of protection from his own relatives, he soon decided that he had better emigrate to Abyssinia and join the exiles there. He asked Muhammad's permission and then took to the road in the direction of the Red Sea. He would have made it to the coast had he not met an old friend, the leader of a group of allied tribes in the western desert. When asked why he was traveling like a fugitive with barely any supplies, Abu Bakr explained, "My people are treating me badly and have driven me out. All I want to do now is travel the land and serve God." The sympathetic chief bid Abu Bakr to accompany him back to Mecca and upon their arrival he announced that Abu Bakr was now under his protection so he should not be harmed. The Quraysh agreed, under the condition that he kept his religious devotions inside his house and that he wouldn't pray or preach publicly.

Other Muslims, however, fared far worse and had little family support to fall back on. The Qur'an acknowledges Muhammad's feelings of helplessness at the suffering of these early Muslims who weathered everything from insults to murder in these words, "There has come to you a messenger from among yourselves. Painful to him are the hardships you suffer." (Qur'an 9:128) To make matters even more untenable, Abu Lahab, Muhammad's hot-tempered uncle and one of his chief detractors, assumed the role of leader of the Hashim clan. Clan solidarity was about to evaporate. For the next few weeks, Muhammad endured being pelted with garbage and dirt and being pushed and shoved in the streets. Once, after a man from another clan threw the entrails of a sheep over his courtyard wall onto him, Muhammad saw the man retreating and called out loudly so his neighbors would hear, "Sons of 'Abd Manaf, what kind of protection is this?"

Looking for succor, Muhammad decided to take his message on the road. If the Quraysh of Mecca would not accept Islam and would continue to try to suppress it, then perhaps another city would allow him and his followers to take up residence and continue preaching. Muhammad's first choice was the city of Ta'if, a small settlement surrounded by fertile plains about half a day's journey to the east. A low-level rivalry had always existed between the predominant tribe of Thaqif, which set up its own small house of idolatry in Ta'if, and the Quraysh of Mecca. Perhaps this tribe would accept Muhammad, his followers, and the new religion.

Traveling alone and telling no one where he was going, Muhammad entered Ta'if in the year 619 and approached the tribal elders there, seeking permission to teach. After several hours, Muhammad surmised that the Thaqif tribe was not at all interested in what he had to say. Before returning to Mecca, he asked the people he had talked with not to tell they had rejected him, lest his enemies tease him about his failure. Rather than agree, the Thaqif elders called their servants and the people in the streets to drive him away. Muhammad was pelted with stones and chased from the town in disgrace.

Exhausted and bleeding, Muhammad stumbled down the road back to Mecca. Soon he spied a small wall that belonged to 'Utbah and Shaybah, two prominent Meccans, and he took shelter in its shade. He prayed to God for guidance, saying,

> My Lord, to you I complain of my weakness and lack of
> ability, my being scorned by others. Most Merciful of the
> Merciful, you are the Lord of the oppressed and my Lord
> as well. Who have you given me to? To strangers who
> insult me or to an enemy that dominates me? If you are
> angry with me, I don't mind, but your pardon is the most
> important thing I desire. I seek the help of the light of your
> visage that dispels darkness and sustains both this world
> and the next. In that I take refuge. I pray that your wrath
> does not befall me nor your displeasure overtake me. To
> you alone belongs the right to blame and to chastise until
> your pleasure is met. There is no power or strength save
> in you.

The owners of the wall, who happened to be sitting nearby, watched the weary man in silence. Muhammad, who was nearly fifty years old at the time, had gone from being a well-respected citizen of Mecca to a pariah, all because of religious differences. Feeling sorry for him, they decided to send their young slave, Addas, to give him some grapes. The boy approached Muhammad and handed him the gift, but before Muhammad ate them, he said, "In the name of God." Then he gratefully enjoyed his unexpected refreshment.

Addas remarked, "The people of this land don't speak like this," for saying grace was not an Arab custom. Curious, Muhammad asked the boy where he was from and what religion he followed. Addas explained that he was a Christian from Nineveh who had been enslaved. Muhammad asked, much to the boy's surprise, "Are you from the country of Jonah, the son of Matta?" "You know of him?" Addas asked excitedly. "Yes," answered Muhammad, "we are brothers. He was a prophet, and I am a prophet, also." Addas smiled in delight and kissed Muhammad's forehead and hands. The boy's owners, knowing what fate befell those who joined Muhammad's religion, called out from where they were resting, "Addas, watch out! Don't let this man lure you away from the religion of your forefathers, for it is better for you than his."

The news of Muhammad's humiliating excursion to Ta'if caused a firestorm of gossip in the streets of Mecca. The Quraysh were delighted that their rivals had rejected Muhammad so soundly. In their minds, this rejection affirmed the rightness of their cause. Abu Jahl began following Muhammad's movements about the city, belittling and berating him. The Muslim community could do little to help him. Meeting in congregation was difficult and dangerous, and many Muslims remained in their homes after dark out of fear of being mugged or assaulted.

Muhammad endured and carried on, teaching the major precepts and moral codes as Gabriel gave them to him. Beyond merely believing in one God and praying to him daily, Muhammad was molding a cadre of followers whose habits were vastly different from their peers. He taught them how to greet each other, how to use proper personal hygiene, how to curb the influence of sin, and how to gain confidence from the stories of the struggles of ancient prophets. The uniqueness of Islam was what kept a small trickle of converts streaming in. Typical of the revelations of this time is the following passage (Qur'an 81:1–29):

> When the sun is covered in darkness, when the stars fall, when the mountains pass away, when the livestock heavy with young are abandoned, when the wild beasts are herded together, when the seas rise, when the souls are sorted, when the baby girl buried alive is asked for what crime she was killed, when the books are opened, when the skies are laid bare, and when hell is set ablaze and paradise is brought near, then, every soul will know what it has prepared.
>
> But no! By the rotation of the stars and the orbit and setting of the planets, by the night as it falls and the morning as it passes, certainly, this is the speech of an honored messenger. He has authority and status before the Lord of Dominion, and he is to be obeyed and trusted.
>
> Your companion is not delirious, nor is he deceived, for he certainly saw the [angel of revelation] on a clear horizon. He doesn't hesitate in disclosing knowledge of the

*unseen, nor is this the work of an accursed force. So which
way will you go? This is no less than a reminder to all of
humanity, for everyone who seeks the straight way. But
not as you will, as God wills. The Lord of all Creation.*

Muhammad had always addressed the pilgrims visiting Mecca
during the sacred months when the Arabs suspended their feuds.
But with the renewed interest of Abu Jahl and even Abu Lahab in
persecuting him, even this activity became arduous. Every time
Muhammad would approach an arriving group of religious suppli-
ants seeking to venerate their idols in the Ka'bah, one or another
of his critics would call out loudly that a madman was trying to
address them.

Realizing the futility of such public spectacles, Muhammad
began secretly visiting the encampments of desert tribes in the territories outside Mecca, asking the elders to listen to and consider
his message or at the very least to allow him to preach freely among
their people. In tribe after tribe he was soundly rejected. What
would the Quraysh think of their tribe if its members converted to
a monotheistic religion? The loss in prestige and economic benefits would be too great. The elders of one tribe, the Banu 'Amr,
were a little more brazen than the rest: They agreed to convert on
the condition that they would rule the Muslim polity upon
Muhammad's death. When he replied that only God could decide
who would succeed him, they withdrew their offer.

By the year 621, the situation in Mecca looked intractable.
Muhammad and the Quraysh were locked in a fierce battle of wills,
and attrition was occurring on both sides. For every idolater who
embraced Islam, a Muslim was killed, persecuted, or forced underground or into exile. With most taboos against interclan conflict
lifted against the Muslims, the members of different lineages of the
Quraysh tribe felt free to harangue Muhammad and his weaker followers. Some conversions, such as those by 'Umar, Hamza, and
Abu Bakr, did the Meccans more damage than others, but the
dominant Meccans' relentless pressure seemed to prevent their
position from deteriorating further. Their customs, idolatry, and
abuse of human rights were no longer enough to cause people to

consider Islam's alternatives. Islam seemed doomed to go nowhere. The minority Muslim group wasn't in danger of being wiped out, but neither could it achieve stability and permanence.

Muhammad tried his best to carry on his duties as leader of the movement, and he made it a point to maintain good relations with his relatives, as was frequently called for in the Qur'an. He even succeeded in bringing some of them into the fold. Abu Talib's widow and her daughter, who was known as Umm Hani, embraced the faith and often invited Muhammad to their home to visit. Hubayrah, Umm Hani's husband, didn't convert, but he was always a gracious host.

Near the end of one such social call, Muhammad led the Muslims of the house in prayer and was about to go home when his cousin invited him to stay the night in the guestroom. After a few hours of rest, the Prophet awoke and decided to take a leisurely walk to the Ka'bah, because he loved to visit it at night when he could pray and meditate free of harassment. While he lingered there, he felt sleepy again and lay down nearby in the outer courtyard. A short time later, something nudged him awake. Seeing no one in the darkness, he became convinced he was in the presence of Gabriel. A moment passed, and the angel appeared.

Muhammad later recounted, "Gabriel took me by the arm and led me to the gate of the Ka'bah. A white animal that looked like a cross between a mule and a donkey stood there. It had wings at its sides and every stride of its legs was as far as the eye could see." Muhammad was asked to mount that fantastic creature, called *Buraq*, and together, with the angel flying by his side, they set off at top speed through the air in the direction of Jerusalem far to the north. The Prophet, who must have been quite unnerved, could look down and see the passage of caravans on the roads below as well as mountains, towns, and the various encampments of the desert tribes.

A short time later, they arrived in Jerusalem and alighted upon the ancient Temple Mount, whose ruins were a testament to the great glories of past prophets and whose direction was where a Muslim was taught to face in prayer. When Muhammad dismounted on that moonlit night he found himself face to face with the prophets of old. Abraham, Jesus, Moses, David, and many others were brought back to earth in spirit to greet him, the last of God's messengers to the world. They arranged themselves in ranks and stood behind Muhammad as he led them in prayer. After the ritual had ended, two goblets were presented to him, one filled with milk and the other with wine. He took the milk and drank it, whereupon Gabriel told him, "You have been guided to the right way, and you have guided your people to the right as well, Muhammad. Wine is now forbidden to you."

The sacred rock on the Temple Mount in Jerusalem from which Muhammad ascended to Heaven.

Gabriel instructed Muhammad to remount the Buraq, and from the sacred rock of the Temple Mount the pair shot straight up into the sky on a fantastic journey that had been undertaken by only a few mortals before: Jesus, Enoch, and Elijah. Muhammad found himself being transferred from the world of substance into an otherworldly dimension known as the *Akhirah*, or Afterlife, where heaven lies. His amazement kept him from panicking or questioning what was happening. He later commented that he felt an overwhelming sense of wonder. As earthly forms were stripped away, he saw Gabriel in his full splendor: an angel with wings that spanned from horizon to horizon. Passing upward through each of the seven layers of paradise, he again saw the prophets he had led in prayer before, though he saw them now as beings of perfection and light. Each of the prophets from Adam to Jesus greeted him and called him a brother before sending him on his way higher. The heavens in which they resided were visions of scintillating colors, of shimmering lights filled with celestial beauty such that no tongue can describe. No longer did time have any meaning; Muhammad saw the beginning and the end commencing all at once. "When Adam was still between water and clay," he once said, "I was already chosen to be a prophet."

Onward and upward Muhammad was taken, past the gates of each heavenly level until he reached the pinnacle beyond which is God, Himself. The Lote Tree of the Outermost Edge came into view as a towering spectacle of rainbow colors enshrouded in the form of a tree that grows out of the very throne of God. Behind and above it was space no one, angel or human, could ever penetrate and knowledge no one could attain. Only God alone knows what secrets lay there. As Muhammad sat on his mount, the power and presence of God descended upon the Lote Tree, exuding a dazzling display that Muhammad could not turn away from. The full crescendo of light, the bursts of color, and visions of space and time caused Muhammad to be spellbound to the core of his very being. He didn't know it then, but having the great honor of seeing the next world would give him the spiritual stamina and conviction to carry his message forward on earth in the face of seemingly insurmountable obstacles.

The command was issued to Muhammad that he and his followers must observe ritual prayers fifty times a day. In addition, he received the most complete statement of the creed of Islam in a new verse (Qur'an 2:285) that stated,

The messenger believes, as do the faithful, in what God
has revealed to him from his Lord. Each one believes in
God, his angels, his books, and his messengers, without
making any distinction between any of his messengers.
They say, "We hear and we obey. Grant us, O Lord,
your forgiveness for to you is the ultimate return."

After absorbing what had been entrusted to his heart, Muhammad was led by Gabriel back down through the layers of heaven. As he passed by Moses' level, though, Moses convinced Muhammad to go back and ask for a reduction in the number of daily prayers required, because he had prior experience with the Israelites and he found their religious stamina wanting. Muhammad returned to the Lote Tree and beseeched God for a reduction in the number of prayers, and God cut the number by half. When Muhammad passed Moses again, Moses again counseled him to ask for further reductions, for his people were weak and couldn't bear it. Muhammad's next (and last) request brought the number of daily prayers down to five. Muhammad later remarked that he felt too shy after that to ask for more reductions in the number. Thus God announced that five daily prayers performed by a true Muslim would be counted as fifty in his sight.

Gabriel returned Muhammad to the physical world just as quickly as they had left it. They landed on the sacred rock of the Temple Mount in Jerusalem as if it were an entry portal into the other realm. From there they flew at top speed back to Mecca. Along the way, Muhammad observed several southbound caravans and even stopped to coax a lost animal back to its owner. Just before dawn broke, Muhammad was back in his resting place near the Ka'bah. He got up and returned to Umm Hani's house and lay down, exhausted, in the guestroom. When the people of the house awoke, Muhammad led them in prayer and afterwards told his cousin, "Umm Hani, I prayed the night prayer with you in this valley that you see. Then I went all the way to Jerusalem and prayed there.

Now I prayed the morning prayer here like you just saw." Stunned, she grabbed his cloak to prevent him from leaving and strongly urged him not to tell anybody what he had just told her. Perhaps she was frightened that people would take this statement as a sign that he was mentally ill or possessed or that they even might try to attack him. "By God I will surely tell them," he exclaimed resolutely.

> *Was Muhammad's journey to heaven a journey in spirit or in body? Muslim scholars have debated this question for centuries. The conflicting reports of the night could support either position. Umm Hani, the prophet's cousin, stated that Muhammad never physically left her house, giving rise to the notion that his soul transmigrated into the next realm. Only the spirit, some suggest, could undertake such an arduous trek. Others hold strongly to the view that he was physically taken and point out that Umm Hani was sleeping that night and so didn't know if he was present or absent. In addition, Muhammad's ability to physically open a caravan camel's water jar and to help a man find a lost mount suggests a bodily presence. Regardless of the means, Muslims hold that the 'Isra and Mir'aj, or Night Journey and Ascension to Heaven, was the most important event (after the first revelation of a Qur'anic passage) that happened to the Prophet while he was in Mecca.*

That morning Muhammad walked straight to the Ka'bah, already filled with pedestrians and merchants scurrying to their market stalls. There he announced that he had journeyed to Jerusalem and back again, all in one night. People stopped what they were doing and immediately began to listen in disbelief. When the Quraysh tribesmen understood what he was saying, they began to jeer and curse him. A caravan took nearly a month to reach Syria and another month to return, and here Muhammad was claiming he undertook the whole journey in one night! His enemies were instantly exultant. Now they felt that they had irrefutable proof that Muhammad, and by extension his message, was a mockery. Cries of "madman" rose through the streets as the news was passed from house to house. The situation began getting out of hand as the Meccans began excitedly teasing Muslims, saying that their prophet was crazy. A few recent converts renounced their faith and returned to the religion of idolatry.

A handful of prominent Meccans rushed to Abu Bakr's house and said, "What do you think about your friend now? He's telling us he went to Jerusalem last night and prayed there and then came back here to Mecca." Abu Bakr at first refused to believe these men were being honest. When they assured him of their truthfulness and said that Muhammad was near the Ka'bah telling his story, Abu Bakr made a statement that would forever after earn him the nickname of *al-Saddiq,* or the one who affirms the truth. He told the men, "If he is saying it, then it's true. Why is that so unimaginable? He tells me that revelations come from heaven to earth in any hour of the day or night, and I know him to be speaking the truth, and that is even more fantastic than what you're ridiculing."

Abu Bakr joined the throngs on their way to the courtyard of the Ka'bah and repeated his belief in Muhammad's story along the way. When he arrived, he found that some in the crowd were beginning to believe Muhammad because he was accurately describing caravans that were due to arrive in Mecca and several had come into town by then. One recent arrival told of a voice from the clouds that helped him to find his lost camel in the night. Another camel with a water jar having a broken seal was examined, because Muhammad said he had stopped for a drink from it on the way back. Abu Bakr pushed his way through the circle and asked his friend to describe Jerusalem, because everyone knew Muhammad had never been there. After Muhammad accurately described the Temple Mount, the city's walls, and several prominent buildings, Abu Bakr was satisfied that his earlier affirmation had been correct. As the morning began to turn into afternoon, the crowds returned to their daily duties, undoubtedly either deeply impressed or chafing at the ammunition this incident would provide in the struggle against Muhammad's message.

Throughout the very public debate, Muhammad never mentioned anything about his journey to heaven. That was private information he would later reveal to Abu Bakr and the other Muslims. In the coming years he would give more details to them about what he saw of heaven, which would form the basis of a large amount of religious literature on the nature of the next life. The 'Isra and Mi'raj is celebrated and commemorated by Muslims to this day as one of the greatest honors Muhammad received from God, namely, the chance to enter paradise and see its wonders while still remaining a living, breathing mortal. The Quraysh, however, saw this event in quite a different light. They saw that events would likely spiral out of their control and debated more earnestly what to do about Muhammad and his religion.

Muhammad was a very sociable man and often visited the homes of friends, relatives, and followers. To the people of Mecca he was one of their own; whether they supported him or not, people had known him as an ordinary citizen for four decades before he ever claimed to receive revelations from God. Even as a religious visionary, he always had an air of familiarity. This history with the Meccans made the opposition and persecution Muhammad suffered at the hands of some of his relatives that much more painful, especially now that he was alone with no spouse to lean on and take comfort in. Three of his daughters were with him, but they couldn't provide the intimate counsel and succor of a wife. Barakah, his constant companion from his earliest days, was living on her own now, having married at Muhammad's insistence a few years before. Zayd and 'Ali were gone by this time as well, though 'Ali hadn't married yet.

To fill the empty space he felt in his heart, Muhammad often paid visits to his old friend Abu Bakr. There he could relax and talk and forget about the troubles that met him in the public eye. Both Abu Bakr and his wife, along with several of their children, had converted in the first years of Muhammad's preaching. His daughters, in particular Asma' and the younger A'ishah, would later play key roles in the defense of Islam.

A'ishah had been born after her family had accepted Muhammad's call and thus grew up in a Muslim household, listening to the rhythms of the Qur'an and the moral dictates of her parents. Although she was only nine or ten years old, she was precocious, intelligent, and strong-willed. Muhammad had dreams during this time in which the angel Gabriel was carrying her wrapped in sheets. He was told, "This is your wife." Repeating the mantra that if it were a true dream from God then it would happen, he kept these visions to himself because he was far older than she and her father had already promised her in marriage to the son of another man named Mut'im. He also still cherished the memory of his late wife with whom he had spent a quarter of a century, and thus made no moves to marry again.

Only at the insistence of his voluntary housekeeper, Khawlah, did he reconsider his hesitation. She bluntly suggested to him that he should remarry because it wasn't good to be alone. He asked her whom she had in mind and she replied, "Either A'ishah, the daughter of Abu Bakr, or Sawdah, the daughter of Zam'ah." Sawdah was a recently widowed returnee from Abyssinia, whose relatives were only grudgingly supporting her, as they opposed Islam. The alternate suggestion of A'ishah confirmed in his mind that God was making his prior dreams coalesce into concrete reality. Muhammad asked Khawlah to arrange both marriages, and she heartily agreed.

Abu Bakr, when he was told of the request, immediately went to Mut'im and asked him to rescind the match they had made for their children. He amicably agreed. Thus Muhammad married an older widow to provide support for her, and a few months later, the youthful A'ishah was betrothed to him. The final marriage ceremony didn't take place for several years so she could gain maturity; she continued to live with her parents until then. Neither A'ishah nor her parents objected to the match, and such an age difference was not uncommon in those days.

Polygamy, or more properly, polygyny, was common in most of the world in the seventh century. In Arabia and elsewhere, women who were co-wives had no protections, and men could marry an unlimited number of women. Islam laid ground rules that made it nearly impossible for the religious-minded man. A Muslim man must treat each wife equally in all respects. In addition, taking a co-wife must be done for a noble reason, not to satisfy one's own physical urges.

Muhammad would marry eleven more times after his long-term monogamous relationship with Khadijah, each one either to provide support to widows, strengthen ties, or prove religious points to break Arabian superstitions. The Qur'an also limits the number of wives a man can marry to four, but this law wasn't revealed until after the last of Muhammad's marriages. With all of his duties as a prophet, Muhammad rarely saw any of his wives for very long.

These changes in Muhammad's personal life did not make his daily struggle to keep his persecuted following together any easier. By now he had accepted the conversion of several hundred people, both native Meccans and individuals who had come in from the countryside, and he had no way of protecting them. With his worst critic, Abu Lahab, now his clan leader, he was unsure how he could protect himself. The most prominent leaders of Mecca, including Abu Sufyan, Ummayah bin Khalaf, Abu Jahl, and Abu Lahab, seemed to have the upper hand and were keeping intense pressure on the Muslims and making life unbearable. (Even Abu Bakr was soon forced to release his own tribal protector from his oath.) After his humiliating rejection by Ta'if and the surrounding tribes in the desert, Muhammad was running out of options. He did, however, begin to report strange dreams to his inner circle of a land dotted with date palms. He wasn't immediately sure what these dreams meant, though. He did know that he had no desire to immigrate to Abyssinia, because he felt sure his mission was there in the Arabian Peninsula.

To the north of Mecca, approximately a week's journey by caravan, lay the sprawling city of Yathrib, a cosmopolitan settlement of mud brick houses surrounded by fertile plains that allowed for the large-scale cultivation of dates and other agricultural products. Though not a major stop on the caravan route north, it was, nonetheless, the frequent object of prolonged visitation by travelers. Unlike Mecca or Ta'if, however, it had no central governing body, nor any large shrines to the gods attracting pilgrims from far and wide. In fact, idolatry was just one of many religions to have found a home in the city. Idolatry, Judaism, and, to a much lesser extent, Christianity all had a presence there.

The single largest contingent of citizens was made up of Arab idolaters from the tribes of Auws and Khazraj. Members of these two rival factions often fought with each other, wreaking havoc on their economic potential and resources. The next most prominent group was made up of Jewish settlers who were divided into three tribes known as the Nadir, Qaynuqa, and Quraiza. They remained mostly aloof from their Arab neighbors, preferring the safety of their fortresses and venturing out only for absolute necessities

either involving trade or maintaining their large date palm plantations. They owned many slaves who worked the plantations.

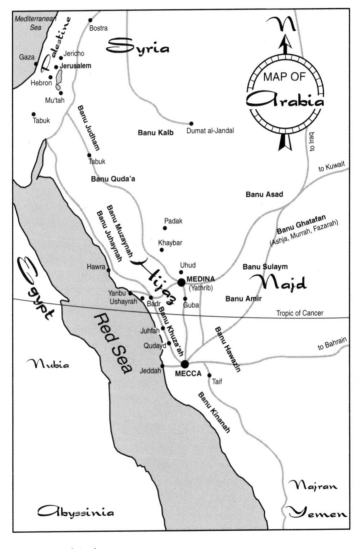

Central Arabia.

The Jews had good reason to be distrustful of their neighbors. Several times in the past, Christian raiders from Syria had attacked the city intending to wipe out the Jews, whom they blamed for the crucifixion of Jesus. While the might of the Jewish warriors was sufficient to repel such incursions, the Jews' vulnerability was exposed when the Auws and the Khazraj joined in a secret pact with the Syrians. Through a ruse, the Arabs had caused the Jews to fall victim to a trap laid by the Christians, resulting in the deaths of many of their finest young men. Since that time, the Jews hated their Arab neighbors. Realizing that the Jews could never hope to achieve military victory against the combined forces of the two Arab tribes, the Jewish elders embarked on a strategy of dividing and manipulating them to keep them at each other's throats. This strategy proved to be very successful.

In about the year 619, the Auws and Khazraj were goaded into fighting each other over petty factional issues, and a series of three small battles took place in and around the city. A delegation of six men from one of the tribes quickly traveled to Mecca and sought the advice of the Quraysh on how to unify their people. While there, they happened to meet Muhammad near the city center. Prior to this meeting the Jews of Yathrib had often predicted that a prophet was coming who would destroy the Arabs and make the Jews ascendant. This prediction had always alarmed the Arabs, who had an almost superstitious regard for the Jews' ancient knowledge and secret scriptures. When Muhammad said that he was a prophet sent from God, the delegation desired to have a more in-depth discussion with him.

After the visitors listened to Muhammad and what he had to say, one of them exclaimed, "My companions, this is much better than what you originally came for." Another said, "By God, this is the prophet by whom the Jews had threatened us with. Let us claim him before they do." A third man excitedly addressed Muhammad, saying,

> We have come from our people, the Auws and Khazraj,
> who are alienated from each other and who hate each
> other. If only God would allow them to meet you so they
> could unite under your leadership. If that ever happened,
> you would be the strongest man in Arabia!

The six men, all believers in Islam now, undertook the long journey home, energized at the new prospects that lay before them for their people.

Meanwhile, back in Yathrib delegations from each Jewish tribe encouraged both Arab factions to continue their fight, citing honor and tradition, and soon a terrible slaughter had occurred throughout the city. In what was later called the Battle of Bu'ath, the Auws tribe reeled from an initial assault but then quickly got the upper hand. Their enraged warriors raced after the retreating Khazraj, killing everyone in their path and burning the houses and orchards of their foes. They would have exterminated them completely had one man named Abu Qays not called out, "They are your coreligionists! It would be better for you to let them live for they would make better neighbors for you than the foxes (the Jews) and beasts of prey in the desert (the Bedouins)."

The Auws halted and withdrew from the Khazraj areas of the city, and when the full extent of the devastation became apparent, each side was given pause. Both tribes were so weakened that they could not possibly oppose the feared Jewish usurpation of the city alone. In addition, the ancient customs of the Arabs dictated that the Khazraj would one day have to avenge their ignoble defeat. That revenge would probably spell the end of both tribes.

Taking a page from the history of Mecca, where Qusayy had unified the city under his sole command in the distant past, the Arabs of Yathrib began to contemplate the institution of a monarchy so that a single man could rule the city and settle its disputes. The choice fell to a Khazraj leader named 'Abdullah ibn Ubayy, who had not taken part in the battle against the Auws. Though he never wielded any real power, he nonetheless provided a nominal figurehead to look towards as each tribe eyed each other warily. In spite of the newly agreed-upon truce and the tentative efforts at establishing a central leadership, Jewish ascendancy in Yathrib was almost complete. This change was mainly on account of their undamaged military might and economic prowess. From that point forward, they would chastise the Arabs more boldly and assume a greater role in the affairs of the city.

In 621, during the annual annual pilgrimage months, a group of twelve men representing both of the main Arab tribes of Yathrib journeyed to Mecca and camped at a place called 'Aqabah on the outskirts of the city. As was his practice, Muhammad went out to meet people and happened upon their encampment. He greeted the men and proceeded to engage them in a conversation about religion. As some of the men had already heard of Islam from a few converts in their city, they listened intently, and each of the twelve resolved to accept the new faith. Muhammad then asked the men to take an oath, which one of them later described as follows:

> We pledged our allegiance to the Messenger of God on the night of the first Oath of 'Aqabah, promising that we would not make others equal with God, that we would not steal, commit fornication, kill our [unwanted female] children, nor engage in slander. We agreed to obey the Messenger in all that is right. He said to us, "If you fulfill this pledge, then paradise is yours. If you commit one of these sins and receive punishment for it in this world, then that will serve as its restitution. If you hide it until the Day of Judgment, then it will be for God to decide if he will punish or forgive you."

Muhammad chose one of his trusted companions, Mu'sab ibn 'Umayr, to return with the new converts to Yathrib to teach them the tenets of Islam and the chapters of the Qur'an that had been revealed up until that point. Mu'sab was an excellent choice. Before his conversion, he had been an idle child of wealth who indulged in great luxuries at his family's expense. He had since redirected his life toward prayer and simple living. While in Yathrib, he succeeded in converting many Arabs of both tribes to Islam, including several prominent clan leaders. After eleven months of preaching and teaching, he returned to Mecca ahead of the coming pilgrimage season with good news for Muhammad: A large contingent of converts would be coming to meet him. In his dream Muhammad had seen a land of palm trees offering its shelter to him. Now he began to feel hopeful that Yathrib was the place where he would find refuge for both him and his followers.

The annual pilgrimage to Mecca was a time for both business and devotion. Many travelers combined the two pursuits, bringing trade goods to the markets of Mecca and later paying homage to the gods of the Ka'bah. That such an inordinately large group from Yathrib arrived in Mecca that year was of no real concern to the Meccans because the city was bursting at the seams with overflow crowds at this time. The group of seventy-three men and two women who came to see Muhammad made their camp in a valley and waited for nightfall. When the time came, they gathered at 'Aqabah and met him on the hillside nearby, the same place where twelve of their comrades had converted in the previous year.

Muhammad had already discussed at length with a few of his trusted relatives his plan to acquire the protection of the Auws and Khazraj through the converts among them. It was not unusual to seek outside alliances if one's own tribe was weak or uncooperative. 'Abbas, his uncle who had not yet converted, accompanied him to 'Aqabah with the concern that his clans of Banu Hashim and Banu 'Abd Manaf should have their interests protected. He didn't want either of his small clans to become embroiled in a war with the rest of the Quraysh tribe if the tribes of Yathrib suddenly abandoned Muhammad. He addressed the people, of whom the Khazraj were the largest component, saying,

> People of Khazraj, Muhammad, as you know, is one of
> us, and we have protected him from our people who dis-
> agree with him over his religion. He is immune among his
> people and has status in this land. He insists, however, on
> joining you and becoming one of you. If you are sure you
> will fulfill what you have called him here for, and that you
> will protect him from all his opponents, then you are free
> to take on this responsibility. If, however, you are going to
> desert him and betray him after he has gone with you,
> then it is better that you leave him now.

The people affirmed their resolve to listen to Muhammad's offer carefully. 'Abbas sat down, satisfied. Muhammad then recited some passages from the Qur'an and spoke movingly about the importance of true faith in God. When he had finished his sermon, he asked the assembly to protect him as they would their own

families. Al-Bara' ibn 'Amr, who was a prominent Khazraj chieftain and who had already previously converted to Islam in Yathrib,
stepped forward and said,

> By the One who has sent you with the truth, we swear
> that we will protect you as we protect them. Accept our
> pledge of allegiance, Messenger of God, for we are a peo-
> ple who know how to fight, a knowledge that has been
> passed down among us from father to son.

A man from the smaller Auws contingent, recalling that the
weakened tribes were recently forced into a deal to be subservient
to the Jewish tribes of Yathrib said, "Prophet of God, there are
treaties between us and other men that we will be breaking. If God
gives you victory, will you then return to your own people and
leave us?" Muhammad announced, "My blood is your blood, my
ruin is your ruin. I am of you, and you are of me. I will fight those
you fight and befriend those you befriend."

The people rose to their feet to give their oath, but one of their
number stopped them with this earnest warning:

> People of Khazraj, do you know what your swearing of
> allegiance to this man means? You are swearing to some-
> thing that will force you to fight all others. If the loss of
> your wealth or leaders would make you turn him over to
> his enemies, it is better to leave him now. If you ever did
> it, by God it would be disgraceful both in this world and
> in the next. If you think you can really fulfill your prom-
> ise to him, even in loss and death, then take him, for he is
> good in this world and in the next.

The crowd answered saying, "We take him regardless of a loss in
wealth or leadership." Then they asked Muhammad what the
reward would be for their obedience, and he replied, "Paradise."

What followed was a long procession, lit by torchlight, of people offering their hand to Muhammad, swearing a bayya' or pledge
of allegiance to abide by his authority. After all the men and
women had finished offering this Second Oath of 'Aqabah,
Muhammad instructed them to choose twelve representatives who
would act as their governing body when they returned to Yathrib.
The Prophet explained the significance of the number twelve as

mimicking the number of disciples Jesus had. Nine men of the Khazraj and three of the Auws were selected.

Just then, a Meccan man who had ostensibly gone out from his home on an errand but had stopped to eavesdrop on the whole affair sounded an alarm and cried out toward the nearest houses of the city, "Quraysh! Muhammad and his defectors are planning to attack you!" This situation was the first test of the new converts' courage, and they held their ground firmly, pledging to go on the offensive if Muhammad so ordered. After a few tense moments in which no other noise issued from the direction of the city, the Prophet was satisfied that no attack was forthcoming. He told his eager followers that God had not ordered him to fight, so they should return to their tents.

The next morning, after the Meccans found out about the previous night's meeting, they sent a contingent of warriors to the camps of the visiting people from Yathrib and searched in vain for any Muslim converts. They also berated the leaders of the clans gathered there for covenanting with Muhammad against them. The Muslims, who were mixed in with the idolaters from Yathrib, merely remained silent as their fellows proclaimed their ignorance of any such action. Later in the day, the Yathrib Muslims quickly headed back to Yathrib before the Meccans could mount an effective assault. One of those present at 'Aqabah the night before, a man named Sa'd, was captured, however, and the Quraysh dragged him back to Mecca in chains and tortured him until some friends of his paid a ransom for his freedom.

Muhammad was now in a very precarious position. Although he had the express protection of many clans from Yathrib, his guardians were a week's journey away. When the Meccans realized the significance of Muhammad's bold move and that Islam would no longer be within their power to suppress, they decided upon a course of action that would, in their minds, finish the issue forever. They resolved to kill Muhammad. This new resolve would set into motion a chain of events that would culminate in one of the most intense manhunts Arabia had ever seen.

Chapter 7

From Mecca to Medina

They plan and God plans though God is the best of planners.
—Qur'an 8:30

For thirteen years, the ever-swelling number of Muslim converts in Mecca had to endure increasing religious persecution. Harassment, loss of property, torture, and even murder had been their lot for far too long. With the Second Oath of 'Aqabah, a new place of refuge opened up for them. Although Abyssinia had been an available avenue of escape for some, the distance and cost of crossing the Red Sea made it impractical for most. A few people had previously emigrated to Yathrib after the first oath, but not until Islam was accepted publicly by two of Yathrib's main factions did people feel safe enough to settle there, a city still well within reach of Mecca.

At the Prophet's urging, Muslims soon began discreetly packing up their belongings and heading northward either by attaching themselves to existing caravans or by moving in groups of twos and threes. Families often traveled separately so as not to attract too much attention. Over the next several months, the Muslim population in Mecca began to decline rapidly. Among the first to go were many of Muhammad's relatives from the Banu Hashim clan. Others from the Banu Asad and Banu 'Abdel Muttalib clans went as well. It didn't take long for the leaders of the Quraysh tribe to figure out what was going on; empty houses and half-filled tenements were evidence enough. When the plans of several prominent converts from well-connected families became known, the elders had special cause for concern.

The commoners' escape wasn't the problem. The problem was Mecca's, and by extension the Quraysh's, reputation. The Meccans felt that they would be embarrassed before the rest of Arabia if it were known that their own children had to leave the city to be safe, as indeed many young men and women of the Quraysh had already converted to Islam and been persecuted. Groups of armed clansmen soon began patrolling the countryside, and whenever they would encounter Muslims fleeing to Yathrib, they would rob them of their wealth if they were commoners or detain them and bring them back to Mecca in chains if they were from one of the noble families. Abu Jahl joined one such party and captured his half-brother. Dragging him back into the city in humiliation, he called out, "People of Mecca! Do to your fools what we have done to ours!" Escaping the city became an increasingly arduous and dangerous enterprise.

Muhammad did not join in the immigration, and many were unsure if he would leave. He did privately ask Abu Bakr to delay his departure with the words, "Don't rush away, for God may give you a companion." Accordingly, Abu Bakr arranged for a Bedouin to keep two of his camels prepped and ready to leave at a moment's notice. Muhammad may well have wanted to wait until the bulk of his followers had escaped so as not to open them up to wholesale slaughter from the Meccans. As long as he remained behind, he could continue to give the Quraysh something else to focus on besides the endless streams of refugees. Whatever the reason, he mentioned to several of his associates that God had not given him permission to go.

His physical presence also heartened those who remained behind, who were now under intense pressure to recant their Muslim beliefs. Though many resisted, a few did apostatize. One such man was 'As Hisham, who had been captured as he tried to rendezvous with his cousin, 'Umar, who was waiting outside the city with loaded camels. Hisham was harangued relentlessly by his father and brother until he finally agreed to renounce Islam. The Quraysh took these and other small successes as a sign of their continuing influence, but they didn't count on the element of deception. Verses of the Qur'an (Qur'an 39:53–54) were soon revealed that said,

> O My servants who have acted unwisely towards your-
> selves, don't despair of God's mercy. God truly forgives
> all sins for He is the Forgiving and Merciful. Turn to your
> Lord in repentance and surrender to Him before the pun-
> ishment comes upon you and you won't be helped.

Hisham received a smuggled copy of these lines recorded by 'Umar, who had sent them with a courier from Yathrib. When Hashim read the words he resolved to convert again, and this time he kept his renewal of Islam a secret. Many others followed suit.

The Meccans had always assumed that they would eventually prevail against Muhammad and his monotheistic beliefs. He was, after all, one of them and living among them, so he could be dealt with in any manner that was deemed necessary. His followers were also mostly locals who would surely return to idolatry in time. As the Muslim population of Mecca dwindled and their population in Yathrib increased, however, the Meccans soon realized that Muhammad was poised to found a rival political entity, and this development alarmed them greatly. How could they protect idolatry and prevent further conversions if an expanding power lay just to their north, astride the main caravan route to Syria? Worse still, if Muhammad went to Yathrib, would he raise an army to attack them?

Late in the year 622, Quraysh elders held a secret meeting in their community hall to discuss the options open to them. One suggested that they lock up Muhammad to see if he would eventually recant his beliefs. The gathering quickly struck down this idea as futile. Hadn't they tried all manner of subterfuge and persecution to convince Muhammad to desist? Another suggested exile: Muhammad could be sent away to some distant land, and the problem would soon be forgotten. Again the notion was dismissed as playing into Muhammad's hands. After further debate, the elders became inclined to listen to Abu Jahl: They should kill Muhammad and end his religion once and for all.

This option presented a number of difficulties that had to be worked out, the most important of which was tribal revenge. Even though many people in Muhammad's own clan, the Banu Hashim, were Muslims, not all were, and related clans also felt he was one of their own for better or for worse. This clan loyalty was the code of the Arabs. If someone killed Muhammad, civil war could erupt in Mecca. The Quraysh had to act soon, however; Muslim influence was rapidly growing in Yathrib.

An ingenious scheme was hit upon whereby every clan in Mecca would provide a strong young warrior to help kill Muhammad. That way, the two or three clans that considered Muhammad one of their kinsmen would be powerless to take revenge. They couldn't go to war against two dozen other clans in Mecca, and therefore would have to accept blood money as payment for their loss. It seemed like the perfect plan. (This plan also eerily echoed Muhammad's wise solution twenty-five years earlier to have the leaders of every tribe replace the Black Stone in unison!)

Arabia, a land ruled by custom rather than by a legal system backed by a civil authority, had several commonly accepted methods for settling disputes, including murder. Although the option of revenge killing remained open if one's tribal or clan member was murdered, a second form of redress involved the payment of blood money, a fine that a perpetrator's family would pay to a victim's family to settle the score. Before 'Abdel Muttalib, the amount varied, but after his experience appeasing the gods to save his son's life, the amount was fixed at one hundred camels. Islam outlawed revenge killing but not the concept of paying a fine to the family of the deceased. Capital punishment could be applied only if the defendant was found guilty in a court proceeding, and the bereaved family could either call for the death penalty or request payment. The latter choice ruled out any jail time.

Muhammad learned of the plot against his life by the time the noonday sun had risen over the mud brick houses of Mecca. Keeping himself from panicking or acting unusually, he headed in the direction of his closest friend's house. He never visited Abu Bakr's home at that hour, so everyone understood immediately why he was there. Muhammad told Abu Bakr that it was time to leave and that they would be traveling together. While Abu Bakr's family bid him a hasty farewell, Muhammad, trying to appear as unconcerned as possible, returned home to put his affairs in order. He met his nephew 'Ali and asked him to return some money to a few people who had entrusted him with their savings. (Even though he was reviled by much of Mecca as a religious rebel, most people still trusted him to hold their money, because his reputation for honesty had never been in question.) Then he waited with his new wife Sawdah, his daughters Umm Kulthum and Fatimah, and his old friend and caretaker Barakah, who was visiting at the time.

As night fell, the assassins of the Quraysh began to gather in a nearby alley. The young men held their swords at the ready and eagerly anticipated the glory they would receive after the deed was done. Their plan was simple: They would jump over the wall of Muhammad's house together and slay him in the darkness. When they were assembled, they crept as one to the outer wall of their victim's home and were about to enter when the sounds of women's voices chatting and laughing were heard. One of the men suggested that it would be embarrassing if word got out that they had burst in upon a bunch of women in the private area of a house. They decided to wait in ambush outside the front gate and kill their prey when he went out for his early morning walk, which had always been Muhammad's habit. They crouched down in hastily assigned positions and spent a tense night lying in wait.

'Ali and Muhammad were soon aware of the men hiding outside. The Prophet took a large green cloak from his closet and handed it to 'Ali, who was about twenty-three years old, saying, "Sleep in my bed tonight and wrap yourself in this green cloak of mine. Remain sleeping with it covering you and you won't come to any harm." Then Muhammad began reciting from Chapter Ya Seen of the Qur'an and kept on reading until he came to the line which read, "We have covered them so they cannot see." (Qur'an 36:9) Without another word, Muhammad slipped out, passing unnoticed by the watchers to where he was to meet Abu Bakr. Along the way he passed by a man who knew him but was unaware of the plot, so no alarm was raised.

Meanwhile, the assassins kept their vigil, confident that Muhammad was still inside. One of them had even crept up to the window to peek inside, discerning a sleeping figure wrapped in a green cloak on the bed. Soon dawn would come, and the swords of the finest young men of Mecca would come crashing down on the man their elders told them to kill. As the sun rose lazily and the first light shone over the desert mountains to the east, the assassins became worried. Muhammad had not come out yet. They were shocked and surprised to see 'Ali pass through the front door leisurely, wearing a large green cloak. Their bungling of the plan was further confirmed when a man who had seen Muhammad leaving the night before came and told them that he was not in his home. Realizing that their quarry had slipped away, they sounded the alarm, and all of Mecca was ablaze with fury and consternation. Hunting parties were quickly arranged, and men swarmed over the desert searching for any sign of the fugitive between their city and Yathrib. They were again the victims of deception because Muhammad was nowhere near where they were looking.

When Muhammad and Abu Bakr left from the back window of the latter's house and ran to their waiting mounts, they immediately headed south, away from the direction of Yathrib. Muhammad looked back at Mecca as he sped away in the darkness on a camel and said, "Of all the places on God's earth, you are the closest to me and the closest to God. If it wasn't for my people driving me out I never would have left you." Muhammad's affection for his hometown was still deep. But he had an unshakable faith that God would protect him. He also had a plan. Along with Abu Bakr's son, 'Abdullah, they made for a little-known place on the road to Yemen, a small cave in the side of a hill called Thawr that had been used once or twice for shelter by travelers, but was too small and inaccessible to gain any notoriety or interest and thus was a good hideout.

Abu Bakr and Muhammad entered the cave with their supply bags, and 'Abdullah, as instructed, returned with the camels to Mecca. A freed servant of Abu Bakr named Amir led a flock of sheep to the cave and then back to Mecca to cover over any tracks. No one knew where the fugitives were hiding except Amir and his feet he will find us." Muhammad whispered back, "Abu Bakr, how can you be afraid for two men when the third among them is God?" The warriors were further convinced that the cave was unoccupied after they saw tree branches all around it. They left to search in another vicinity. Abu Bakr crept forward and saw in amazement the three natural deterrents that had saved their lives. He let fall from his lips a grateful, "Praise God. God is most great."

After three days of hiding, Abu Bakr and Muhammad felt it was safe to travel because 'Abdullah reported that the knot of searchers was growing thinner and further away. 'Abdullah and Asma' brought several large bags of supplies, and Abu Bakr and Muhammad prepared to start the next leg of their harrowing journey. A short time later, Amir, accompanied by a Bedouin guide Abu Bakr had hired before, arrived with three camels. Neither Amir nor the Bedouin were Muslims, but they were trustworthy. The Bedouin guide was to lead them northward through the trackless wastes and hills of the desert for the next two and a half weeks in order to elude capture. As the men made ready to mount their animals, Asma' realized that she had forgotten to bring rope with her to tie the supply bags. Thinking quickly, she removed her belt, ripped it in two, and then used it to lash the largest bag to its carrier.

Abu Bakr offered the finest camel to Muhammad, who refused to take it, saying he would not mount a camel that wasn't his. Abu Bakr offered it as a gift, but the Prophet insisted on paying him for it, and Abu Bakr, realizing that Muhammad was leaving behind all his worldly property in Mecca, acquiesced, noting that his friend wanted to begin the next phase of his life on the right footing. Amir was to ride with Abu Bakr on the same camel to assist them on their journey. Together, Muhammad, the Bedouin guide, Abu Bakr, and Amir set off towards the new sanctuary of Islam: Yathrib. This epic journey would forever afterwards be known to Muslims as the *Hijrah*, or Migration. It marked the end of the Meccan period and the beginning of what would be called the Medinan period—after Medina, as Yathrib would be called—a time when Islam would come into full flower as well as be endangered as never before.

The journey to Yathrib was long and hard, made all the more so given that the party had to avoid all main roads and often hide for hours from the posses that would occasionally appear. Heading deeper south at first, the guide led them in a wide arc that brought them near the Red Sea before finally turning northwards. They rode all night and most of the day, resting during the hottest part of the afternoon when traveling was unbearable. Over hot rocks and burning sands they pressed on, knowing their fate if they were to be caught. They had one close call when a skilled tracker named Suraqah tried to ambush them. As he charged on his horse, however, it kept stumbling and throwing him off. The superstitious man interpreted this problem as a sign that God was protecting Muhammad, and he begged an audience with the Prophet. Before leaving, he promised not to tell anyone that he had seen the fugitives.

As the party inched northwards, they were again alarmed to see a caravan coming their way. Abu Bakr soon recognized it, however, as that of his cousin Talha, with whom he had always had good relations. He was returning from a business trip to Syria and had passed through Yathrib on his way to Mecca. He told Muhammad that all of Yathrib was eagerly awaiting his arrival and that people were beginning to get worried. He gave the dusty travelers new clothes from his stores and bid them farewell. Perhaps by way of comfort but more rightly as a prediction, a verse (Qur'an 28:85) was revealed to Muhammad that told him, "Truly the One Who made the Qur'an binding upon you will one day bring you home."

The party came upon a Bedouin encampment and were invited to rest by Umm Ma'bad, a generous woman who had a reputation for giving succor to strangers. On this day, however, she had nothing to offer except the shade of her tents, for her husband had taken all their best goats out to pasture. Muhammad asked permission to milk her remaining goats, though she assured him that they were too weak to give milk. He placed a hand on one goat's back and said, "In the Name of God"; then he proceeded to produce a full bowl of milk. He gave the bowl to Umm Ma'bad, and then filled three more bowls for his companions before taking one for himself.

After Muhammad and his friends left, Umm Ma'bad's husband came home, and she told him of the visitors who had stopped by. She pointed to the full bowls of milk that they had left behind and explained, "I saw a man who came here with two of his friends. His face was luminous like a full moon, and his demeanor was tranquil. When he wasn't talking there remained a strange dignity about him; when he spoke his words were like sprinkled pearls. His friends obeyed his every request and listened to his every word." "Oh," her husband replied, "that must be the man the Quraysh are looking for. If I had been here I would have joined his religion." "Why don't we do it now?" his wife exclaimed. "Let's follow him to Yathrib and join Islam." The couple packed up their tents and prepared to move on to their new life. They would later meet Muhammad and convert at his hands.

After another week of relentless travel, the scenery began to change, and the slightly more verdant hills of northern Arabia came into view. Even though the heat of the midday sun was bearing down upon them, Muhammad and his friends decided to forgo their usual rest stop and continue. Anticipation of their goal grew with each passing mile. They finally reached the gentle upward slope of a valley wall, and their Bedouin guide explained that Yathrib lay on the other side. They climbed frantically to the top and were delighted to see an open plain before them filled with groves of date palms, small pools, and fertile pastures. Here lay the land of palms that the Prophet had seen in his dreams! Here was where the weary Muslims could find a home and build a new society. Feeling more confident, the group rode into the valley.

Muhammad was informed that the closest settlement just before Yathrib proper was a small town known as Quba, which most of the Muslim immigrants had passed through on their way into Yathrib and where many remained. Every day groups of local and immigrant Muslims would come to the edge of the city and watch for Muhammad's arrival with great anticipation. They had already learned of the bounty on his head and hoped in earnest that their prophet and guide would make it safely. Muhammad told his guide, "Lead us directly to the Bani 'Amr in Quba and not into the city just yet." The Bani 'Amr were a clan of the Auws tribe, and he wanted to greet them and honor their efforts for the cause. It was Monday, September 27, 622.

Quba mosque.

The residents of Quba had already waited under the intense heat of the Arabian sun for most of the day and had returned to the relative coolness of their homes, expecting that again their hopes would not be realized. But as the party of four approached in their new white clothes in stark contrast with the brown of the outlying desert, a Jew who happened to be sitting on his roof called out, "Sons of Qaylah! Your man has come!" Instantly the cry was taken up from house to house as people rushed out to see the arrival of the man they had long expected. Muhammad arrived triumphantly in the town and was immediately surrounded by crowds of cheering people. Raised hands and familiar faces dotted the knots of jubilant spectators as Muhammad recognized many of his companions from Mecca. A group of girls rushed forward and began clapping their hands and singing a song saying, "We are the girls of Banu Najjar, Oh what a wonderful neighbor is holy Muhammad." Muhammad called back to the people that he passed, "Listen everyone, greet each other with peace, feed the hungry, honor the ties of kinship, pray when others sleep, and this is how you can enter heaven in peace."

After the excitement and greetings died down, it was arranged that Muhammad would stay with an old respected man of Quba and member of the Auws tribe named Kulthum, who had already welcomed Muhammad's uncle, Hamza, and his adopted son, Zayd. While in the oasis town, Muhammad founded the first public mosque of Islam and instituted congregational prayers there for the local residents. So as not to slight the Khazraj, Muhammad moved from Kulthum's house and stayed for a day or two with a man of the Khazraj tribe in the nearby village of Sunh so that both tribes could share in the honor of catering to this important guest. 'Ali ibn Abi Talib wandered in from the desert a couple of days later. It had taken him three days to return all the monies that Muhammad had been safeguarding to their rightful owners. Afterwards he spent two weeks walking toward Yathrib. Other last-minute arrivals from Mecca came in a steady stream as well.

During his stay in Quba and Sunh, Muhammad received many visitors. Among these were Jews from nearby Yathrib who wanted to see the celebrated Prophet from Mecca. A young slave named Salman, who was owned by a Jewish plantation owner, also came to have a look. He was originally from Persia, but he had run away from his father so he could go to Syria and become a Christian. His last job had been to serve an elderly bishop who told him a new prophet was going to arise in Arabia and that he could be found in a city of date palms. Sadly, he was kidnapped and sold into slavery on his way to the land of the Arabs. While working atop a palm tree one day, he overheard his Jewish owner discussing the arrival of Muhammad. That night he excitedly went to join the long line of visitors to determine if this was, in fact, the Prophet he so longed to find. After administering a series of tests that the bishop had told him to conduct, involving the giving of gifts and alms and whether Muhammad would accept them or give them to others, Salman was convinced that Muhammad was the Prophet of God. Later Muhammad and his companions would buy Salman's freedom by planting a whole grove of date palms, as stipulated by his master.

After four days, Muhammad prepared to enter the metropolis of Yathrib itself. Accompanied by his closest companions from Mecca and an honor guard that soon grew to over a hundred warriors of the Auws and Khazraj tribes (a sign that they took their oath to protect Muhammad seriously), he set off towards the main city. After a brief stop to offer a congregational sermon in a nearby valley (for it was a Friday, the Muslim Sabbath), the Prophet remounted his camel, and the procession began anew. All along the road as Muhammad and his entourage drew ever closer to the city's precincts, men, women, and children lined the way cheering and waving, "The Prophet of God has come! The Prophet of God has come!"

Following the pace set by Qiswa, Muhammad's camel, the ever-swelling procession of people slowly moved past the stately groves and gardens south of Yathrib. Muhammad politely declined the numerous requests from spectators to visit their homes and pressed on. When Muhammad and his companions reached the city limits, the expectant throngs that met them let out a cry of delight. Evidently wanting to outdo the girls of Quba, a chorus of girls from Yathrib let loose a song of their own that went,

The white moon rose over us from the valley of Wada'.
Now we owe it to show the Lord thankfulness whenever a
caller calls to us. O you who have been sent among us, you
came with a direct command, and you have brought to our
city nobleness, so welcome to you, the best caller of all.

From that day onward, the city of Yathrib was renamed by common usage to *Medinatun Nabi,* which meant "the city of the Prophet," though it was usually called Medina for short.

As Muhammad approached the city center, the crowds shouted greetings and earnest invitations to stay in their homes. Every leader and commoner in the city wanted the Prophet as his honored guest. The leaders of the Bani Salem clan even took hold of the reins of his camel and declared, "Messenger of God! Come with us! We are the most numerous, best supplied, and the strongest." Muhammad, whose wisdom in similar circumstances was displayed so long before in the dispute over the placement of the Black Stone, announced, "Let go of the camel. She is under God's command!" So it was decided that the camel would choose where Muhammad would stay so no human would feel slighted. No one disagreed with this compromise, and the camel was allowed to wander freely. At first it headed toward the neighborhood where Muhammad's mother's distant relatives lived, then it abruptly altered course and passed by several houses that belonged to those who made the First Oath of 'Aqabah. After a few minutes of further sauntering, it sat down on a vacant lot. Suddenly the camel stood up again, walked in a wide circle past one nearby house, paused briefly, and then sat back down again in the vacant lot.

Muhammad dismounted and asked who owned the land. He was informed that it was the inheritance of two orphans, and just then the pair appeared from the crowd accompanied by their guardian. They announced that they wanted to donate that land to build a mosque, but Muhammad, seeing that they were poor, refused the gift and insisted on paying a fair price. After the price was settled, the community joined hands to build their much-anticipated religious center along with some apartments for the Prophet and his family.

The construction of the mosque took about seven months, during which time Muhammad joined in the work and laid bricks with the best of his fellows. The simple structure was made of mud bricks, wooden poles, and a roof of palm leaves, though most of the walled-in courtyard was left open to the sky. It was large enough to accommodate a good-sized crowd and remained unaltered for the next nine years. The Prophet's new apartments were built in a separate structure next door and were connected to the main mosque area by a doorway. A room was dedicated to poor or homeless Muslims to sleep in at night. The mosque was lit for part of the evening by burning torches made of bundled straw. It would grow to be the most important place for the community to gather to meet, pray, talk, and rest.

While the construction was going on, the Prophet stayed in the house of a man named Abu Ayyoub Khalid, by whose door the camel had hesitated before finally settling in the empty lot. In addition, as if by premonition, Abu Ayyoub had already unloaded Muhammad's baggage and had it stored in his house! His spacious home had two floors, with the master bedroom located on the upper floor. Abu Ayyoub insisted that his guest sleep on the second floor, but the Prophet wanted to sleep somewhere on the first floor, making it easier to meet with people at all hours. Accordingly, Abu Ayyoub cleared out a space on the first floor and furnished a comfortable bed for Muhammad.

That night, Abu Ayyoub and his wife became worried. They felt uneasy about sleeping above the Prophet and were afraid of coming between him and any revelation that might descend upon him from heaven. The next morning they told him their fears and begged him to sleep on the second floor, saying they would never want to sleep above the Messenger of God. Muhammad told them it was all right and that he still preferred the first floor. For a few weeks, Abu Ayyoub and his wife remained nervous, but they finally began to relax. Then one night Abu Ayyoub accidentally broke a jar of water, and it spilled all over the floor. He and his wife quickly mopped up the water, worried that it might leak through the floor onto Muhammad, who was sleeping directly below. The next morning they asked him if he had felt any dripping water in the night, and he laughed and assured them he had not. Abu Ayyoub again insisted that he wouldn't feel at ease unless they switched floors. Finally, the Prophet agreed to sleep on the second floor, and Abu Ayyoub and his wife were relieved. In later years, Abu Ayyoub said he had never had a better and more pleasant sleep than when he was sleeping on the first floor, under the Prophet of God.

The Muslims of Medina were made up of two groups. Those who escaped Mecca were called *Muhajirun*, or Immigrants. The native converts of Medina were called *Ansar*, or Helpers, for the assistance they had given to Islam. The Muhajirun were generally poor, given that many of them had escaped Mecca with little more than the clothes on their backs. Many of the men slept in the mosque at night or in the streets while the women and children congregated in the homes of sympathetic bystanders. Although he could have lived like a king, the Prophet generally shared in the deprivations of his followers.

One day Abu Bakr left his small rented house and was walking towards the mosque. 'Umar ibn al-Khattab came out of his quarters, saw his friend passing by, and asked him where he was going.

Abu Bakr replied, "I'm hungry, and I don't have any food in my house." "The same reason got me out of my house," said 'Umar. Just then, they both saw Muhammad coming out of his own apartment. He came up to them and asked, "Why are you both outside on such a hot day?" After they told him, the Prophet replied, "By God! The same thing got me out of my house. Come on, let's go see Abu Ayyoub." At his home the hungry trio were graciously given a simple meal. The Prophet said, "Dates, bread, and meat!" He shed a few tears and said, "This is an indulgence that you will be asked about on the Day of Judgment. So when you eat, say, 'Praise be to God who has satisfied our hunger.'"

The condition of the Muhajirun was so difficult in those first few weeks that Muhammad had to take decisive action. He gathered the Muslims together one morning in the mosque and announced that the two parties would be joined together in brotherhood. Every local family would adopt an immigrant and share half their possessions with him or her. The Ansar happily responded, and immigrants were parceled out to them and given goods and property. Soon every poor Muslim from Mecca was given the means to earn a livelihood. The Muhajirun, for their part, brought with them a wealth of religious knowledge to share with their hosts. This mutual exchange built a strong bond of brotherhood in the hearts of these two different communities and helped to alleviate the suffering of the poor.

Was Muhammad an extremist? Misconceptions about Islam today might give that impression, but despite the misinterpretations of some militant Muslim groups, Muhammad himself was actually a religious and political moderate. He initiated no wars (though he did often act in preemptive self-defense), he called his followers to respect the rights of women, he honored all treaties, he guaranteed minority rights, he championed education, and he warned that nations were destroyed when people went to extremes. He even forbade people from excessive praying and fasting, pointing out that life should include family and recreation. As a testament to the tolerance he preached, Islamic history has had no Holocausts, Inquisitions, bloody Crusades, or other large-scale tragedies on its record.

In a short time, the Muhajirun became prosperous and achieved a measure of stability. Some, such as Abu Bakr and 'Umar, engaged in trade and rebuilt the fortunes they had left behind in Mecca. Others took jobs ranging from sharecropping to herding. New arrivals were sheltered in the mosque until they could be paired up with local sponsors, and a tithe was taken from the most affluent Muslims to support their upkeep. Economically the Muslim community's situation was improving. Most of the families of the immigrants finally made it to the city as well, bringing joy and a sense of normalcy to many.

Muhammad knew that he had to unite the disparate groups of the city if Islam were to be allowed to thrive. Fresh in his memory was the fear of persecution for him and his followers. He didn't want anyone to fear any longer if they chose to accept Islam. The Auws and Khazraj were generally not a concern, given that the number of idolaters among them was dwindling rapidly and conversions were picking up. However, a faction led by the erstwhile yet unconfirmed king of Medina, 'Abdullah ibn Ubayy, only grudgingly converted so as not to appear unpatriotic to his tribe. He and his followers would cause a great amount of mischief later.

Beyond the Arabs, however, the three Jewish tribes, the Banu Nadir, the Banu Qaynuqa, and the Banu Quarayza, had to be brought into a common security pact. Rival power bases and distrustful partners were one of the main causes for the city's woes in the past. If Muhammad could bring Arab and Jew together in a municipal bond, the city would be much more stable and prosperous. When he had first arrived in Yathrib, the Jews had given Muhammad a respectful welcome. Indeed, they had hopes that he would join their religion and strengthen their position with the Arabs and the Christians to the north. Muhammad returned their cordial greetings and paid courtesy visits to the homes of several prominent rabbis. For the moment Jewish opinions of Muhammad were still in flux, and their leaders were open to many of his ideas.

The grand pact Muhammad forged with the Jews is known as the Compact of Medina. This lengthy document, considered the world's first constitution, delineated the reciprocal relationships between the Muslims and the Jews, along with a statement of the rights of each party in the civil functioning of the city. The main thrust of the document was in creating a shared sense of identity as citizens of one state. This shared identity by no means meant that Jews were asked to give up their religion or to accept Muhammad as a prophet. The pact merely stated that Muslims and Jews would have equal status before the law and that if a person from one group were wronged, it was up to both groups to help him or her. In the case of invasion, both sides had to participate in the defense of the city, and neither side could make a separate peace with the enemy.

The model of an Islamic state as fashioned by Muhammad was built with the understanding that people of differing religions share many of the same goals and can be included equally in the weaving of one diverse society with mutual benefits. The Jewish tribes soon agreed to the provisions of this pact, and it was confirmed as the city charter that all groups had to honor. The most important stipulation for Muhammad was that he, as the Prophet of God, would be recognized as the final arbiter in disputes that could not be settled by others. Thus Muhammad was confirmed by common consent to be the ruler of the city, yet the ruling power was widely dispersed among the leaders of every local group. Day-to-day affairs were handled locally, and only matters of state such as security, religious freedom, teaching, and interfaith relations got Muhammad's attention. In addition, Muhammad had a circle of talented advisors consisting of his most important companions whom he consulted often. This system would evolve further into something of a quasi-representative democracy that would allow for the wide participation of ordinary citizens. Medina was now an evolving, vibrant state, encompassing many religious entities and disparate groups.

What the Meccans had feared most was coming to pass. Islam now had an independent power base of its own and was quite out of their immediate reach. The Quraysh were not without options, however, and their hatred of Muhammad and his religion would propel them to further conflict, armed violence, and subterfuge that would span the length of the Hijaz. The Qur'an would continue to provide guidance to Muhammad and his followers as they entered their most difficult conflict: the fight for the soul of Arabia.

men. The unprecedented transformation of an entire society was begun in earnest.

Islam was undergoing a metamorphosis of sorts as well. In Mecca, the main thrust of revelation had been concerned with the esoteric: opposition to idolatry, improving personal morality, and establishing a personal relationship with God, but the Medina revelations established regulations for public and social life. The Qur'an, as it evolved, laid down new rules for the conduct of business and commerce. It institutionalized the heretofore optional fast of the month of Ramadan, making it obligatory for all who could perform it. The compulsory welfare tax known as *zakah*, a 2.5 percent tithe on one's savings to be paid yearly for the benefit of the poor and needy, was also established. The five daily prayers were now held in congregation in the mosque to overflow crowds, and the Prophet utilized the newly established Friday noontime sermon to expound further upon Islamic regulations in a variety of spheres of life.

The changes Islam was asking people to make in their lifestyles were often quite unusual for that time and place. Many of the new regulations were implemented gradually, for the Arabs were a people of longstanding customs, and no sudden changes would have succeeded. One good example of this gradual change is the three-step process that resulted in the final ban on alcohol consumption. The first verses of the Qur'an to comment on the Arabs' love for wine were revealed in Mecca and said that intoxicants were a tool of Satan to be avoided. This pronouncement caused some Muslims to curtail their drinking habits and gave others pause for reflection. Later on in Medina, in response to the inebriated condition of some people in the mosque during prayers, a verse was revealed that said that no one should perform his or her prayers with a mind clouded by drunkenness. Given that the five daily prayers were held at specific intervals throughout the day, people still found it hard to achieve total sobriety. Showing up at the mosque even slightly inebriated soon became a cause for shame, and alcohol consumption dramatically declined. Finally, a few months after that, following a drunken rampage by Muhammad's uncle, Hamza, a verse from the

Qur'an came that forbade completely the consumption of anything that intoxicates or impairs a person's clear thinking. The streets of Medina flowed red with wine as people dumped out all their stores. Muhammad went so far as to forbid the possession of the special goblets that were used for alcoholic beverages.

Muhammad was altering the character of his flock in many other ways as well. Even mundane activities such as eating and drinking did not escape his notice as he worked to impose a single standard of etiquette. Table manners were heretofore up to each individual, and personal hygiene in Arabian society was appallingly poor. Muhammad taught people to wash their hands before eating, to eat from their own section of the large communal plates, to not gulp liquids, and even to brush their teeth several times a day, a practice that was generally unknown in Arabia. He also taught them to say grace before their meals and to thank God afterwards. These and other manners seem normal in our own time, but they were quite new to the Arabs in the seventh century.

In the personal sphere, the chance to be reunited in safety with husbands and parents who had fled to Medina caused another exodus of Muslims from Mecca. Like the earlier group who left Mecca, these Muslims had to leave their homes and properties behind, which the Quraysh quickly seized, but their families in Medina now had the means to support them. It was against Arab custom to attack women and children, so even though some family members had fled Mecca under the threat of persecution, those left behind were generally not harassed. One notable exception was Umm Salamah, a woman who was forcibly detained by her clan in Mecca while her husband's clan assumed custody of her child. It was some time before she could reclaim her child and join her husband in Medina.

With the recent arrival of Sawdah, Muhammad was also establishing a stable household once again. His long-awaited marriage with A'ishah also took place. Abu Bakr bought a beautiful red striped wedding dress for his daughter in honor of the occasion, and after a simple ceremony, A'ishah went to live in her own private apartment adjoining the mosque. Being only around twelve years old or so, she nonetheless was graced with maturity, intellect, and charm. She spent her days in leisure, entertaining visiting friends and walking the streets of Medina in search of adventure. Her fine memory and attention to detail caused her to become a sought-after teacher on Islamic issues as the years progressed. Sawdah, who already had an apartment of her own, didn't encroach upon her co-wife's domain. She did, however, take A'ishah under her wing and guide her in her role as a wife.

That both women had their own space was in keeping with the Islamic code that dictated a man must treat each wife equally; each wife gets her own private apartment or house. Indeed, the practice of plural marriage was also an area upon which Islam would soon cast its eye. The first regulations were in the realm of fairness. Any man who had more than one wife could not favor one over the other. Muslim men were further instructed that having only one wife was the ideal, as it was very difficult to be fair. Muhammad was monogamous with his first wife for almost three decades and only took co-wives after her death to support widows or build alliances. His marriages were not due to desire or lust, as some have charged; he set up strict rules protecting the rights of women, married mostly older widows, and was rarely able to see his wives due to his various preoccupations as a prophet.

Islam did not outlaw the practice of plural marriage, but it modified and restricted it greatly. In Arabia before Islam, there were no agreed-upon rules concerning plural marriage. Islam applied the following rules:

- *A man will be held accountable to God if he does not treat each wife equally in all respects to affection and physical well-being.*

- *A man is counseled to have only one wife, as this is better for him.*

- *A man cannot marry more than four wives. (This stipulation was revealed after the last of Muhammad's marriages.)*

- *No woman can be forced into marriage against her will, and the authorities can annul any marriage that is forced. (This regulation was quite an advancement for women in a society where they were used to having no say in whom they married.)*

In time, Muhammad would marry several other women, and his wives would be considered scions of the community with the special status of *Ummul Mu'mineen,* or Mothers of the Believers. This status meant that they were authorities on Islam and could be consulted on matters of faith. Both men and women sought the counsel of these women. So as to protect their honor, the Qur'an asked them to cover their faces with the ends of their veils when in the presence of men whom they were not married or related to. Although the use of the *niqab,* or face veil, was mandatory for the rest of Muslim women, who only were exhorted to cover their hair as a sign of modesty, several women began to employ the niqab as well to show their greater piety, a practice that persists to this day in some cultures.

The Muslims of Medina passionately believed that Muhammad was a genuine prophet. When a new Qur'anic passage was announced, Muslims immediately put it into practice. The Medina of Muhammad had no religious police or enforcers to ensure the conformity of the community to Islamic values. There were no public beatings for infractions of the dress code or over the length of the beard. The spirit of tolerance in Islam was at its best. The operative verse in the Qur'an that guided the earliest believers stated that "There is no forcing anyone into this way of life. Truth stands clear from error." (Qur'an 2:256) Muhammad also directly instructed Muslims to treat people of other religions with respect. Once while Muhammad gave a sermon on the rights of non-Muslim neighbors, one of his companions commented that he was afraid Muslims would be asked to make their Jewish neighbors heirs to their property. Such was the nature of Islamic tolerance towards diversity.

Some people among the Arab population resented Muhammad's perceived intrusion on the public life of Medina. Led by the almost confirmed (and hence thwarted) king of Medina, 'Abdullah ibn Ubayy, this group wanted to preserve their pre-Islamic customs and only pretended to acquiesce, because they thought if they were patient enough they would outlast the new religion. Ibn Ubayy made no secret of his displeasure with Muhammad and remained aloof to the Prophet's entreaties.

Once Muhammad was passing by Ibn Ubayy's fortress and saw him sitting in the shade of a wall with some friends. The Prophet hailed him out of courtesy and took a seat, whereupon he began to explain something of Islam to the gathering. After he finished his discourse, Ibn Ubayy responded by saying,

> *Nothing could be better than these teachings of yours, if only they were true. Stay at home in your own house and preach to anyone who comes to see you, but don't preach to people who aren't interested to see you or hear what you have to say and don't enter someone's gathering with words he doesn't want to hear.*

Muhammad was taken aback and hurt by the stinging rebuke, though another man in the circle broke in and replied, "No, please do come to us with your words and join us in our gatherings and in our homes for we love this kind of talk and the bounty and guidance God has given us." The voice was that of one of Ibn Ubayy's friends, 'Abdullah ibn Rawahah, whom the sullen chieftain had always thought he could count on. Muttering that he could not resist if his own friends deserted him, Ibn Ubayy withdrew to his house.

Muhammad left as well, morose at the disaffected nature of Ibn Ubayy, and visited a friend who had fallen ill. When Muhammad explained why he looked so somber to his friend, who was also a clan leader of the Khazraj tribe, the friend counseled him to be kind to Ibn Ubayy because the arrival of Islam prevented him from being confirmed king of Medina. Thereafter Muhammad gave special consideration to Ibn Ubayy and spoke to him kindly. Because of Muhammad's considerate treatment, Ibn Ubayy and his followers eventually began to come to the mosque regularly to pray. Their lack of genuine commitment to Islam was apparent to many, however, and they caused much mischief. They came to be called the *Munafiqun*, or hypocrites.

Without mentioning these people by name, the Qur'an ominously noted their presence when the longest chapter of the Qur'an, the Chapter of the Calf, began to be revealed. The operative passage (Qur'an 2:14) stated:

> *Among people are those who say, "We believe in God and the last day," but they don't really believe. When they meet the believers they say, "We believe," but when they're alone with their evil associates they say, "We are really with you, we were only mocking them."*

This secretive clique took every opportunity to cast doubt in the minds of the sincere and questioned any new doctrine incessantly. The Qur'an acknowledged this tactic and asked people, "Would you question your messenger as Moses was questioned in ancient days?" (Qur'an 2:108) The hypocrites would pray loudly in the mosque in a showy way and then hold clandestine counsels in the night to plot and plan their next moves against Islam. They tried to remain camouflaged in the community, however, and fomented no public rebellion. Their true motives would be revealed later, on a day when the very survival of Islam would be at stake.

One of the main changes to the practice of Islam in Medina was the concept of public worship. The five daily prayers of Islam are performed at set times throughout the day, as determined by the position of the sun. The first prayer is said before sunrise, followed by the noon, afternoon, sunset, and late-night prayers. Because Muslims had been unable to gather freely in Mecca, they had never established a way to call the faithful to the mosque for prayer. People would show up based on their own reading of the sun, and latecomers often disrupted the concentration of those who had already begun their devotions. A way had to be found to alert people of the time uniformly and bring order to what was supposed to be a solemn ritual.

The Prophet first proposed appointing a man to blow a horn from a high wall, as was the practice of the Jews. He soon discarded this idea and considered a wooden clapper such as was used by the Christians of the day. A local craftsman fashioned a large instrument and delivered it to the mosque, but Muhammad didn't feel it was appropriate, and it was never used. Muhammad mulled over what to do. Then one morning a man named 'Abdullah ibn Zayd came to the mosque and told the Prophet that he had had a dream in which he saw a man wearing green garments. The apparition told him to put aside the clapper he was holding and to call people with the human voice instead. 'Abdullah then recited the words he was taught in the dream. He said "*Allahu akbar*" four times. This phrase meant "God is greater." Then repeating each of the following phrases twice, he continued, "I bear witness that there is no god but

God. I bear witness that Muhammad is the Messenger of God. Rush to prayer. Rush to success. God is greater. There is no god but God."

Muhammad listened and then exclaimed excitedly that this dream was a true vision from God. He told the man to seek out Bilal, the freed Abyssinian slave, and teach him the words, for he had a powerful voice. When the time for the next prayer came, Bilal climbed onto the roof of the highest house near the mosque and called out in his strong and melodious voice the *Adhan*, or Call to Prayer, which still rings out from the minarets of Muslim cities to this day. When 'Umar heard the lines floating over the city streets, he joined the throngs who converged upon the mosque to see what was going on and announced to the Prophet that he had had a dream the night before in which the exact same words were recited. Bilal was placed in charge of the prayer call and continued to summon the faithful for the next twelve years.

The fact that Bilal was black did not prevent Muhammad from choosing him for this honor, for even though Arab racism was legendary, Islam made its position on the subject known from its earliest days. Like almost every other aspect of Muhammad's teachings, Islamic belief in the equality of all people regardless of race was new to Arabia. Of course, racism wasn't just a problem in Arabia. Every civilization wrestled with the issue. In China, people from the furthest plains were considered subhuman. In India, the highly rigid caste system made permanent slaves of millions. Europeans also identified other races harshly, equating them with demons and such.

Muhammad called upon his followers to rise above color and racial prejudice: "You are all the children of Adam, and Adam was created from dust." The Qur'an made its own case clear by saying, "O Humanity! We created you from a single pair of a male and a female and made you into nations and tribes so you can come to know each other. The noblest among you in the sight of God is the one with the most piety." (Qur'an 49:13) The Prophet put these teachings into practice from the earliest stages of his mission, embracing people of every color, race, and social status. In an early speech he said, "There is no superiority of a white over a black or a black over a white."

One day Muhammad went to a respected family of Med
had a daughter of marriageable age. He asked them if thei
ter would like to marry Bilal. Both the mother and father started
offering excuses and indicated that they would rather not have
their daughter marry him. The Prophet then informed them, "Isn't
it enough for you that Bilal is a man of Paradise?" They thought
about the import of the words and asked their daughter, who
agreed to the match.

Arabian custom had always dictated that women should take no
public role in religious or political activity. The superiority of men
over women in all respects was also a widely accepted notion.
Muhammad changed that notion by asserting that men and women
were equals before God in every sphere. One telling Qur'anic passage reads, "For believing men and women, for devout men and
women, for truthful men and women, for patient men and women,
for humble men and women, for charitable men and women ... for
them has Allah prepared forgiveness and a great reward." (Qur'an
33:35) Women engaged in business, teaching, studying, public discourse, and all other areas of community life in Medina, with no
restriction other than the oft-repeated advice that no unmarried
man or woman should be alone together because Satan would be
the third among them.

How did women fare in the mosque? Although Muhammad did
mention that a woman receives more reward for praying at home,
in keeping with the realization that women in his time had many
responsibilities and often found it difficult to get out of the house,
he nevertheless did not forbid women from attending mosque services. At every prayer hundreds of women lined up behind the rows
of men. (The placement of women in the back rows was for prac-
tical considerations and did not reflect a demotion in status. The
frequent bowing of the Islamic prayer ritual would distract the
members of both sexes if the congregation were mixed.) Muhammad commanded men thus: "Do not prevent the female servants of
God from going to the mosque."

In these early days of Islam, women participated fully in the
educational life of the community and were as eager as the men to
learn the Qur'an and the values of their adopted way of life. One

day a delegation of several women met the Prophet and complained that the men were taking all of his time and that the
instruction of women was being neglected. The Prophet promptly
announced that one day a week would be set aside for women's
classes exclusively, and he honored this practice until there were
enough female scholars to look after the intellectual needs of his
female followers. What made Muhammad so accepting of women,
even though Islam today is so often perceived as stifling gender
equality? Muhammad was surrounded by independent women and
was used to their participation in business, social affairs, and major
decisions. He was principally raised by women as well, with
Halimah, Aminah, and Barakah molding his values and attitudes
towards women. His playmates as a boy consisted of both boys and
girls, and his wife of three decades was wealthier and of a higher
status than he was, and he always treated her with respect. After
he assumed the role of a prophet, his basic attitude did not change,
and he accorded the women of his family and community the
utmost honor. To examine the record of Muhammad and his mission is to gain a new respect for the improvements he made in the
lives of both men and women.

The Qur'an enshrined a new status for women and gave them
rights that they could have only dreamed of before in Arabia, so
why the seeming disparity between what once was and what now
appears to be? The answer lies in the deterioration of basic Islamic
education that occurred in the Muslim world after the disasters of
the Mongol invasions and the Crusades in the eleventh through
thirteenth centuries. The Mongols laid waste to half the Muslim
world and forbade the practice of Islam among their conquered
subjects for a hundred years, and the Crusaders decimated the
Muslim heartlands of Palestine and Syria, leading to a void of great
learning centers. Cultures that arose since that time have been
characterized by customs and local cultural leanings more than
genuine Islamic values.

In those first few months in Medina, Muhammad made it a point
to open a dialogue with the local religious and political leaders of
the three Jewish tribes. He would engage them in discussions on
interfaith issues as much as he would speak to his own followers.

Being the custodians of an ancient religion, the Jews were not looking to convert, but they listened politely. They were still undecided in the beginning about who and what Muhammad represented and harbored hopes of co-opting him for their purposes.

As the months passed and the differences between Islam and Judaism became apparent, however, the Jews began to realize that Muhammad was not going to join their religion. Eventually, a certain measure of distrust developed, but the Jewish elders had already given permission to their community members to attend Muhammad's teaching sessions. After getting a firsthand look at how persuasive Muhammad and the Qur'an were, however, they began to fear that some of their number might convert to the simple and direct teachings of Islam. These concerns were not unfounded. One of the top rabbis in the settlement converted to Islam and publicly called upon his brothers to follow suit. This alarming development, coupled with their sagging hopes for attaining dominance in Medina, caused a rift between the Jews and the Muslims that would not be easy to heal. Where once there was guarded optimism about the meaning of Muhammad's mission, now there was scorn and open derision.

An unknown artist's rendering of Medina in 1790. At that time the city was surrounded by thick ramparts.

The Qur'anic revelations, as they continued to unfold, also began to look at Judaism in a new light. Whereas earlier stories of the prophets of old, many of them held sacred by Jews, spoke of their trials and sacrifices in the cause of God, newer passages questioned the Jews' disobedience to God and even to the laws of Moses. Furthermore, the Jewish claim of being the chosen people of God was also questioned in verses that described the covenant as being superceded on account of the Jews' rejection of God's many messengers to them. While maintaining that there was indeed once a special relationship between the Divine and the Children of Israel, the Qur'an put forward that God had moved beyond that covenant and had turned his attention to other people, notably the Christians. This assertion didn't help interfaith relations between the Jews and Muslims. Muhammad held that Jesus was an authentic envoy from God who had been sent to call the Jews back to true faith. (Judaism did not accept any role for Jesus.) The further leap was made that because the followers of Jesus didn't fulfill their duty to God, the mantle of God's favor was now upon the followers of Muhammad. The Qur'an was merely God's last revelation to the world.

The Muslim proposition was presented earnestly and often in every public forum. Their leaders began to engage him in public debates over religious issues in their scriptures, which Muhammad, being an illiterate Arab, could not have known about. In particular, they would ask him to relate the histories of events that had happened centuries or even millennia before. Entire chapters of the Qur'an came to Muhammad in response to these challenges, including the complete renditions of such stories as Cyrus the Great, Moses, Joseph, and Abraham. Privately, the Jews initiated a campaign of slander and innuendo against Muhammad's every pronouncement and attacked his integrity and judgment. More insidious plans involved the false conversions of several rabbis whose mission was to disrupt Muhammad's classes with theological debate. During one such meeting, an undercover rabbi asked, "If God created everything, then who created God?" Muhammad answered with a verse from the Qur'an that said, "Tell them, 'He is One God, the Eternal Absolute. He neither begets nor was He begotten and there is none equal to Him.'" (Qur'an 112:1–4) Muhammad later publicly expelled a group of false converts from the mosque when they were caught plotting together in a dark corner.

Finding that they could make little headway in tearing down Islam theologically because the new faith's simple, direct doctrines made most debate futile, the various Jewish leaders looked for other ways to advance their own agenda. One community leader of the Banu Qaynuqa, Sha's ibn Qays, was passing by a group of Auws and Khazraj tribesmen leisurely talking and became incensed. In the past, the two tribes were enemies, and the Jews had always exploited this rivalry to their benefit. Sha's asked one young man of his tribe, who was skilled in poetry, to join the gathering and start reciting the odes composed by both groups after the Battle of Bu'ath. Old memories quickly resurfaced about glory, revenge, and deeds of valor. The members of the two tribes, moved by the rhythmic verse, went from reminiscing to shouting at each other. Both groups, passions enflamed, called their tribesmen to arms and soon dozens on each side had rushed out into a nearby plain and eyed each other with swords drawn and taunted the other side to strike the first blow.

Muhammad rushed to the scene with as many of the immigrants as he could find and stood between the two sides. "O Muslims!" he cried. "Will you behave like you used to in the days of Ignorance, even though I am with you and God has guided you to Islam, honored you with it, and helped you to leave your old customs so you could be saved from disbelief and united together as one?" After his conciliatory plea, both sides sheathed their swords and wept at their folly, finally embracing and resolving to resist such passions for tribal chauvinism in the future.

The Jewish leaders didn't know what to do with Muhammad after that. They could not discourage his followers with sophistry or divide them with old disputes, and even a few of their own community members had now converted. Seeking one last angle, a group of rabbis went to Muhammad and told him that a true prophet had to live in Jerusalem, for that was where the prophets of old resided. In addition, they reasoned that because the Muslims faced Jerusalem whenever they prayed, along with the Jews, surely that was where he belonged. Muhammad listened attentively but made no decision. A short time later, a new revelation came to him that instructed Muslims to change their direction of prayer to the Ka'bah in Mecca, due south. The verses were revealed while the congregation was praying in a small local mosque, and as Muhammad recited them, he turned to face the new way, and his flock did likewise. That mosque is now named the Mosque of the Two Directions. The Muslim community reacted with joy at this change because many privately believed that the ancient House of Abraham was a more fitting place to turn in unison.

Seeing that their relevance to Muhammad was rapidly receding, a delegation of Jewish elders approached Muhammad and suggested that if he changed the prayer direction back to Jerusalem, then they might be inclined to follow him. Muhammad refused the request, and the status quo resumed, with the Muslims and the Jews eyeing each other warily. As both sides were bound by treaty to respect each other's civil and religious rights, the hostility remained verbal and invisible for the most part.

An interesting event happened during that first year in Medina to broaden the religious debate beyond merely a Judeo-Muslim affair. A delegation of sixty priests and tribal leaders from the Christian region of Najran, a land in the deep south of Arabia, rode into Medina wishing to learn more about the man who claimed to have a new message from God. Perhaps their curiosity was heightened by the fact that several of their people had converted a couple of years before when they met with him in Mecca. An impromtu Congress of the Three Religions was organized, in which representatives of Judaism and Christianity met in an open forum with Muhammad and some of his followers. The meeting was lively as each side attempted to make its position known. One of the main topics was the nature of Jesus. The Jewish rabbis asserted that Jesus was not the Son of God, preferring to give that title to Ezra, one of their most important forebears, who salvaged their religion after the Babylonian captivity. They also postulated that Muhammad could not be a true prophet, for only a Jewish man could ever be so honored by God. The Christians vigorously defended the divinity of Christ and his plan for salvation while Muhammad laid out his proposition that Jesus was a messenger from God, though he was not God. He further expounded upon the Islamic belief that history revolved around a chain of prophets sent by God to guide the many nations of the world.

At one point in the proceedings, Muhammad challenged the Jews and Christians to read from their books on the subject of God and Jesus, and both sides politely demurred. Although Muhammad had never read any book before, he told them that their own books would bear witness against them. Muhammad concluded his remarks by reciting this passage of the Qur'an that said, "People of the Book, come to a fair understanding between us and you that we don't worship anything but God, that we don't make partners with Him and that we don't make anyone a lord besides God." (Qur'an 3:64)

As the meeting drew to a close, the Jewish delegation, which already had a wealth of experience in debating Muhammad, withdrew and returned to their sector of the city. The Christians remained, and Muhammad felt that they might be inclined to accept his message. After consulting among themselves, however, their chief spokesman, Abu Harith, explained that they had to decline Muhammad's offer of conversion on economic grounds. The people of his region had long had the favor of the Byzantine emperor in Constantinople and feared that he would withdraw his largesse if they left his religion. "What prevents me," he explained, "is what those people have done to us. They have honored us, enriched us, and made us influential. If I disagreed with them, then all that would be gone."

Undaunted, Muhammad entered into a treaty of peace and friendship with the Christians, and a document was signed that contained, among other things, the following points:

- Christians have the right to safety in their lives and property, and Muslims will respect those rights.
- No churches will be harmed, nor will any monasteries be closed nor priests impeded from their work.

- The Christians will not have to provide any supplies for the Muslims if there is a war with an enemy nor will their religious symbols be harmed.

- No Muslim will interfere in the practice of the Christians and their religion.

The Christian delegation amicably asked for Muhammad to send one of his teachers with them to explain Islam to their fellow countrymen, given that it seemed that they would be permanent neighbors. The Prophet assented and sent a trusted companion who would remain in Najran for many years. In addition, Muhammad sent word to a prominent community of Zoroastrian fire-worshippers on the eastern Arabian coast and invited their participation in a treaty of mutual respect as well. The pact was similar to the one signed by the Christians, and thus was Muhammad establishing a network of budding alliances among the more advanced religious traditions. The Quraysh in Mecca, meanwhile, took note of what was happening in Medina and discussed their options carefully.

Part Three

The Struggle for Survival

Chapter 9

The Great Battle of Badr

*Consider the treaties of the Quraysh, those treaties that
protect them on their caravans through winter and summer. They should obey the Lord of this House, because
He is the one who provides them with their provisions
against hunger and their security against fear.*
—Qur'an 106:1–4

The dominant Meccan tribe of Quraysh, with all its various
clans, had caused enormous amounts of suffering to the followers of Muhammad when Islam was in its formative years. Even
though the Prophet forbade Muslims to fight back, many converts
underwent torture and murder for the sake of their faith. When the
persecution became too great, Muhammad sent some of his followers to Africa for refuge, and later he had to flee to Medina with
the threat of murder hot on his heels. Although an official state of
war did not exist between Medina and Mecca, there certainly was
an understanding that the Meccans hated Islam and Muhammad
wanted to abolish idolatry and neither side would accommodate
the other.

Muhammad's escape and adoption by recognized tribes of
Medina meant that the Meccans temporarily had to halt their
campaign against him and other Muslims, at least outside their
immediate borders. A trickle of new converts to Islam in Mecca

still provided ample targets for their aggression. Those converts who could not flee were set upon mercilessly by their families and neighbors. Many converts had to hide their faith and perform their rituals in secret. A few were from the upper classes, but most of the converts were commoners or servants. In time Muhammad would utilize all these people as sources of information and gain valuable insight into the plans of his enemies. He would come to rely on sympathetic non-Muslim Meccans as well. For example, his Uncle 'Abbas, who had not yet converted and remained in Mecca, began to send messages occasionally when great events would take place in Mecca. This information helped the Muslims tremendously.

Whereas Mecca was bristling with armed men and the economic strength to back them up, the Muslims in Medina were just beginning to gather strength. With a mosque, relative safety, mass conversions, and a base of operations, Islam could begin to stand on its own as an independent power—if it had the time to do so in peace. Muhammad wisely began to use his diplomatic skill to prepare for the next phase of his cold war with the Quraysh, realizing that it would only be a matter a time before Mecca would try to reach him in his new sanctuary. The Muslims were still only a tiny fraction of the total population of Arabia, and they were not even a majority in Medina yet with its mix of Arab idolaters, Jews, and Muslims.

Muhammad's main task in his first year as a statesman was to initiate the network of treaties and alliances that protected his community and served his needs in the event of open hostilities with the Meccans. Evidence of this strategy and its effectiveness is apparent in the stipulations he included in the agreements made with the Jews of his own city, the southern Christians, the eastern Zoroastrians, and several outlying tribes all around Medina. He even succeeded in cementing a few alliances with tribes living along the western coast of the peninsula. These tribes controlled the main trade routes from Mecca to Syria. The Meccans took note of these alliances.

Given the nature of the bitter relationship between the Muslims and the Meccans and that the Quraysh had already struck the first blows in their campaign against Islam for thirteen long, arduous years, Muhammad's plan to strike back at the enemies of his religion was understandable. Revenge was not necessarily the issue, for the Muslims had already shown great patience and forbearance in their previous trials and tribulations. The verses of the Qur'an explained that the main focus for the believers in their struggle would be in two areas: getting justice and promoting religious truths. Righting wrongs, such as the seizure of the emigrants' homes and properties, or punishing the Meccans who engaged in murder and torture were powerful incentives to act. In addition, with the changing of the prayer direction from Jerusalem to Mecca and the focus of Islam increasingly oriented on putting a stop to the idolatrous desecration of the ancient shrine of Abraham, it also became patently clear that Mecca had to eventually be reclaimed for monotheism. A show of strength on the Muslims' part would also impress the embittered Jews of Medina and the various outlying Arab tribes, showing them that Muslims were a potent force and could back up their words militarily.

Accordingly, about seven or eight months after his migration to Medina, Muhammad sent his Uncle Hamzah to confront a large patrol of Meccan cavalry near the coast of the Red Sea. (The Meccans, cognizant of the fact that Muhammad's position could threaten their caravan routes, had already begun expanding the areas of their operations.) The Muslim force numbered about thirty riders, all of them immigrants from Mecca. The Quraysh contingent, under the command of Abu Jahl, consisted of nearly three hundred men. The imbalance might have looked extremely advantageous to the Quraysh, but in Arabia, martial bravado bred a sense of fearlessness that enabled men to fight even overwhelming foes. In addition, the concept of martyrdom was already well entrenched in Islam, and those who died fighting in God's cause were automatically promised paradise. On the other hand, Arab idolatry had no afterlife in its theology, so death in battle offered no reward. This outlook may have made the Meccans less inclined to fight fiercely. Nevertheless, no fight took place that day: A man friendly to both sides intervened and persuaded them all to go home.

Islam's conception of religious martyrdom is much more developed than that of Christianity. According to Muslim beliefs, any person who dies or is killed in the path of God automatically goes to paradise where they receive unimaginable delights. A martyr's body is not ceremoniously washed, as are other deceased individuals, in order to honor his or her sacrifice. On the Day of Judgment, Islam teaches, the martyrs will be absolved of their sins and will ask God to return them to earth to die for his cause again, so great is their conviction that their cause is just and righteous. To qualify as a martyr, one cannot desire wealth or fame; one has to be killed by the enemy and not commit suicide, which condemns a person to Hell; and one must obey Islamic rules for armed action, which forbid harming noncombatants, women, children, animals, and trees. In recent years, some political movements have tried to bend or circumvent these rules, causing a great deal of turmoil.

At about the same time, Muhammad sent another force under the command of a prominent companion named 'Ubaydah ibn al-Harith to meet a Meccan patrol led by Abu Sufyan. The Muslims numbered sixty; the Meccans numbered about two hundred. The two forces met in a valley and made menacing moves against each other. Only one arrow was fired from the Muslim side, and both groups withdrew with no further action taken. A smaller expedition a few weeks later led by Sa'd ibn Abi Waqqas also ended in no engagement with the Meccans. All these moves and counter-moves, coupled with the alliances of both sides, made northern Arabia resemble a great chessboard. Sooner or later someone would attempt to take the other side's pieces.

Muhammad did not participate in any of these early forays, but in the year 623, he embarked on a new strategy of taking the fight to the Quraysh. The only vulnerable targets within striking distance were the caravans the Meccans sent to and from Syria along the main roads north and south. For years the Quraysh had counted on a system of treaties with tribes all along the caravan routes to keep their wares safe. Muhammad's ability to win over some Arab tribes to his side made the Meccans' route more precarious.

In the spring and summer months, caravan traffic increased, and Muhammad chose that time to act. In September, he learned that a great train of over two thousand camels was lumbering southwards back to Mecca from Syria. Its leader was Umayyah ibn Khalaf, one of the worst tormenters of Muslims in Mecca. The chance to strike back at him and to seize some of the wealth that Mecca depended on was too inviting to pass up. Although reports of the exact position of the caravan were spotty at best, Muhammad nonetheless led a hastily organized expedition of two hundred men and set out in search of the prize. They missed their objective, however, and returned to Medina empty-handed.

In October, news of another great caravan came to the Muslims' attention: This caravan was heading north toward Syria and was led by Abu Sufyan. Muhammad led the same number of men as before to prepare an ambush in a place called 'Ushayrah, located at a bend on the main road that curved gracefully outward from Mecca heading in an arc along the shore of the Red Sea. Muhammad's forces waited there for a whole month and again had no luck: The caravan had passed just before they arrived. Undaunted, the Prophet made a friendship pact with two local tribes and again returned home, feeling that he might yet have another chance at Abu Sufyan's caravan when it began its return journey southwards several months later.

The Meccan leadership was aware that their caravans to Syria were vulnerable as they passed near Medina, so they arranged for more numerous armed guards to accompany them. The Meccans also began sending out even more patrols to cover the space between their city and Medina and had encountered Muslim soldiers, as was previously mentioned. Although no fighting had occurred as of yet, the Quraysh were eager to strike a blow and demoralize the Muslims of Medina. Muhammad had only been back in Medina for about ten days when a tribal leader named Kurz al-Fihri, who was an ally of the Quraysh, led a group of raiders in an attack upon a herd of cattle on the outskirts of the city. The Prophet raised a hasty pursuit force and tracked the rustlers to a valley named Safawan, near the famous oasis of Badr. They never found the enemy, however, and returned home having missed their prey yet again.

After this provocation, Muhammad deemed that more dramatic and concerted efforts were called for. But with the close of summer, Meccan caravan traffic would begin to shift to the winter pattern and thus head southwards towards Yemen, effectively out of reach of his forces. A new revelation (Qur'an 22:39–40) came to Muhammad that helped bolster his call for expeditionary volunteers:

> Permission to fight is given to those who were attacked,
> for they have been wronged. Only God is able to give
> them victory. They are those who were driven out of their
> homes unjustly and for no other reason than that they
> said, "Our Lord is God."

Although every Muslim from Mecca already knew they were at war with the Quraysh, this clear pronouncement of the validity of their resistance helped mobilize the local Auws and Khazraj converts to take greater risks.

Bold moves needed more reliable intelligence gathering, however, so Muhammad sent out a patrol under the command of 'Abdullah ibn Jahsh with a sealed letter to be opened only upon reaching an appointed place. Together with his patrol of eight men, he rode for two days and then opened the document. He was told prior to leaving not to force any of his men to go with him farther after that. The note simply said, "As soon as you read this paper, proceed to Nakhlah between Mecca and Ta'if. Find out for us where the Quraysh are moving and what they are doing." All of the men agreed to follow these orders except for two who decided to scour the hills around Mecca searching for some of their camels that the Quraysh had seized earlier. Both men were intercepted and captured. They were ignominiously taken to Mecca and held as prisoners.

Meanwhile, 'Abdullah led his six remaining men to the appointed location and set up observation posts overlooking the main road to Yemen. In the late afternoon, they spotted a small caravan of donkeys with only a few attendants minding it. Their instructions were to observe and not to engage any enemy targets; moreover, it was the last day of one of the traditional sacred months when the Arabs observed a general truce. Should they attack such an easy treasure trove or wait? 'Abdullah convinced his men to move on the caravan, and in the process they killed one man and took two others prisoner. A fourth man escaped to Mecca and sounded the alarm, but no pursuit could overtake the captured booty now. As 'Abdullah led his prisoners and their donkeys northwards, the Meccans spread the news far and wide that the Muslims had violated the great sacred month, a convention that had been honored in Arabia since time immemorial. Despite their public appearance of outrage, what they really hoped to get out of the situation were valuable propaganda points. This incident could help them discourage many Arab tribes from entering into treaties with Muhammad, for how could the tribes trust a man who broke with tradition?

When 'Abdullah returned to Medina he was greeted with disappointment by the Prophet, who knew full well the position of custom among the Arabs. He scolded the men saying, "I did not instruct you to fight during the sacred months." He then ordered the captured caravan to halt and took no part in the official division of the booty, even though the Qur'an officially allotted one fifth of any spoils taken to be given to him to support the cause of Islam. The two detainees were lodged in a local dwelling under guard, and the baggage was sequestered to await further consideration. 'Abdullah soon found himself the object of scorn from his peers for taking such a bold move without permission.

Indeed, the impending public relations disaster made the Muslims appear off-balance. When the Arabs heard the news of the violation, many questioned the motives of Muhammad and his followers. That Muhammad did not order the attack mattered little; the voices of dissent and anger all along the Hijaz were not interested in the details. The Jews of Medina seized upon this incident as well, hoping it would foment a war between the Muslims and Mecca that would very likely spell disaster for Muhammad. The Muslims themselves were also feeling uneasy and did not know how to interpret what happened. The attack had taken place around the time of sundown, and according to the custom of the day, sunset was the official calendar end of a day, so it might have occurred technically during the first day of the next month, one that was not sacred. Only guidance from the Prophet would still their misgivings.

A few days afterwards, in the mosque Muhammad recited the following revelation (Qur'an 2:217):

> They ask you about the permissibility of fighting in the holy months. Tell them, "Fighting in them is wrong, but to impede people from following the cause of God, to deny God, to desecrate the Holy Sanctuary, and to expel people from it is a greater wrong in the sight of God than just fighting in a holy month." Persecution is worse than killing. They will never stop fighting you until they have succeeded in turning you away from your religion.

Thus the answer was given that because the Quraysh had done far worse to the Muslims, fighting back in a sacred month was no great sin. The Muslims felt their side had been vindicated, and 'Abdullah was reinstated in the good graces of the community. The Prophet then accepted his share of the booty to be used to support the mosque and its functions. The detractors of the Muslims failed to come up with a convincing counter-argument to this new explanation.

A short time later, a delegation arrived from Mecca asking for the return of their two captured men. The prevailing custom in those days was to pay a ransom for someone's freedom. Rather than accept a monetary offer, however, Muhammad said, "We will not accept your ransom for the two captives unless you return our two men whom you have captured, namely Sa'd ibn Abi Waqqas and 'Utbah ibn Ghazwan. If you kill them, we will likewise kill your two men." The Meccans agreed to these terms, and soon the two Muslims who had been taken while looking for their camels arrived in Medina. Of the two Meccan captives, one returned home, and the other converted to Islam and decided to stay in Medina.

For nearly five months, Abu Sufyan managed a caravan of over two thousand camels, each loaded to the hilt with merchandise from all over the world. Passing through rugged terrain and bandit-infested lands, he had safely led his caravan into well-settled and well-policed Syria, which was under the control of the Byzantines at the time. Abu Sufyan was well pleased with the performance of his traders and was sure that the great caravan he had led would return to a hero's welcome. Indeed, nearly every man of Mecca who could afford to do so had bought a share in this enterprise, and it was one of the grandest expeditions Arabia had seen in a long time. Through business savvy and prime deal-cutting, Abu Sufyan had increased the value of the goods under his care several-fold. With autumn on the wane, he prepared his caravan for the long, slow journey home with one thought on his mind: Would he be safe from attack? He had only narrowly missed attack on his way north from Mecca; would he be so lucky on the way back?

This thought also occupied Muhammad's thinking. In war, the supplies and economic resources of the enemy are fair game, and weren't many of Abu Sufyan's camels carrying the goods of Mecca that were stolen from the Muslims in the first place? Determined not to miss the caravan a second time, Muhammad sent out two swift scouts to locate and report on its whereabouts. The pair traveled to a point on the main road named Hawra, which was due west of Medina near the Red Sea. There they hid among the tents of a friendly local chieftain until the object of their search came into view. After a little while, thousands of camels strung two by two passed through the area, with bales of silks, jewelry, pottery, clothes, vestments, spices, gold, and other treasures strapped to their backs. The prospect of such a trove tantalized the two young men, and they waited impatiently for the caravan to pass before scurrying back to Medina with the train's exact location.

Mecca was quite unaware of all these plots against its valuable cargo. The Meccans felt confident that, through a combination of expanded patrols and their leaders' expertise, no great disaster would befall them. Hadn't Muhammad's forces shown ineptitude in capturing caravans before by only being able to take one small and poorly guarded donkey train? The only unusual occurrence that disturbed the peace of an otherwise typical week in Mecca was the warnings of Muhammad's aunt, 'Atikah, who had such a realistic dream that she had to tell others about it. She spoke of a nightmare that included a disaster that would befall the Quraysh, touching every house. Abu Jahl began mocking her and her family, saying that it had already produced a male prophet with whom they were now at war—was the clan of 'Abdel Muttalib going to bring forth a female prophet as well? No one took her warnings seriously.

Meanwhile, in Medina, Muhammad had decided not to wait for word from his scouts, fearing that any reports they would provide would arrive too late. If he drove his forces hard, he might be able to find the long-winding caravan by simply cutting a straight line to the southwest. With this plan in mind, he called his followers together and announced, "Out there is the caravan of the Quraysh. Mobilize your forces now and try to capture it. Maybe God will give it to you as booty." Of the throngs of people present, many Muslims responded to the call; many others, mostly from the native convert population, declined because they were not used to such adventurous forays. A few non-Muslims asked to join in, but Muhammad would not allow them to accompany him unless they converted first. A few did so.

As the Muslims prepared to march, however, one stealthy enemy of Islam (most likely a hypocrite or a Jewish dissenter, though the person was never found out) quickly sent word to Abu Sufyan about Muhammad's plans. When Abu Sufyan heard the report, he became alarmed. He had less than forty fighters at his disposal and would be powerless to prevent the capture of his caravan if he were intercepted. Given the pace at which fully laden camels can travel, outrunning Muhammad's forces wasn't an option. Thinking quickly, Abu Sufyan hired a local man named Damdam to send word of his predicament to Mecca. Damdam rode hard for several days to reach the outskirts of the city. Following Abu Sufyan's instructions, he tore his shirt, cut his camel's ears, broke its nose, and turned the saddle around sloppily. Thus attired in an air of desperation, he sped into the city standing on his camel's back. He began shouting wildly at the top of his lungs, "Help! Help! Quraysh! Muhammad and his followers are attacking your caravan! You may yet be able to stop them!"

This dramatic display was designed to cause an uproar in the streets, and it worked. Thousands of men and women began shouting and clamoring in anger and confusion. Abu Jahl raised his voice over the tumult and urged his countrymen to rise and defend their property. So many Meccans had a stake in the caravan that any thought of loss made them hot with rage. A few dissenters called out, however, that if Mecca sent its finest warriors away for several weeks, the Kinanah, a rival southern tribe, might take advantage of the situation and attack Mecca. A chief of the Kinanah tribe happened to be visiting Mecca on business, and he pledged on his honor that his tribe would not take advantage of this situation.

Abu Jahl's proposal was heartily accepted by the crowds and later confirmed in an emergency meeting of the clan elders. In short order an army of one thousand men, fully equipped for battle, was organized and ready to move. Within a day or two, this fearsome force took to the road northwards, following the main coastal trade route. Nearly every chief of the combined clans of Mecca (none wishing to appear cowardly) rode with the army, though Abu Lahab sent a man who owed him money in his stead. This display of raw power replete with javelin throwers, mounted cavalry, lancers, and numerous slave attendants was designed as much to impress the surrounding tribes in the Hijaz of Mecca's vast power as to defend the caravan. Referring to the poorly defended donkey train taken by 'Abdullah ibn Jahsh, one of the Meccans quipped, "Does Muhammad think that this caravan will be like the one they ambushed before?"

For his part, Muhammad put off his army's departure from Medina as long as he could because he didn't want to leave his daughter Ruqqayah, who was gravely ill. Finally he instructed Uthman ibn Affan, who had recently married his daughter, to remain behind and see to her. At the head of 305 men who were so poorly equipped that every three soldiers had to take turns riding a camel, the Prophet set out on an intercept course to capture the Quraysh caravan. A white banner led the column, and two black banners, one representing the immigrants from Mecca and the other the helpers from Medina, followed. Muhammad insisted on sharing his camel as well and so walked part of the way. It was also the fasting month of Ramadan in the year 624, and the Muslims were forbidden to eat or drink during the daylight hours. This fasting made the effects of the hot desert sun that much more oppressive.

The planned ambush point was a small complex of wells at the oasis of Badr. Caravans on the main road arriving from Syria invariably had to stop there because the next available water sources were much farther away. At first, the Muslim army traveled without detection, and then they encountered a lone Bedouin traveler. He could have been a Meccan spy or could have at least informed the Meccans of the Muslim position. Muhammad questioned him at length before telling the man he could leave, determining that he was not a threat. Before exiting, the curious desert dweller asked the Prophet, "Where are you from?" Not wanting to give away his people's identity, Muhammad paraphrased a verse from the Qur'an by saying, "We are from water." Thus the puzzled Bedouin could not provide any information to the enemy. After several more days of hard marching, the Muslims finally made camp a few miles from Badr. Muhammad then sent two scouts ahead to reconnoiter the oasis and its surrounding Bedouin encampment and to gather any news that they could from the local people.

The scouts pretended to be drifters and casually approached the oasis that sat astride the main trade route. Several tents belonging to local residents dotted the surrounding area under and outside the shade of the tall palm trees. Walking down a hillock to one of the wells to draw water, the scouts overheard two young women arguing about a debt one owed to the other. The one promised her friend that she would have the money when the great caravan came in a day or two because she would draw water for its men and receive a handsome salary. The scouts were relieved that Abu Sufyan's venture hadn't arrived yet and rushed back as fast as their camels would take them to tell the Prophet.

Had they waited only a few more hours, they would have seen a solitary rider approaching the wells who looked as if he were searching for something. It was Abu Sufyan himself, who rode ahead to see if the wells were safe to enter. After inquiring about any strangers, he was directed to a spot on a small hill where two men had earlier tethered their camels while they went to draw water. Abu Sufyan examined the fresh camel dung he found there and noticed some date stones in it, a sure sign that these animals had come from Medina, which was known for its endless supply of the fruit. Sure that danger was near, he made all haste back to his caravan and ordered it to turn away from the main road and instead to take a secondary, more circuitous road that hugged the shore of the Red Sea.

Just before the scouts arrived back in the Muslim camp, news reached Muhammad that a large force from Mecca was on its way to rescue its caravan. Given the grave turn of events, Muhammad felt compelled to call a council of war. He asked the gathered officers what they thought he should do. Abu Bakr and 'Umar both were for advancing upon the enemy. After meeting and—with God's grace—defeating the Meccan army, they still might have time to take the caravan. Having already taken to the road in search of their prey, the general consensus among the leaders was that, whether it was an attack against an army or a caravan, they were willing to proceed. A recent convert named al-Miqdad said,

> Prophet of God, move ahead towards the object that God
> has shown you. We are with you. By God, we will never
> say to you, as the Jews said to Moses, "Go alone, you
> and your Lord can fight, while we stay here and await
> your return." Instead we will say, "Go forward, you and
> your Lord to fight, and we are with you."

A thoughtful silence followed al-Miqdad's pronouncement, and then Muhammad reiterated, "Speak, men, and give me your advice." Thus far only immigrants had spoken in support of the mission. Muhammad wanted to gauge the feelings of the helpers, who had pledged themselves at 'Aqabah and were his main source of protection now. Realizing that it was their turn to speak, a man of Medina named Sa'd ibn Mu'adh stood up and said,

> We have believed in you and confirmed that what you
> brought us is the truth. We made an agreement with you to
> hear and obey. Go ahead with whatever you decide, for we
> are with you. By the one who sent you as a prophet, if you
> were to lead into the sea, we would go in it with you and
> not one of us would remain behind. We aren't afraid that
> you might make us face an enemy tomorrow. We will hold
> firmly and stand our ground and press forward against the
> enemy in solid ranks. We hope that God will let you see us
> in action and that you won't be disappointed, rather you
> will be proud of us. Lead us forward with God's blessings.

Muhammad beamed at their loyalty and announced, "Go forward then and be confident, for God has promised me one of the two, either the caravan or the Meccan army. By God, it's as if I see the enemy lying supine on the ground." When the two scouts finally returned with the news that the caravan was expected in Badr shortly, the Muslims prepared themselves for the next day's events. Whether it would be a battle with a superior foe or the rout of a semi-defenseless caravan, only God knew.

Muhammad, feeling a great sense of excitement, rode ahead of his men towards Badr. He saw an old Bedouin man who did not know him and asked him if he had heard anything about an army from Mecca in the area. The grizzled settler responded that a force was in the vicinity somewhere. Hoping that his troops could get their hands on the caravan first and thus slip back to Medina before any engagement, Muhammad returned to his encampment and sent three more scouts back to Badr after nightfall to get additional information.

The scouts, led by 'Ali, managed to capture two teenage servant boys who were drawing large amounts of water at an hour when such activities were unusual. When they arrived back at camp, Muhammad was praying, so some of his companions began questioning the youths. When the boys wouldn't answer, some of the men began to rough them up, and the boys started saying whatever they thought their captors wanted to hear. When Muhammad completed his prayers, he exclaimed with displeasure, "How amazing! When they are telling the truth, you beat them. When they are telling you lies, you leave them alone." Muhammad asked the boys how many Meccans were in the army. They replied that they didn't know, so Muhammad asked them how many cows the army cooked each day, and they answered nine or ten. From this answer, the Prophet surmised that there were around a thousand men in the enemy camp. He also learned that nearly all of the top leaders of the Quraysh were in attendance and eager for a fight.

Neither army knew the exact whereabouts of the other, and it was some time before further information became available to the Prophet. He ordered his men to set up camp just outside the oasis of Badr and wait, hoping the caravan would soon come into view.

The locals, who had already heard reports about two armies seeking to clash in their neighborhood, promptly fled. The next morning the Muslim forces readied themselves uncertainly. When word finally arrived that the caravan had escaped the vicinity by another road and that it was now hopelessly out of reach, Muhammad had to make a decision. Should the Muslims await the certain appearance of the Meccan army, or should they withdraw without meeting the enemy like previous Muslim forays? Many of Muhammad's companions surmised that the Muslims would look foolish if they were to return to Medina without engaging anyone or anything, especially after assembling such a large force. Following a lengthy discussion, Muhammad and his officers resolved to occupy the oasis and see what moves the Quraysh would make.

Even though the decision had been made, some of the native Muslims of Medina were worried about the prospect of a battle. Most of them had no experience in combat. In contrast, the Meccans were able to field a body of warriors with vast martial experience. With the hope of getting easy riches fading away, the morale of many of the men also began to sag. The Qur'an answered their concerns with the following new revelation (Qur'an 8:7):

> Now that God has promised that "one of the two" would
> fall to you, you wish it was the weaker of them, which has
> no strength to resist. Rather than easy booty, God desires
> that truth shall prevail, that justice should be done, and
> that the unbelievers should be scattered.

God's own prediction of victory helped to sway the troubled hearts of Muhammad's army. That night the men slept peacefully, and in the morning many commented on how rested they felt.

And what of the caravan, the weaker of the two forces? It was now quite safe. Abu Sufyan sent a swift runner to the Meccan army to inform its leaders that everything was under control and that the army could now return home. Armies in Arabian history often avoided war when it was convenient, so shame should not have been an issue. Indeed, some Meccan leaders were in favor of returning, but Abu Jahl, whose hatred for Muhammad was unquenchable, stood up and passionately pleaded for the army to move forward and engage the Muslim force. With fiery appeals to their bravery and honor, he won over most of the clan elders to his position. Only one chief returned to Mecca with a few fighters, leaving the overwhelming bulk of the army intact. Abu Jahl sent the courier back to the caravan and instructed him to tell Abu Sufyan that the army intended to go to Badr and spend three nights celebrating so that the rest of the Arabs would note their determination and continue to fear their strength. Obviously, Abu Jahl expected that Muhammad would withdraw now that the easier target had escaped. If he didn't and there was a fight, so much the better.

Muhammad chose to array his forces near the first well he encountered. One of his companions, al-Hubab, noting their exposed position, asked, "Messenger of God, is this the place where God has guided you, for if that's the case we won't budge an inch from it, or have you chosen this place for strategic reasons?" The Muslims followed Muhammad's orders no matter what they were, but they were not too shy to ask him if his decisions had come from God or from his own estimation; Muhammad had emphasized that when he relied on his own judgment, he could make a mistake as well as many man. Only when certain knowledge came to him from God could no alteration be made.

Muhammad answered that it was his opinion that the well he had chosen was a good spot. Al-Hubab was a much better strategist and suggested that they move to the well that would be closest to the enemy, thereby preventing it from accessing the wells and drawing water for its men. Keeping in mind that the Muslims were fasting and couldn't drink anything until sundown, al-Hubab further proposed that they fill the wells in with sand as a precaution, leaving only a large nearby cistern filled for the benefit of any wounded or exhausted Muslims who would have to drink.

The Prophet agreed, and Muslim soldiers were put into action covering the wells and making makeshift fortifications. Afterwards a small booth was made for the Prophet so that he could escape back to Medina rather than falling into Meccan hands in case the battle went poorly. Such was the loyalty of his men that they would rather die than see him captured. The tent-like structure was unnecessary, however; Muhammad was not the type to remain in the rear when his people needed him. After making some final preparations and plans for the placement of the men, the Muslims awaited the enemy.

The Meccan army set up its base of operations behind a hill just outside the oasis. The Meccans intended to use the natural landscape to their advantage, keeping the Muslims unaware of their true number and protecting their camp from a frontal assault. As the morning sun ranged higher in the sky, the leaders of the Quraysh marched with their men around to the front of the hill and arranged their ranks to face the wells of Badr. Before them they saw the army of Muhammad, standing in formation in front of the soaring palm trees with their white shirts and turbans and swords at the ready.

Meccan spies had already informed Abu Jahl that the Muslims numbered no more than three hundred and had scanty provisions and supplies. Most didn't even have any armor, and the Muslims had few horses, so a cavalry assault would not be a danger. Abu Jahl felt confident that his seasoned fighters would make quick work of their foe. Not everyone in his ranks shared his confidence, however; some still felt uneasy about engaging the Muslims in battle. Weren't they a determined foe who would fight to the death? Nearly every Meccan noble was present, and if many of the nobles died, then it would leave a vacuum of leadership. Although the concerned clan elders were afraid to speak up for fear of Abu Jahl's wrath, one man named 'Utbah ibn Rabi'ah called out,

> Men of Quraysh! We surely won't achieve anything by meeting Muhammad and his companions in battle. If we beat them, every one of us would recognize in their dead a cousin, an uncle, or a neighbor of his own clan and tribe. Let us go home and leave Muhammad alone among the tribes of the desert. If they kill him, your purpose will be achieved. If they don't, you won't have to suffer the ill effects.

Filled with battle lust, Abu Jahl fumed and sent for the brother of the man who had been killed during 'Abdullah ibn Jahsh's raid the year before. He called to him when he came into view, "Your

ally, 'Utbah, is shamelessly calling men to go back to Mecca even
as you see your enemy with your own eyes. There is your enemy!
You must avenge yourself! Rise up and avenge the slaying of your
brother!" The man raised his sword high in answer to the taunt
and cried, "Ruination! My brother shall be avenged! To battle!" A
collective shout rang out from the Meccans as they raised their
idols high on poles and cried for revenge and slaughter. The javelin
throwers waved their weapons in the air, the horses stamped their
hooves, and the men unsheathed their swords.

Muhammad and his soldiers eyed the scene before them
uneasily. They were outnumbered three to one by an enemy fully
equipped with the deadliest armaments Arabia could muster. The
thought of the time-honored code of Arab honor and its tradition
of torturing and dismembering captured enemies must have sent
shivers through the inexperienced Muslim ranks. The Prophet did
what he could to steady them, reminding them of their duty to
God and God's promise to help them if they would only be true in
faith. He walked along their rows, straightening their lines and
encouraging each man until he felt they were ready. He then raised
his hands to heaven and prayed, "My Lord, here is the Quraysh in
all their power seeking to attack your prophet. My Lord, give us
victory, the victory that you have promised me. If you let this group
of men perish today, who will be left on earth to worship you?"

Abu Bakr, standing near his friend, replaced the cloak that had
fallen off Muhammad's shoulders and replied, "Messenger of God,
don't take it so hard. God will fulfill his promise to you." The
Prophet lost himself in thought for a moment and then regained
his senses, exclaiming that he again saw a vision of the Muslims
winning. He rushed back in front of his men and, seeing the enemy
just a bow shot away, encouraged his men to stand firm. He quickly
taught them a battle cry if fighting broke out: "Strike, victorious
ones!"

Suddenly, the fearsome warrior al-Aswad al-Makhzumi burst
forth from the Meccan lines and charged at the cistern the
Muslims had reserved. Hamza rushed onto the plain of battle
to meet him, and both sides watched awestruck as the men
exchanged blows. Hamza swung mightily, parrying a sideswipe, and

struck al-Aswad in the leg, severing it completely. A final blow dispatched the attacker, and Hamza retreated to his post to the shouts and cheers of the Muslims.

The Meccans looked on stunned for a moment, and then three of their top leaders strode forward into the middle of the plain separating each army, challenging the Muslims to individual duels. The three were 'Utbah ibn Rabi'ah (no doubt wanting to save face for his call to withdraw before), Shaybah, and Shaybah's son, Walid. Several eager men from Medina rushed out to meet them, including one of the first men to take the pledge of 'Aqabah, but when the Meccans saw them, they jeered at them saying, "We have no quarrel with you; we want to face our own people." As the youths scurried back to their lines, a crier from the Meccan side shouted, "Muhammad, send out our peers of our own tribe to fight us!"

The Prophet asked Hamza, 'Ali, and another immigrant named 'Ubaydah to go forth. They confidently stepped out and walked towards their foes. They unsheathed their swords and met their Meccan counterparts in a fight to the death. Hamza quickly dispatched Shaybah while 'Ali, wielding a sword with a double blade at the end, struck down Walid. Then both of them rushed over to help 'Ubaydah, who had received a mortal blow to the leg before wounding his opponent, 'Utbah. The pair made quick work of the Meccan and then carried their disabled comrade back to their lines.

Seeing all three of their champions fall, the Meccans let out a collective groan of anger and disgust. Suddenly, two arrows shot out from their ranks and felled two men where they stood, one an immigrant and the other a helper. Muhammad quickly announced, "By the one who holds power over Muhammad's soul, the man who fights them today, firmly and persevering, God will let him into Paradise." The Muslims let out a cheer and felt their courage peak. Muhammad scooped up a handful of gravel, walked to the front of the Muslim position, and flung the gravel at the Quraysh as a challenge. He then ordered a general charge as the Quraysh rushed madly to overwhelm the Muslim lines like a wave rushing over a patch of sand. The Muslim lines held firm, though, as the Meccan horses and men crashed wildly against them.

The Muslim plan was to try to pick off as many of the enemy's leaders as possible. They were easy to spot because they rode prominently on horseback in the finest armor. Prior to the battle, Muhammad had beseeched his men to try to avoid killing people who had been fair and kind to him while he was in Mecca, but distinguishing who was who became increasingly difficult as the mass of bodies tangled in the close combat. Dead men choked the shifting space between the warriors' positions. The Meccan cavalry found itself hemmed in by its own undisciplined soldiers, and horses began to stumble and throw their riders.

Bilal caught a glimpse of Umayyah ibn Khalaf, his former owner who had tortured him so badly before, surrounded by a group of Muslims trying to subdue him and his son. The former slave let out a battle cry, "Umayyah! The chief of idolatry! Death to me if he escapes!" Then he charged furiously through his own men and struck down his nemesis. Meanwhile, each Muslim leader became a rallying point around which the rank and file would congregate. They spun forward in little rotating islands through the seething mass of dark-robed Quraysh, giving no heed to their small numbers or to the danger on all sides. Soon even Abu Jahl lay dead, wounded in the face as was predicted by the Qur'an in Mecca many years before. As the Muslims surged forward chanting, "God is one! God is one!" the Meccan warriors began to lose heart and retreat. Clearly the momentum was now against them.

Muhammad, surrounded by some of his men, was in the middle of the battlefield encouraging the Muslims to advance. At one point, he threw dirt in the faces of an advancing party of Meccans, and his act of defiance emboldened his men to overwhelm the superior force. In small groups, the Meccans began to break from the battle and retreat towards their camp. Soon the Meccans, now leaderless, began turning and running from the Muslims at top speed. The Muslims let out a chorus of cheers exclaiming, "God is great!" and pursued the terrified Meccans into and past their encampment. When the battle was over, the remnants of the Meccan force, bedraggled and confused, made their way back home in shame. There was no talk of regrouping and counterattacking because they had no one to lead them.

The outnumbered and ill-equipped Muslims had beaten an army three times larger and suffered only fourteen deaths. The Meccans, however, in addition to losing their camp and all its wealth and supplies, had almost fifty casualties, including nearly all their leaders. Seventy Quraysh were taken prisoner and gathered on the battlefield under guard. In explaining the miraculous Muslim victory, the Qur'an stated (Qur'an 8:9 and 8:17),

> *Remember when you implored the help of your lord and*
> *he answered you: "I will help you with a thousand angels,*
> *ranks upon ranks." ... It wasn't you who smote them, it*
> *was God. When you threw the pebbles, it wasn't your*
> *act, but God's, in order to test the believers by a gracious*
> *trial from himself, for God hears and knows all things.*

God's help, Muhammad announced, allowed them to win. Angels had put fear in the hearts of their foes and strengthened their resolve so that they fought with almost superhuman prowess.

The Muslims buried the fallen Quraysh warriors in a large pit on the battlefield and spent the rest of the day and evening burying their own dead and collecting the considerable booty. Later that night, Muhammad walked among the freshly dug graves and addressed the Meccan deceased. "People of the grave! 'Utbah, Shaybah, Umayyah, and Abu Jahl! Have you now found that what your Lord promised is true? I have found what my Lord promised me, have you?" Some nearby companions asked him, "Are you talking to the dead?" Muhammad replied, "They hear me no less than you do, except that they are unable to answer me."

Then he noticed one of his companions looking despondent. It was one of the sons of 'Utbah who had been a convert from the early days of Islam. "Are you sad about what happened to your father today?" Muhammad asked him. "No, by God," Utbah's son, Abu Hudhayfah, answered. He then continued,

> *I haven't scolded my father's memory or mourned his fate.*
> *I always knew him to be a wise and good man, and I had*
> *hoped he would eventually convert to Islam. When I saw*
> *what happened to him on the battlefield, I thought of his*
> *undying devotion to the idols despite what I had hoped for*
> *him. In the end I'm just feeling sorry for him.*

The Prophet consoled him for his loss and praised his resultant bravery and prayed to God to give him strength.

The next morning, the weary but proud Muslims began to distribute the booty, as was the custom. There were swords, camels and horses, and a great deal of traveling gear. Several of the men began to argue, however, pointing out that some had taken greater risks in the battle than others. The Prophet stopped the squabbling at once and ordered that all the booty be kept together until he could decide how to parcel it out. After assembling for the long march home, the victorious army mounted freshly captured camels and horses and set off with a long line of prisoners trailing behind. The Prophet did not allow the guards to rope or chain the prisoners excessively, and he ordered that they be given food in equal amounts to the Muslims.

> Much sensationalism has sprung from the misinterpretation of Islamic law concerning slavery. In fact, Islam shies away from the terms slave and master, and Muhammad forbade their use. A Muslim soldier's captured enemy can be a servant for him, but they can only be obtained through war. Kidnapping, waylaying, or impressment are illegal in Islam. According to Islam, captured enemies have the right to fair and humane treatment and the right to be set free upon payment of a fine or ransom by relatives. If no ransom is paid, that servant has the right to be fed and clothed according to his controller's own living standard. If the servant is ever struck in anger, Islamic law stipulates that he can sue for freedom. Forcing servants to convert to Islam or overworking them are forbidden. Servants also have the right to pay their way to freedom. In the end, the Qur'an called the freeing of slaves an act of essential righteousness.

After three days' travel through the desolate brown desert, the Muslims made camp in the Valley of Safra, only a couple of days from Medina. There the Prophet began dividing the spoils. He gave an equal portion to all, save any Muslim horsemen, who got a double portion for the greater risks they took in their maneuvers. He set aside equal portions for the heirs of the deceased. He also assigned a portion to those Muslims left behind in Medina to act as guards and watchmen to keep an eye on enemy raiders and the local Jews, who seemed ready to revolt at any time. Later in the journey, two men who had murdered and tortured Muslims back in Mecca were found among the prisoners and brought before the Prophet for judgment. One of the men, Nadr, stood trembling and called out to his fellow prisoner, "Muhammad is surely going to kill me. He looked at me with eyes that had the judgment of death in them." The other man spat back, "You're a coward."

Then Nadr saw Mu'sab, a distant Muslim relative of Muhammad's, standing nearby and beseeched him to intervene on his behalf. Mu'sab answered, "You used to speak all kinds of slander against the book of God and his prophet. You also used to persecute and torture his companions." Nadr begged for help, saying that he would have treated Mu'sab nicely if the Quraysh had captured him, but Mu'sab rebuffed him saying, "By God, I don't believe you. I am not at all like you. Islam has cut all of my ties to you." Nadr and another blatant abuser of human rights, 'Uqbah, were then executed. The rest of the prisoners were treated humanely and were not harmed.

Just after the battle, Muhammad sent two messengers back to Medina to bring the good news to the people there. One of them, his adopted son Zayd, rode Muhammad's own camel, Qiswa. As the messengers entered the city, each in a different district, they proclaimed loudly the news of the Muslims' great success. They also mentioned the number of Meccans who had been captured and the names of the clan elders who had fallen. Muslims, Jews, and the few remaining idolaters in the city came rushing from their homes and filled the streets. The Muslims were celebrating; however, the embittered Jews and idolaters were somber and sullen-faced, for they had secretly hoped the Quraysh would win.

A group of Jews began disputing the reports, saying that if Muhammad were indeed alive, then he would have ridden his own camel into the city and not sent it ahead. Soon the Jews began chanting, "Muhammad is dead, and his companions were defeated!" They also said that Zayd had lost his mind in the heat of battle and was now hopelessly insane. A few more reports came in from arriving travelers that confirmed the news of the Muslims' victory, and the Muslims rejoiced even more heartily.

One Jewish leader, realizing that the Muslim victory squashed his people's chances of regaining ascendancy in Medina, lamented in an assembly, "Death for us is better today than life. What kind of life can we live now that the best men of Mecca, their lords and kings, are dead and defeated?" Now many among the Jewish community felt that it would be impossible to dislodge Muhammad and his religion, given the rout of their potential allies. Their hatred of Islam was so strong that they would praise idolaters over Muslim monotheists. The Jews of Medina considered Muhammad a dangerous imposter who, like Jesus before him, would call for people to dismiss Judaism. Local politics and the desire to dominate Medina, which the Jews still knew as Yathrib, also played a role in the Jewish opposition to Islam.

The next day the Muslim army entered Medina with great fanfare. Never before had the Muslims had so much to celebrate. As the men dispersed to their families with the captured booty and the promise of even greater security for their community, a tremendous sense of joy descended upon the city. A long passage of the Qur'an was revealed that spoke of the lessons of the Battle of Badr and exhorted Muslims to remain on their guard. Another day of confirmation of the Muslims' good fortune came when the long prisoner train entered the city the following morning. Sixty-eight of Mecca's finest warriors were now the humbled prisoners of the Muslims. This turn of events seemed like incontrovertible proof that God was on the Muslims' side and that they would win over their foes in the end. The captives were parceled out to be held in the custody of various companions under conditions of house arrest until their fate could be decided.

While the celebration continued in Medina, Mecca was filled with laments of loss and humiliation, which were laying the seeds for yet another confrontation. Muslims, still basking in their victory, had no cares at all, but time would soon demonstrate how things could change. Didn't the Qur'an itself explain this situation in a telling verse? It said, "We alternate conditions among nations so God can bring out those with faith, and so he can appoint witnesses from among you." (Qur'an 3:140)

Chapter 10

The Battle of Uhud

Believers! Don't betray the trust of God and His Messenger,
nor misappropriate knowingly things that are entrusted to
you. Realize that your possessions and your descendants
are only a test and that the greatest reward lies in God.
—*Qur'an 8:27-28*

Mecca was in quiet mourning for her lost sons. Her grand army had marched out to protect a caravan of unimaginable value, but while the merchandise was now safely within their possession, many of its guardians were now dead or imprisoned in Medina. Just before the bedraggled men returned home, a rider who had gone on ahead entered the city to bring the woeful news of defeat. The people he initially spoke to refused to believe him; it was inconceivable that any ragtag force Muhammad could muster would overcome Mecca's best and strongest warriors, especially with their enormous advantages in men and equipment. As the ragged column came into view over the plain, however, disbelief turned to fear and sorrow as wives, fathers, and other relatives asked the returnees about missing loved ones.

The Meccan warriors were indeed in a pitiful state. They had traveled on foot for nearly a week, with scant provisions or shelter. As the names of the dead or missing were announced, cries of sorrow rang out in the streets. Not wanting to appear weak, however, the remaining Meccan leaders decided against paying ransom for any of their prisoners, no matter how painful this proposition would be. They didn't want to hand another victory to Muhammad by enriching his followers. Meccan women resolved not to mourn publicly lest the Muslim women would hear of it and gloat.

Abu Lahab, the one high-level leader who didn't accompany the foray, was filled with wrath and vitriol and began cursing the Muslims ceaselessly. While visiting someone's home, he was informed that one of the household slaves had recently converted to Islam. He immediately set upon the slave, beating him mercilessly in front of his mistress. The lady, who had already secretly converted herself, picked up an iron bar and whacked Abu Lahab over the head, shouting that he had no right to beat her slave. He withdrew and within a few hours developed a violent fever that raged for a week, culminating in his sudden death. Thus was fulfilled the prophecy that Muhammad had made so many years before, when he called down the wrath of God upon the Meccan nobles who humiliated him while he was out for a walk with his daughter Fatimah. The others had fallen at Badr.

Back in Medina the Meccan captives were on everybody's mind, for they were a constant reminder to the Muslims of just how much they had suffered over the years at their hands. Indeed, when the line of prisoners was marched into the city a day after the main army arrived, the Prophet's own wife, Sawdah, came out to assail them. One man she knew, who had his hand tied to his neck because he was particularly troublesome, was Abu Yazid Suhayl ibn 'Amr. She taunted him saying, "Abu Yazid! Did you surrender all by yourself? You're pitiful. What a shame that you didn't fall on the battlefield in a heroic manner." Muhammad had to call her aside and ask her, "Sawdah, are you inciting the man further against God and his prophet?" She realized the sharpness of her tongue and apologized.

The Meccan captives were held under guard while their fate was decided. Many trembled in fear, knowing that common Arabian custom regarding defeated enemies was ruinous ransom, painful torture, or even death. Although Muhammad had receiveds a revelation informing him that capturing prisoners for worldly benefit was wrong, he had already decided, at Abu Bakr's insistence, to hold the men, so he told the Muslims that God would allow his decision to stand. The Prophet's companions were divided about what to do with the men. Among the prisoners were the most violent persecutors of the Muslims of Mecca. 'Umar ibn al-Khattab, known for swift justice for wrongdoers, believed they should all be killed outright, rather than live to fight Muslims another day. He urged the Prophet, "Messenger of God, these are the leaders of the deniers of truth. If you kill them, then God will give Islam a great victory because of it." Abu Bakr, who was less stern than his fellow companion, counseled the Prophet to spare the men and accept ransom in order to defuse further Meccan anger. Many of the prisoners were relatives of the Muslims. Perhaps, Abu Bakr reasoned, a few of them would accept Islam.

In the end, Muhammad called the Muslims to the mosque and announced that Abu Bakr was like the angel Michael, who was a herald of God's mercy, and like Jesus and Abraham, who prayed for mercy for their enemies. 'Umar, on the other hand, was like Gabriel, who delivers God's just condemnation, and like Noah and Moses, both of whom prayed for God to decimate their foes. By publicly recognizing the validity of both men's opinions, Muhammad skillfully assuaged any ill will that might develop from his decision about the prisoners. Keeping in mind that the Muslims were poor, especially those immigrants who had left most of their property to the Meccans when they fled, Muhammad declared, "You have families to support. Don't send any of your captives away until you have been paid for their release. If they try to escape, then strike them down." One Meccan captive, a professional poet who had made a career of inciting others against the Prophet, stepped forward from his guardian and said, "I have five daughters to support. Please give me to them as a charity on your part, Muhammad, and I promise I will never fight you or slander you again." The man was freed, but he later broke his word and fought against the Muslims once more.

Relatives of the captured Meccans soon broke ranks with their leaders' directive and came to Medina to seek the release of their family members. Muhammad was instructed to tell the prisoners before they left that, "If God finds good in your hearts, He will give you better than what you lost and He will forgive you, for God is merciful and forgiving." (Qur'an 8:70) This statement may have seemed puzzling to the Meccans as they departed, but it showed that Islam still had a place for the people of Mecca if they chose to join it. When one man named Suhayl, who was famous for his elo-quence, was released, 'Umar felt that he was more dangerous than the strongest warriors and asked the Prophet if he could knock out his front teeth to keep him from speaking in public again. Muhammad said that he was not allowed to disfigure any creature that God had made, for God would then do the same to him. Even prisoners had rights to humane treatment in Islam, and this treat-ment was another one of those new concepts that set Muslims apart from the rest of Arabia.

While Muslims excitedly collected payments of sums that ranged between one and four thousand dirhams for the release of the men they held, the Prophet was dealing with another personal loss. He learned when he arrived back in Medina that his sick daughter Ruqqayah had passed away. In sadness he prayed for her and counseled Uthman, her widower, to be patient. Now he had only three daughters: Umm Kulthum, Fatimah, and Zaynab, the latter who was still living in Mecca. Events would soon unfold, however, that would bring some measure of joy back into their father's heart.

Zaynab's husband, Abul 'Asi ibnul Rabi, who was still an idol-ater, was among the captives taken at Badr. When Ruqqayah and Umm Kulthum had been divorced by their husbands in anger as a way to publicly humiliate the Prophet, Abul 'Asi stood firm beside his wife, despite their religious differences. When Zaynab found out that he was being held, she sent money for his ransom, includ-ing a necklace that had once belonged to her mother, Khadijah, who had given it to her daughter on her wedding day. Muhammad, who learned what had happened when he noticed the necklace in the treasury, felt overwhelmed by grief and melancholy. He told his companions, "If you think it's possible to let her have her captive and to return to her the payment she made, then do so." It was done as he asked. Before allowing Abul 'Asi to return to Mecca, however, Muhammad asked him to leave Zaynab because of their religious differences, and he agreed. Muhammad secretly sent three of his companions back to Mecca to retrieve Zaynab and bring her to safety in Medina.

Some months later, Abul 'Asi was delegated to take a shipment of money to Syria on behalf of the Quraysh. When he traveled past Medina, he and his cargo were captured by a Muslim patrol and taken into custody. He managed to sneak out of his guardian's house late one night and found Zaynab's door. He begged for her intervention, and in the morning she was able to convince the men who had captured him to both return his money and let him go. Abul 'Asi then made a swift trek back to Mecca. He returned all the money to its owners and publicly asked if anyone was owed anything further. When no one in the crowd spoke out, he instantly recited the Muslim confession of faith, "I declare there is no god but God, and I declare that Muhammad is his servant and messenger." Then he told his stunned listeners in the marketplace, "By God, I didn't join Islam before only because I feared that people would say I ran off with their money. Now that everyone is paid back and my reputation is clean, I declare my conversion." He immediately left the city and headed back to Medina where the Prophet allowed him to remarry his daughter Zaynab. Another marriage was in the offing as well. After a year or more of mourning, Uthman eventually was wed to Muhammad's daughter Umm Kulthum, and thus he came to be known as the Possessor of Two Lights, on account of his having been married to two daughters of the Prophet.

Muhammad's youngest and favorite daughter, Fatimah, was now a fine woman in her early twenties. She was devoted entirely to her father and was so outgoing and positive that her beaming face seemed to radiate light. People even began calling her by the nickname al-Zahrah, which means "the Shining Person." She also had a close physical resemblance to her father. Once A'ishah, Muhammad's other current wife after Sawdah, remarked, "I've never seen anyone in God's creation resemble the Messenger of God more in speech, conversation, and manners than Fatimah .... When the Prophet saw her approaching, he would welcome her, stand up, kiss her, take her by the hand, and then set her down in the same place he had been."

Fatimah was also very beautiful and soon marriage offers began pouring in from all quarters of Medina, though she refused every suitor. Then a young man named 'Ali ibn Abi Talib gained the courage to go to the Prophet and ask for her hand in marriage. When he approached Muhammad, however, he became nervous and tongue-tied. He stared at the ground and said nothing. The Prophet then asked, "Why have you come? Do you need something?" 'Ali still couldn't bring himself to say what he wanted. The Prophet then inquired thoughtfully, "Perhaps you came to propose marriage to Fatimah?" "Yes, I did," replied 'Ali shyly. The Prophet smiled and said, "Then welcome to the family." Then he asked 'Ali what *mahr*, or dowry, he had for Fatimah. 'Ali answered that he didn't have anything to give. The Prophet then reminded him that he had a shield that could be sold. So 'Ali sold the shield to Uthman for four hundred dirhams. 'Ali was returning back to the mosque to show the Prophet the money he had for Fatimah when Uthman came after him and told him, "I am returning your shield to you as a present from me on your marriage to Fatimah." 'Ali and Fatimah were married, and the Prophet himself performed the ceremony. The proud father of the bride prayed, "O Lord, bless them both, bless their house, and bless their children."

Islam requires that a groom pay a dowry to his intended bride before marriage. This mahr, or marriage gift, is not a payment to the woman's family; she alone receives it. The bride can demand any sum of money or material good, though if the amount is too high, she can accept partial payment on her wedding day and let the man pay in installments. This money is a form of insurance for her; in the event of a divorce, the man is not legally allowed to seize her property. Although Islam mandates alimony and palimony payments to the divorced woman, this extra money provides that a woman need not fear a drastic reduction in her standard of living. If a woman initiates the divorce, the Muslim family court judge may ask her to remit a portion of the mahr to her husband to compensate him. In any case, the Qur'an counsels men to forgo this award as a charity if they so choose.

Life for the newlyweds was sweet yet difficult. 'Ali worked as a water carrier, and Fatimah ground corn for a fee. One day she said to 'Ali, "I've ground corn until my hands are blistered." 'Ali, who was also tired, replied, "I've carried water until my chest hurts." Then 'Ali got an idea. "God has given your father some captives of war, so go and ask him to give you one as a servant." She went to the mosque to ask, but she felt shy when she saw her father and didn't say what she really wanted. Later she and 'Ali both went and asked together. The Prophet replied that he had an obligation to help the poor Muslims first, allowing them to collect ransom payments, so he couldn't grant their request. Later that evening, the Prophet visited them in their home and told them,

> Shall I teach you something that is far better than what
> you asked me for? Words which Gabriel taught me? You
> should say "Glory to God" ten times after every prayer.
> Then follow it with "Praise God" also ten times, and then
> "God is great" ten times also. Then before going to bed at
> night, you should say each one thirty-three times.

This ritual and others like it contributed to a large and growing number of faith-reinforcement exercises that Muhammad encouraged his followers to recite.

After the last of the Meccan men returned home from Medina (the poorest ones having been released for free by Muhammad), the Meccans felt that they could now mourn their loss in public. Many women shaved their heads and whipped themselves, following the customs of their people, and the men beseeched their idols for revenge and listened to woeful stories of the battle told in verse. The concept of vengeance was so ingrained in Arab society that it was a foregone conclusion that action would eventually be taken. The poets recited prose lamenting the dead and vilifying the Muslims, while the new clan chiefs struggled to fill the shoes of their dead forebears. Hind, wife of Abu Sufyan and daughter of the fallen 'Utbah, vowed that she would not mourn the deaths of her father, brother, and uncles until she had her vengeance against the Muslims. She also resolved not to sleep with her husband until such time. Seeking to demonstrate his own bravado, Abu Sufyan promised not to bathe until he had defeated Muhammad.

Mecca soon found an ally in the Jews of the Banu Qaynuqa tribe in Medina. Already angry that their influence was on the wane in a city they had once come close to controlling, and mindful of the vast differences in doctrine between Judaism and Islam, the leaders of this tribe of Jews began to send secret envoys to Mecca to incite the people there to attack the Muslims again. One Jewish elder, Ka'b ibn al-Ashraf, was keenly interested in getting the war back on track. Hadn't the Jews been able to gain ascendancy before by pitting the Auws against the Khazraj? Wouldn't the same tactic work between the Meccans and the Muslims? Ka'b had cried that Muhammad's victory was like a deathblow to him, and he was the most vocal in encouraging the Meccans to remember their dead. After returning from one trip to Mecca, the emboldened Ka'b even publicly proclaimed to Muslim men that many of their wives had been unfaithful to them while they were away.

Realizing that Ka'b was calling for a renewed war against the Muslims and enraged at the affront to their women's honor, a group of Muslims attacked and killed him in the street one night after coaxing him from his home with promises of a lucrative business deal. His murder, though not sanctioned by the Prophet, heightened the Jews' anger toward Muhammad and Islam. A party of Jewish leaders came to Muhammad to insist on redress. The Prophet replied, "The man that you claim was an innocent victim harmed us greatly and composed slanderous poetry against us. If he would have kept quiet like his brethren, nothing would have happened to him."

Besides the murder, the Jews were still fuming over occasional converts to Islam from their own community. A Jew who was owed a sum of money by Muhammad angrily came one day and demanded full, immediate payment. He was rude and aggressive, intimating that the Prophet was neither prompt nor trustworthy. 'Umar, who was present, became incensed at the Jew's incivility and began to shove him away roughly. Muhammad smiled broadly and asked 'Umar to leave the Jew alone, and then he explained, "We needed something else besides this kind of response from you. I needed to be reminded to pay my debts, and he needed to be told to ask more nicely. There are still three days left for me to repay him in the agreement, but go to the treasury and pay him with an added bonus besides." The Jewish man was given the money that afternoon. He then returned to Muhammad and declared his acceptance of Islam to a stunned audience. He was later asked why he converted and he answered, "Those are not the manners of ordinary men; these are the manners of the prophets." Despite differences in religious doctrine, Muhammad and his companions continued to do business with Jewish merchants in Medina. (When Muhammad died, his armor was in hock to a Jewish shopkeeper.)

Muhammad's reasonable attitude towards his Jewish neighbors did little to temper the anger of the Banu Qaynuqa, however. Their close proximity to the Muslims made their grievances all the more tangible. Even though each group in the city, the Muslims, the Jews, and the idolaters, had its own distinct neighborhoods, there was also considerable interaction and intermingling among the groups as people visited shops and bazaars across the sprawling settlement. The Jews couldn't avoid seeing Muslims and hearing their call to prayer echoing through the air five times every day. This constant interaction presented many opportunities for tension to develop until one day the actions of a particular group of shopkeepers led to a devastating breach of the city charter.

One day a Bedouin Muslim woman came into Medina to see a jeweler about remodeling an ornament. She found a craftsman in the Banu Qaynuqa quarter and proceeded to discuss the job with him, but instead of merely listening to how she wanted the piece to look, the shopkeeper insisted that she remove her headscarf so he could fit the jewelry by hand. She refused and adamantly told him to do the work from her verbal instructions. The man became angry, and while she examined something else in the store, he moved silently behind her and tacked the end of her dress to a nail in the wall. When she abruptly turned to go, her clothes were torn from her body, and she cried in shock at her nakedness. The shopkeeper laughed at her, and a Muslim man who happened to be passing by was so filled with rage that he attacked the Jew, killing him. Nearby Jews surrounded the Muslim and beat him to death. Relatives of the Muslim victim quickly learned what had happened and called on their clansmen to help, and soon a riot erupted in the street. Jews and Muslims fought ferociously. Muhammad rushed to the area and convinced both sides to back down.

Cognizant of the enmity the Banu Qaynuqa had for him, he asked the members of the tribe to stop harassing him and the other Muslims and to respect the treaty they had signed. He said he would do the same and control his people. Jewish tempers were high, however, and one of their leaders shouted, "Muhammad! Don't think you're invincible. The people you fought [at Badr] were weak in war. By God, if you go against us you'll find out what it means to face a warrior race." With the gauntlet thrown, the Muslims could not back down or they would risk being ridiculed as weak and cowardly, so Muhammad ordered a mobilization of his forces. Instead of engaging in a battle, however, he chose a different tactic. For the next fifteen days, his men enforced a blockade of the entire neighborhood of the Banu Qaynuqa by not letting anyone in or out. Thus cut off from their livelihoods, the Banu Qaynuga had to sue for peace.

Muhammad, heeding the Qur'anic prohibition of taking captives merely for worldly benefit, believed the Jewish warriors should be executed or enslaved for breaking the covenant of peace in the city. 'Abdullah ibn Ubayy disagreed, for though he was a Muslim, he still had alliances with the Banu Qaynuqa. He was fiercely insistent, even going so far as to grab the Prophet's shield while he held it and demand that his allies be spared. The Prophet, who had perhaps suggested the harsher option out of anger only, relented and ordered that the Jews of the Banu Qaynuqa leave the city forever. Accordingly, the Jews packed their goods and possessions and left the next day, heading northwards. Eventually the tribe, which consisted of almost two thousand people, settled near Syria and lived peacefully thereafter.

The Muslims took over the many homes and shops that had belonged to the Banu Qaynuga, and the Prophet distributed these to his followers, saying it was part of the bounty of God bestowed upon them. A sense of calm descended over the city, and it seemed as though peace would at long last grace its inhabitants. The two remaining Jewish tribes, the Banu Nadir and the Banu Qurayza, lived outside the city proper in fortresses, still respecting the provisions of the treaties.

But the menace of Mecca loomed on the horizon. The first attack came when Abu Sufyan led a large group of raiders to the fields of Medina and murdered a farmer. They burned his date palms before fleeing southwards in the face of an armed Muslim posse that came after them. To aid in their flight, Abu Sufyan ordered his men to cut loose their food sacks to lighten their horses. Several bags of flour broke open as they fell, spreading a puffy cloud behind them. Rather than impressing the rest of Arabia, however, the tribes ridiculed this puny raid by calling it the Campaign of Flour Dust.

Seeing the growth of Muslim power and influence, many tribes in the countryside around Medina began to fear a loss of revenue. Prior to Muhammad's arrival in the north, the Quraysh had paid protection money annually to the local tribes so that their summer caravans would not be harassed. If the Meccans decreased their shipments or chose another route, these payments would dwindle. Though none of the various tribes, each of which was small and controlled only limited areas, could face the Muslims alone, the tribes attempted to form a grand coalition to fight the Muslims. When Muhammad found out what was happening, he assembled a force of several hundred men and went out in search of these allied forces, which consisted of the Ghatafan and Sulaym tribes. The Muslims were able to capture over five hundred camels as the enemy chose to flee and not to engage the men who had defeated the fearsome Quraysh at Badr. Muhammad led a later expedition against two other tribes that had amassed an army, and this force also fled without a fight to the mountains to the north. A third report came to Medina of an invading force of tribesmen on the march from Bahrain, but the tribesmen retreated as well when they learned Muhammad was leading an army out to face them. Muhammad never hesitated to ride out to meet these threats: The more the Muslims appeared strong and able, the less likely they would have to face new foes in the future.

The Meccans realized that their traditional trade route to Syria was slowly being cut off. From the vicinity of Medina all the way west to the coast of the Arabian Sea, Muhammad exerted his power and influence with impunity. All of the coastal tribes now had to sign treaties with him, and his feared patrols intercepted every Meccan caravan they could find. A meeting of Abu Sufyan and the newly elevated clan leaders, who were all young men with little experience, decided to try an alternate route that swung widely to the east and up into the eastern edge of Syria, near Iraq. Though the route was without the oases and other amenities they were used to, it was at least theoretically safe from Muhammad's grip. Accordingly, in the year 625, the Quraysh, who were desperately in need of a successful venture, assembled a grand caravan to attempt this new path. Its total worth in goods and material was well over one hundred thousand dirhams.

Little did the Meccans realize that a Muslim named Nu'aym happened to be visiting their city and noticed the preparations. When he learned of the caravan's intended route, he hurried back to Medina and informed the Prophet. Muhammad sent his adopted son Zayd to lead one hundred riders to intercept the new prize. When the Meccan guards saw the Muslims glide over the dunes at full speed, they turned tail and fled. The Muslims seized the abandoned camel train and returned to Medina with their loot. They didn't know that this would be the last seizure that the Meccans would tolerate. With the desire to revenge Badr still burning in their hearts, the loss of a caravan of this magnitude impelled the Meccans to take more concerted action than they ever had.

Muhammad had just celebrated his new marriage to Hafsa, the widowed daughter of 'Umar, when news came from Mecca of a large army on the march. The Quraysh had three goals: to take revenge upon Muhammad and his community, to regain their influence over the coastal tribes, and to reestablish a secure trade route north once again. They had been preparing for this new war for a long time. Indeed, all of the proceeds from Abu Sufyan's grand caravan that was saved at Badr were earmarked by mutual consent for weapons procurement for the next campaign against the Muslims. The Quraysh enlisted the aid of several skilled poets and orators, including the poet who had promised Muhammad he would slander him no more, to whip up war hysteria among the clans in and around the city. The Meccans assembled a force of three thousand men divided into three massive columns. The warriors were all locals except for one hundred men from Ta'if. This formidable army was fully equipped with armor and weapons, two hundred horsemen under the command of a talented leader named Khalid ibn Walid, and three thousand camels to bear the rest of the force. So great was the supply train that hundreds of slaves were put to work as porters and cooks.

The men were not the only ones preparing to sally forth to battle, however; many of their wives and daughters decided to come along to encourage their husbands and fathers and to see the grand slaughter that was sure to come. Many men objected to their inclusion at first, pointing out that in the unlikely event that they lost, their own loved ones would be taken captive. Hind, Abu Sufyan's wife, stated flatly, "Indeed! We will accompany the army and watch the battle. No one can stand in our way or force us back into our homes. If the women were there on the Day of Badr to witness the soldiers running away, it never would have happened." Thus Hind attributed the failure at Badr to the absence of women, in whose presence their men would have been inspired to fight harder. No man felt secure enough after that statement to oppose her, so hundreds of women tagged along as the great army began the long march north.

After about a week's traveling, the multitude reached the place where Muhammad's mother was buried. Some of the Meccans wanted to dig up her remains and defile them, but cooler heads pointed out that such an action would set a bad precedent in Arabia and the graves of their own people might be tampered with as well. After another day or so, they were within five miles of Medina. They established base camp at the foot of a small mountain named Uhud.

'Abbas warned his nephew Muhammad of the invasion. Though he clung to idolatry and was a loyal member of Qurayshi society, he also loved his nephew and had great admiration for his principles. 'Abbas described the supplies, strategy, and size of the invasion force. He closed his letter urging his nephew to take great care in his next moves. The courier arrived just ahead of the Meccan force. Time was of the essence. The Prophet showed the letter to his closest companions and held secret deliberations to decide what to do about it. The Meccans were still a full day's travel from Medina, so Muhammad sent two brothers to scout out their location and report back. After their report confirmed 'Abbas's letter, Muhammad announced the frightful news to the community. Panic gripped Medina. Soon reports came in of a huge cavalry force moving closer and closer. Frightened farmers streamed into the city with tales of armed men occupying their fields and seizing their livestock. That night the Muslims set up regular patrols around the city and were in a state of high alert. Several of Muhammad's companions even stood guard over the Prophet as he slept.

The next morning the discussion in the mosque was lively among Muhammad, his companions, and other local leaders. The Prophet believed that they should remain within the city behind fortified walls and repel the invasion through defensive means. Even 'Abdullah ibn Ubayy, who was known as a hypocrite on account of his grudging acceptance of Islam, agreed:

> Messenger of God, we have used this same tactic before.
> We used to fortify the city and shelter the women and
> children in the upper stories of the houses from where they
> could hurl stones down at the enemy while we met them
> with our swords. Our city, Messenger of God, is un-
> touched, for no enemy has ever entered it without being
> defeated. On the other hand, we always found loss when
> we tried to fight outside the city. Please listen to me and
> follow this wise plan which I have learned from the best of
> our leaders who have gone before.

This position would have carried the day, for many in the mosque agreed, but a large number of younger men present had been unable to participate in the Battle of Badr. They wanted to experience the glory of open battle for themselves. They were joined by some vocal veterans of Badr who were convinced that God would bring their side victory no matter how large an enemy they faced. One of these men suggested that the Quraysh would later boast, "We laid siege to Muhammad and his companions inside the walls of Yathrib, and none of them dared to come out and face us." Another man warned that if they didn't go out, nothing would prevent the Meccans from coming and raiding at will. These arguments began to sway those assembled, and the consensus evolved that the Muslim army should go out to meet their foes. Grand talk of vanquishing the idolaters filled the air, and even some of the more cautious were convinced that they couldn't possibly lose. An old man named Khaythamah then spoke in moving words about his own desire:

> Maybe God will give us victory over them, or it will be
> our turn to earn martyrdom. Even though I badly wanted
> to join in at Badr, it wasn't my fate to go, rather it was
> my son's, and God was pleased to let him die as a martyr.
> Last night I saw him in my dreams, calling to me,
> "Hurry, Father, join us in heaven! I have found every-
> thing that God has promised me to be true." By God,
> Messenger of God, I now long to join my son in heaven.
> I am quite old and my hair is graying. Truly I yearn to
> meet my Lord.

Powerful were the invocations of heaven, where, according to the Qur'an, earthly enjoyments ranging from mansions to virginal pleasuremates to the finest foods and gardens await those who fall in battle for God.

Muhammad decided to go along with the majority, in keeping with the tradition of mutual consultation, or *shura*, which he was carefully trying to foster among his companions. He adjourned the meeting with instructions that all preparations for war must be completed before nightfall. He then returned to his apartment to gather his armor. Just before the proponents of open battle left the hall, though, one of the chiefs of the Auws, Sa'd ibn Mu'adh, scolded them for adamantly pushing an option that the Prophet was against. Some of them felt remorse and told the Prophet when they saw him next that they would go along with his original idea if he wanted. Muhammad, who was now dressed for war, declined. "I did suggest something else, but you refused. No prophet will remove his armor once he has donned it until God decides between him and his enemy. Listen then to my command and obey, for if you are steadfast you will achieve victory." This statement was not stubbornness; the Qur'an counseled, "Once you decide on something, then trust in God."

By nightfall Muhammad set out at the head of a column of roughly one thousand men and several dozen women who were to act as field doctors and nurses. The Muslims were slightly better equipped this time, though there still weren't enough mounts to field an effective cavalry. Scouts had already informed the Prophet of the Meccan camp at Uhud, so he set his sights on moving to the other side of the mountain, across from the enemy.

After a few hours' travel, the army stopped to rest in a small village known as Shaykhan, where the Prophet noticed that a contingent of his force looked quite unfamiliar. He recognized none of the men nor their battle standards. He inquired and was told that they were Jews of the Banu Nadir, allied with 'Abdullah ibn Ubayy. Muhammad flatly refused to allow them to participate in the fight, equating the Jewish veneration of their ancient prophet Ezra with idolatry, because some Jews of Medina did subscribe to the view that Ezra was the son of God. Muhammad said, "You don't ask for help from idolaters to fight other idolaters." The Jewish column was commanded to return home. Ibn Ubayy was beside himself in anger but kept it inside, saying only to his close associates that he saw it as a blatant slap in his face and a military blunder. For Muhammad, the principle was more important. As the Muslims resumed their march towards Uhud, one of Ibn Ubayy's advisors questioned Muhammad's decision privately, saying, "Do you see? Muhammad didn't listen to your advice and preferred to hearken to his own boys instead, and now he's driven your allies away." As the army traveled under a full moon across the desert landscape toward its objective, Ibn Ubayy became convinced that the Muslims were making a terrible mistake. On top of that, he felt that his own honor had been slighted.

By morning the Muslims stood at the foot of the far side of Mount Uhud, which was not a terribly imposing peak, but considerably high nonetheless. Muhammad arranged his men into long rows facing the plain that the Quraysh would have to cross as they came around from their side of the mountain. To prevent a rear assault from a narrow pass behind them, the Prophet placed fifty archers on an incline overlooking it. Their instructions were clear: *Protect our rear! We're afraid they might come upon us from behind. Remain where you are placed. If you see us winning, don't leave your places until you see us entering their camp. If you see us getting beaten, don't come and try to help us. Your only job is to shoot the horses with arrows. Horses don't charge where there are arrows.*

His directions to his infantry were equally succinct: No one attacks without his order. Watching from under their black and white banners, the Muslims saw the mighty Meccan army come into view. As more and more warriors rounded the corner of the mountain, the confidence that strengthened the Muslims at Badr came over them again. But as the enemy began to assemble itself into three thick columns bristling with spears and swords, Ibn Ubayy ordered his followers to leave their positions and follow him back to Medina. Shocked, the Muslims were powerless to prevent the rapid departure of these sorely needed men. Three hundred in all deserted their posts and followed their leader away. The remaining Muslim forces numbered now only seven hundred against three thousand Meccan soldiers eager to avenge their defeat at Badr. The Prophet counseled his men to be patient and pondered his options. The hypocrites could be dealt with later, if they returned alive.

At the head of each Meccan regiment were men who dearly wanted to see Muhammad dead. Khalid ibn Walid, the famed Meccan cavalry general, wanted glory and accolades. Abu Sufyan and Ikrimah, the son of Abu Jahl, sought blood revenge. The throngs of Meccan women whipped the warriors into a blood lust by running throughout the lines singing, "Listen, Sons of 'Abdal Dar! This is the land you guard! Strike your enemies down and see that if you move forward we will embrace you. Go and we will spread the rugs for you! Turn your backs and we will avoid you! Turn your backs and we will never come to sleep with you again!" Thus the women made it clear that the Meccans' manly honor was at stake.

It must have been quite a scene for the Muslims to behold: slaves beating on drums, scurrying women with their colorful veils waving in the breeze, and the patron idols of many clans being held aloft on pikes. By contrast, the Muslim women wore simple white garb and remained in the rear of the army, ready to attend to the wounded. The only standards held high were made of plain cloth. With hundreds of horsemen and even whole companies of slave soldiers carrying spears lined up to face the Muslims, one would think that the Muslims would lose heart. But their unshakable faith in God's favor gave them succor, and they began cheering, "God is great!"

Muhammad was swept away in the bravado, and he drew his sword high in the air, challenging any companion to come and accept it if he could fulfill his one rigid command. A dozen men rushed to him, each begging to have the honor to use it, but Muhammad sent them all back to their posts. Then the lithe and experienced fighter Abu Dujanah stepped forward and asked what the requirement for using his sword was. Muhammad replied, "That you must continue to strike the enemy with it until it breaks." Abu Dujanah took out a red scarf and tied it around his head, a sign of his that meant he would fight to the death. Then he took the sword and began to twirl it over his head in a ritual war dance that looped throughout the lines of anxious men. Muhammad frowned and commented, "This behavior would be hateful to God except under the circumstances."

One of the men in the Meccan ranks was a tribesman of the Auws, Abu Amir, who had moved to Mecca in protest against Islam. He had missed the Battle of Badr and so perhaps felt more motivated to prove his valor. Previously, he promised the clan leaders of the Quraysh that he could get his tribe to side with him, and now his time to act came. He called out across the field of packed earth and identified himself, asking his fellow tribesmen in Muhammad's ranks to rebel and turn on the Muslims. The Auws promptly refused to heed him and called back curses upon him. The enraged traitor then ordered his company of slaves to attack, and the Meccan column on the left followed behind as they charged the Muslim lines nearest to them. The Prophet's uncle, Hamza, led his soldiers in a swift counterattack with a cry of "Die! Die!" The clash of armor against armor and spear upon shield soon echoed across that part of the field as a thousand swords glimmered in the sun.

In the Meccan center, which had not yet joined the battle, the standard-bearer of the Quraysh, Talhah, raced forward and challenged anyone from the Muslim side to an individual duel. 'Ali went out to meet him and smote him quickly with his trademark double-pronged sword. The massed center column of the Quraysh army then swept forward in such numbers that the force of their impact caused the Muslim lines to waver. Behind the first rows of pikemen were the swordsmen, and behind them stood Muslim archers trying in vain to keep shooting as the pressure of the Meccan assault intensified. The Meccan women stayed on the heels of their men, demanding their courage and bravery lest they be scorned as less than men. Some of them offered jewelry to anyone who would slay the Muslims who had killed their husbands, sons, or fathers at Badr. Seeing that maneuvering behind the Muslims' lines was impossible, the Meccan cavalry attempted to join the fray, but just as at Badr, it couldn't move effectively in the choked and crowded field of combat.

Typical armament and garb for an Arab fighter in the early days of Islam.

After an initial period of general mayhem, with thousands of men madly swinging their weapons, something unexpected began to happen. The Muslim defenders met the fury of the Meccan attack and held firm. No part of the Muslim line faltered, and as Meccans fell with greater frequency, those still standing began to fight with less conviction. The rank-and-file Muslim looked upon this fight as a win-win situation. The Qur'an taught them, "Whether you die or beat your foe you win either way." It was paradise for the martyr or victory for the victorious. With his prominent red scarf, Abu Dujanah threw himself at the enemy and struck down all who came near his blade. At one point, he saw one masked Meccan fighting a Muslim with his fingernails. As he drew closer he realized that it was a woman and that it was Hind, the wife of Abu Sufyan. Abu Dujanah moved away, not wanting the Prophet's sword to ever shed the blood of a woman.

Other Muslims, following Hamza and 'Ali's lead, began to charge the stunned Quraysh. As the Meccans faltered and were forced backwards en masse, the Muslims surged forward. Something happened, though, that nearly resulted in a tremendous loss of morale for the Muslims. While still in Mecca, Hind had promised an Abyssinian slave named Wahshi that he would be freed if he killed Hamza, who killed several of her relatives at Badr and on whom she desired revenge. Wahshi was an expert with the javelin and didn't need to get close to the feared swordsman to hit him. He later recounted what happened:

> I set out with the rest of the army planning to fight using my javelin, as all my people do, and I rarely miss my target. When the great battle took place, I searched for Hamza and then caught sight of him. He was right in the thick of the fight, standing out as clearly as a black camel in a herd and striking down everyone around him with his sword. I tested the balance of my javelin and then hurled it at him, hitting him in the lower chest with a shot that went completely in. I left him to die without retrieving my weapon until he was no more. Then I took my javelin and walked back to camp and fought no further. I killed

him to win my freedom and I attained my goal. When I
returned to Mecca I was officially freed.

When the Muslims saw that Hamza had fallen, however, they didn't lose heart: They fought even harder. Their battle cries echoed as they followed 'Ali forward and killed the Meccan flag-bearer, instilling a sense of panic in their foes. With their flag no longer flying as successive men who lofted it were mowed down, the Meccans began a disorganized withdrawal, and then broke ranks completely and fled, many even running right through their camp with their women screaming at them and hysteria setting in. A regiment of Muslims eventually broke through and knocked the idol the Meccans had brought with them off the camel that was bearing it. The battle became a rout. Even the Meccan cavalry, which had been bottled up during most of the engagement, began to race away.

The Muslims were now almost in possession of the enemy camp and the Meccans were scattering to the hills. Then a curious thing happened. Rather than continuing to pursue the Quraysh's still overwhelming forces, some of the Muslim soldiers slowed and began collecting the booty left behind on the field of battle. The archers, still stationed on the hill, saw this and wanted to go and get their share of the loot. Their commander reminded them of the Prophet's strict orders to stand fast, but one eager man replied, "The Prophet didn't say we should stay after God had finished humiliating the idolaters." With that nearly all of the archers deserted their posts.

Khalid ibn Walid was having a difficult time steering his mount in the panicked mass of men around him, then noticed the Muslim pursuit bogging down. He quickly saw an opportunity to mount a counteroffensive from the rear now that the pass was virtually unguarded. He gathered his riders and rushed them around the mountain, erupting from the pass behind the now disjointed Muslim lines. The surprise was complete. His men struck down the remaining Muslim archers, and then from that higher vantage point Khalid signaled the rest of the Quraysh to turn and mount a counteroffensive. With a mighty battle cry, he ordered his men to charge into the Muslim rear. Simultaneously, the fleeing Meccan infantry swung around and attacked. The Muslims were caught and overwhelmed in a pincer movement, and many were killed. Muslim even fought Muslim in the confusion, not realizing who was friend or foe. The Prophet himself was wounded in the mouth and had a tooth knocked out by a thrown rock. Two links of his armor stuck in the wound painfully as he fell to the ground.

Now rapidly regaining momentum, the Quraysh forced the scattered and disorganized Muslims back farther as their cavalry pressured them from the rear. Some bold Meccans attacked the cluster where the Prophet was located. Abu Dujanah used his back as a shield to protect the Prophet from Meccan arrows, and other companions formed an impenetrable knot of cold steel around their leader. A Muslim woman named Umm Amarah who had come along to nurse the wounded saw Muhammad under attack and rushed to him. She picked up a fallen bow and shot arrows at the advancing Meccans, and when the last arrow was gone, she stood between them and the Prophet and slashed and struck at them with a sword until she herself sustained many wounds. The Prophet tried to get up, but he fell into a pit that one of the Meccans had dug to trap the Muslims. 'Ali and another man lifted him out of it, and the ring of defenders began to move towards the heights of Uhud as the Quraysh warriors swirled around them.

The Muslims had no escape route except to climb the rocky slopes of Uhud, where they could avoid a two-sided assault. Further confusion set in when a Meccan shouted that the Prophet had been killed in order to demoralize the Muslims further. Many of them raised a cry of lament and ran for their lives. Others saw the Prophet climbing the mountain under fierce attack by the Meccans and rallied their comrades to follow. The remaining fighters made it to the side of the mountain and began furiously climbing higher and higher, with the Meccans following close behind. Though wounded, the Prophet continued issuing orders to his men and told them, "Do not let them attain a higher position than us." 'Umar gathered as many men as he could and confronted the Meccan cavalry, which was trying to force its horses to climb the slope. Through sheer willpower they turned the advance back. The beleaguered army would now be able to make a stand and hold off their pursuers. Fatimah, along with 'Ali, remained with Muhammad, treating and cauterizing his wounds with ash.

The Meccans, realizing the futility of fighting on a steep incline and now possessing the battlefield, began to search through the dead bodies, frantically looking for the body of Muhammad. This search gave most of the rest of the Muslim soldiers a chance to escape up the mountain and join the defenders there. One party of Meccans shouted at the badly shaken Muslims, "Where is Muhammad? Death to me if he lives!" The Prophet grabbed a javelin and threw it, striking the speaker. For the rest of the afternoon, the Meccans made menacing gestures, but they couldn't mount an attack on the Muslim battle line now that it held the high ground. Finally both sides were so exhausted that the fighting subsided. Abu Sufyan rode to the foot of the mountain and looked up at the hundreds of wounded and exhausted Muslims. He smiled in satisfaction and shouted, "A day for a day! Our next appointment will be next year at Badr!" Now they were avenged for their humiliating loss and would be ready to best the Muslims once more.

Meanwhile, the Meccan women, led by Hind, were executing plans of their own. They were so enraged by their near defeat that they began to mutilate and deface the fallen Muslims, cutting off noses and ears to use as ornaments or necklaces, slashing faces and humiliating the dead, and moving over the bodies like ghouls. When Hind found Hamza's body, she ripped open his chest with a dagger and chewed on his liver, fulfilling a vow she had made. The carnage and barbarity of the women was so disgusting that Abu Sufyan publicly chided his wife and sent a message to the Muslims saying, "Your dead were truly mutilated. I swear by God that I never approved of it. How can I be accused of commanding the women to do it?"

The Meccans collected their dead and went back to their camp singing and cheering in the confidence that they had won the day. Feasting, drinking, and telling tales of valor were the order of the night. Not so for Muhammad's army. When the Muslims finally came down from the mountain and saw the condition of their fallen comrades, especially Hamza's nearly unrecognizable body,

197

they were filled with rage. It was unheard of to do such things to dead bodies in Arabia. Muhammad, covering his uncle with his own cloak, vowed, "If God ever gives me victory over them, I will mutilate them in a way the Arabs have never done before." As was often the case when a great event took place, new verses of the Qur'an (Qur'an 16:127–129) came to the Prophet. As soon as they were complete, he read them out loud:

> If you punish, only do so as much as you have been, but
> if you are patient it is better. Be patient for patience
> comes from God alone. Don't feel sad or give in to anger
> because of the cunning of your enemy. God is with those
> who fear him and who are gracious.

With these words of calm, Muhammad retracted his former vow and told his companions never to mutilate the Quraysh.

The weary Muslims buried their dead on the plain in the faint moonlight, digging a grave where they found each body; both men and women participated in the funeral prayers. In all there were seventy martyrs, which was a stunning blow to the prestige and reputation of Islam and a sobering reminder of the reality of death, though the Qur'an always reminded them in verses of the true reality of the next life. The somber Muslims then returned to Medina while the Meccans remained in their camp behind Mount Uhud celebrating and getting drunk.

Every Muslim knew that it was the archers' dereliction of duty that caused their defeat. The infantry could not completely escape blame, however, for they, too, disobeyed orders and failed to press the enemy retreat. Instead they stopped to pick up worldly goods. When the counterattack came, many of the Muslims died with their arms fully loaded. Greed had been their undoing. Muhammad was rightly angry, and he was about to scold his men harshly when another verse (Qur'an 2:159) came to him, saying, "By the mercy of God you will soften towards them. If you were hard on them they would have deserted you. So pardon them, ask forgiveness of them, and consult them still in decisions." The Prophet was not to add to their dejection.

The next morning, a herald was instructed to roam the streets of Medina announcing that everyone who had fought at Uhud the day before should prepare to march out to war again. No one was to join in except them, thus preventing the hypocrites from disrupting the expedition again. The Muslims all responded, regardless of their wounds, and soon Muhammad marched out at the head of his army, heading back towards Uhud and the Quraysh who still lay camped there. It may have seemed a foolhardy decision, but Muhammad wanted to prove that the Quraysh had not beaten his men and that the battle would be continued. If the Meccans returned home thinking otherwise, surrounding hostile tribes would have been emboldened to resume their raids, and Muhammad's own people's morale would suffer further.

The army stopped near Uhud, took up positions on a hill within sight of the Quraysh, and made camp. When Abu Sufyan found out about the Muslim army's new march, he couldn't believe it. Reports suggested that the Muslims sought revenge and that more reinforcements were preparing to come from Medina. To stall for time, he sent a message to the Muslim camp threatening to come and finish them off for good. However, he argued with his fellow leaders and allies about whether it was a good idea to engage them once more, for although many Muslims were killed, the Meccan army had lost hundreds more. The Prophet waited with his army for three days and nights, lighting a huge bonfire to let the world know he was there. Abu Sufyan finally decided against taking another chance with the Muslims and withdrew his army to Mecca, desperately not wanting to jeopardize his one day of victory.

The Muslim fighters began to feel more confident as they watched the Meccans break camp and leave. They knew they had done well during the initial hours of battle until a series of missteps for which they had only themselves to blame snatched victory from their grasp. With their willingness to fight again, however, they felt that they had done their duty and that they could hold their heads honorably once more. The Muslims returned to Medina, and in the coming weeks a number of Qur'anic verses were revealed explaining the lessons of the Day of Uhud and how they might overcome such disasters in the future. They were also reminded that God was still on their side. This thought was a comfort in the days ahead, because terror and trials such as the Muslims had never imagined soon befell them, making Uhud seem like a minor skirmish.

Chapter 11

The Great Siege of Medina

*Have you seen how the hypocrites have told their fellow
disbelieving brethren from among the People of the Book:
"If you are forced to leave then we will leave with you,
and we won't listen to anyone else about your situation;
and if you are attacked we will help you." But God is a
witness that they are liars.*

—Qur'an 59:11

In trying to understand their loss at Uhud, the Muslims relied
heavily upon the words of the Qur'an for both solace and direction. Their shortcomings, as the revelations explained, were
caused by a love for worldly wealth, a lack of obedience to their
commander's orders, and an inappropriate sense of panic when
they thought the Prophet had been slain. The Qur'an addressed
the latter issue by asking, "Muhammad is no more than a messenger. Many were the messengers who passed away before him. If he
dies or is slain will you turn back on your heels?" Islam was meant
to survive the death of Muhammad, and the sooner the Muslims
realized that the better.

The hypocrites, led by 'Abdullah ibn Ubayy, were having a field
day with the defeat. In their eyes, the fact that the Muslims suffered a setback was proof that Muhammad and his cause were a
temporary phenomenon that could eventually be overcome. The

hypocrites had only grudgingly accepted Islam because it seemed to be the trend; they had no sincerity and often pined for the many liberties they had before Islam. From the ban on alcohol to the concept of an afterlife they could attain only through faith and good deeds, they clearly felt that their lives were restricted unfairly. Though they never openly battled the Prophet, their resistance wore down many rank-and-file Muslims. So great was their damage to the cause that the Qur'an itself pointed out their true intentions and warned the believers against them.

Among the hypocrites' actions to undermine the Muslim community, their campaign of spreading misinformation, doubt, and rumor often hit the hardest. They were surreptitious before Uhud, but they became far bolder afterwards. They began telling other Muslims that their friends and relatives would not have died if they had only declined to fight like the hypocrites had. They also questioned the power of God because his Prophet had been miserably defeated, and they also sought to stoke fears of more attacks from the tribes. The Qur'anic revelations, which used to dwell more upon the evils of idolatry or the mistakes of Judaism and Christianity, now focused on answering the charges of the hypocrites (Qur'an 3:165, 168–169):

> *What! When a single disaster strikes you, although you in-*
> *flicted twice the punishment on (your enemies), you ask,*
> *"Why did this happen?" Tell them, "It is from your own*
> *fault for God has power over all things …. The hypocrites,*
> *who sat at home, say, "If only they had listened to us they*
> *would not have been killed." Tell them, "Then keep death*
> *from coming for you if you speak the truth." Don't think*
> *that those who were killed in God's cause are dead. No,*
> *they are alive, finding their provisions in the presence of*
> *their Lord.*

For several months after Uhud, the Muslim position in Medina was unsettled, and the hypocrites capitalized on this situation to strengthen their position. 'Abdullah ibn Ubayy even felt confident enough to attempt to renew some of his old contacts with the Meccans. The Jews of the Banu Nadir also began to grow restive, and an undercurrent of dissent and subterfuge returned to the city.

The Arab tribes living in the countryside felt that they might have a chance against the Muslims in Medina now that they saw the Muslims weren't invulnerable. For two years, scattered converts had made their way to Muhammad's city, which clearly became the center around which Islam revolved. The target, then, was clear: all any tribe had to do was attack Medina.

Inspired by the Quraysh's victory, the clan leaders of the large Banu Asad tribe assembled a force to attack Medina's hinterland and loot and vandalize the farms there. When Muhammad was informed, he tapped a companion named Abu Salamah, still suffering from a wound he received at Uhud, to lead one hundred and fifty men in a daring counterstrike. Traveling by night on unfrequented routes and lying low in the day, the Muslim men soon found the large enemy force encamped near some hills. In the pre-dawn fog, Abu Salamah led a surprise attack and forced the tribal fighters to retreat hastily into the hills. The Muslim defenders returned to Medina with much booty and many tales of great success. Abu Salamah, however, soon succumbed to his wounds, and as he was slipping away, the Prophet sat by his bedside, imploring God to enter him into Paradise. "My Lord, grant forgiveness to Abu Salamah. Elevate him among those who are near to you. Take charge of his family at all times. Forgive us and him, O Lord of the Universe. Widen his grave and make it lighted for him."

Later the Prophet heard that a man named Khalid al-Hudhayli was busily inciting his tribal subclan, the Banu Lihyan, to attack Medina as well. Muhammad sent a single man, 'Abdullah ibn Unays, to reconnoiter and report back to him. After arriving in the clan's large encampment, a component of the large Hudhayl tribe, 'Abdullah asked where he might find the chief, and he was directed toward a group of women. He found Khalid in their company, and the latter asked him who he was. 'Abdullah answered, "I'm a tribesman, and I've heard that you are raising an army to fight Muhammad. I want to join you."

A *typical bedouin camp.*

(*Photo by Luke Powell*)

Khalid relaxed immediately and began talking all about his preparations and how his forces would strike with the utmost surprise and cunning. Sizing up his opponent's vulnerability, Khalid asked the chief to go for a walk to discuss things further. As they were strolling behind the tents, 'Abdullah took out his sword and killed Khalid. The women, who had been watching from a distance, immediately began to cry and wail, but it was too late. 'Abdullah was already headed back to Medina with the good news that a potential plot had been foiled.

A betrayal connected with this incident soon followed. One day men from the small al-Kada tribe came to Medina and asked the Prophet to send some people with them who could instruct converts among them in the ways of Islam. Muhammad cheerfully complied; he never turned down an opportunity to send missionaries where they were needed, especially if they were requested. A short time later, six Muslims set out with great fanfare for their new assignment deep in the Hijaz.

Along the way they stopped for the night at an oasis near the lands of the Hudhayl tribe. Their guides betrayed them to the locals, who rallied their men and encircled the oasis in silence. Desire for revenge burned in their hearts as they still mourned for their fallen chief. The six Muslims were awakened by battle cries in the darkness. By the light of their dying campfire, they saw that they were completely surrounded by hundreds of armed men. They drew their swords and were about to fight when one of the attackers called out, "We don't mean to kill you. We want to sell you as captives to the people of Mecca. Put down your swords, and we promise we won't harm you." Knowing what unthinkable fate would befall them if they were brought to Mecca, they decided that they preferred a quick death fighting on their feet. They were no match, however, for the throngs of men around them, and three of the Muslims were killed in the ensuing struggle. The surviving three were bound and taken to Mecca. Along the way one of the men broke free and attempted an escape, but he was killed.

In Mecca, the Quraysh eagerly purchased the two prisoners and relished the chance to publicly execute them to avenge the deaths at Badr two years before. One of the condemned men, Khubeyb, was bought by the family of Harith, a Meccan who had been killed at Badr. He was held in a certain woman's house for a few weeks before his sentence was carried out. He impressed the people who lived there with his honesty and good manners, and they almost forgot he was their prisoner, though he was kept in a locked room. One day Khubeyb asked the woman of the house for a knife so he could shave, and she sent her young son to take it to him without thinking. Khubeyb took the knife and then held the boy saying, "Doesn't your mother fear treachery?" Then he merely let the boy go and resumed his shaving. When the day of his execution by crucifixion came, the members of the clan gathered around to witness their revenge. He asked to be allowed a last Islamic prayer. They granted his request, and when he had finished, he declared, "I am dying as a Muslim. I don't care if my headless body drops to the right or left. Why should I? My death is in the way of God. If he wills, he can bless every part of my mutilated body."

The second prisoner, Zayd ibn al-Dathinah, was bought by the family of Ummayah ibn Khalaf. The family burned with rage and showed no mercy. Abu Sufyan called to Zayd on his death march,

"Wouldn't you rather be safe at home and Muhammad was in our hands instead?" Zayd answered, "What, Abu Sufyan? What are you saying? I would rather die than have the Prophet's foot step on a thorn in the streets of Medina." Abu Sufyan remarked, as he watched the barbarity that followed, "The gods be my witness. I have never known anyone to show as much love as do the companions towards Muhammad."

When the Muslims heard of the cruel deaths suffered by their compatriots, they were filled with sadness. A Muslim poet named Hassan ibn Thabit composed a poem in their honor and called to the Muslims to remember their brave example. The guides' betrayal that resulted in this terrible loss drove home the feeling in Medina that the climate for Muslims was becoming precarious once again. Muhammad explained the change in their fortunes as a way for God to test their resolve and sincerity. "Be sure," said the Qur'an, "that we will test you with hardship through fear, hunger, poverty, death, or loss. But give good news to those who persevere; who say, when stricken with adversity, 'To God we belong and to him we return.'" (Qur'an 2:155–156) Little did they know to what extent they would be tested, for the Meccans were sending messages to every tribe in north and south Arabia, encouraging them to attack Muslims wherever they found them.

Weeks later a chief of the prominent Banu Amr tribe, Abu Bur'a Amir ibn Malik, came to Medina and met Muhammad to discuss political matters. Although he refused to convert at Muhammad's invitation, he did agree to allow the preaching of Islam in his territory. Before returning home, he asked the Prophet to send some Muslim teachers to his tribe. The Prophet demurred at first, considering the fate of his previous missionary group. After repeated assurances of safety, however, Muhammad agreed to send seventy of his followers to Abu Bur'a's people. They departed the city within a few days.

Upon arriving at a place called Bi'r Ma'unah on the border between the lands of the Banu Amr and the Banu Sulaym, the Muslims sent a letter of introduction to a local clan chief and asked permission for an audience. The chief didn't even bother to read the letter, and instead exhorted his fellow tribesmen to kill all the

Muslims. When his own tribe was hesitant to cross the pledge of one of their most respected elders, he sent a message to another tribe, and soon a force surrounded the Muslims in their camp and killed all but two. One was taken captive, and the other escaped by playing dead.

The captive, Amir ibn Umayyah, was freed within a few days by the tribesman who had custody of him in order to pay for a blood-debt his mother owed. As Amir was returning to Medina, he saw two men on the road and thought they were from the group that had ambushed his party. He waited until they made camp for the night and then crept upon them and killed them in the dark. Unbeknownst to him, they were allies of the man who had freed him. When he finally saw the Prophet again he was told that the community as a whole would have to raise the blood money to pay the relatives of the two victims in compensation. Meanwhile, the Muslims grieved for their large number of lost companions for a whole month, while the embarrassed Abu Bur'a killed the clan chief who had brought his word into doubt.

The situation in Medina became even more problematic when one of the two remaining Jewish clans in the area, the Banu Nadir, took up the cause of working against Islam. Muhammad knew his community was in a delicate situation; if it became common knowledge that the Banu Nadir (and possibly the hypocrites) would likely revolt if the Muslims were distracted by attacks from outside forces, any tribe might try to force this result through a surprise invasion. Muhammad decided to try to expose the true intentions of the Banu Nadir and their allies. The question was, how to do it?

The Prophet surmised that, according to the terms of the city charter, the Banu Nadir had to help raise the funds to pay the blood money for the two men who had been accidentally killed by Amir ibn Umayyah. The problem was that the deceased were from the Banu Amr tribe, and the Jews were allied to them as well. To resolve this issue, Muhammad took ten companions to the Banu Nadir quarter just outside the southeastern edge of the city, where the Jews had built several large fortresses surrounded by a warren of tenements, homes, orchards, and shops. The surprised clan elders received Muhammad graciously and asked him and his men to sit near a wall outside one of their homes, insisting that Muhammad have the shadiest spot.

While the Muslims waited, the Jews who had received them stood whispering nearby. They were discussing the murder of Ka'b ibn al-Ashraf (discussed in Chapter 10), and at one point the conversation was loud enough for the Muslims to hear. Muhammad felt uncomfortable when he saw Ka'b's son, Amr ibn Jahsh, sneak into the house. Suddenly the Prophet stood up and left. His companions assumed he would soon return. He didn't. The Jews grew increasingly nervous as time passed. They began to speak to the Muslims, babbling and flattering them, emphasizing their commitment to the treaty. The Muslims realized their leader wasn't returning, and they excused themselves. They didn't know that Muhammad had narrowly escaped assassination. Amir ibn Jahsh had poised a heavy rock on the roof above where Muhammad sat and had been about to drop it on Muhammad's head.

Muhammad had gone straight to the mosque, where important announcements were always made, and called as many people as he could. The ten who had accompanied him to meet the Banu Nadir also arrived. Muhammad explained to the crowd what had almost happened to him, denouncing the villanous attempt on his life. The men who were with him before began to realize their folly and naiveté. A message was sent to the leaders of the Banu Nadir: "Get out of my city. You have broken the agreement between us by plotting to kill me treacherously. You have ten days. If any of your people are found in the city after ten days they shall die."

The Banu Nadir were shocked. They tried to persuade the messenger, a longtime acquaintance, to speak to Muhammad on their behalf. They chided him saying, "Son of Maslamah, we never expected that such an order would be carried by an old friend of ours. You are a man of the Auws tribe and our ally against the Khazraj." The messenger replied curtly, "Times have changed and so have the affiliations." As the Banu Nadir began to the see that Muhammad was serious, they discussed their options. Their property was considerable: large homes, orchards, fertile farmland, herds of animals. How could they give it all up?

Hope came later in the day when two messengers from 'Abdullah ibn Ubayy arrived with a weighty proposal. He told them to remain in their fortresses, and if Muhammad attacked, he would send two thousand Arab and Jewish fighters from among his allies who would join the battle. Together they could crush the Muslims. He was so confident that he even promised that he would share in their fate of exile if they lost. The Banu Nadir debated for another day. Could Ibn Ubayy be trusted? He had promised before to help Muhammad at Uhud and withdrew. Moreover, when the Muslims were besieging the Banu Qaynuqa, he offered to help them and then backed down. The third Jewish tribe of Banu Qurayza would probably not help because they were still committed to their covenants. Could the Banu Nadir stand alone? Further messages from Ibn Ubayy implored them to hold fast, but the consensus was moving towards flight.

One elder suggested that they could merely move in with their Jewish cousins at the fortress city of Khaybar, some days' travel to the north. When harvest time came, they could send men to the orchards and carry on as they had, albeit with some distance between them and their crops. Their head chief, Huyayy ibn Akhtab, angrily put a stop to such proposals and said, "No. I will send Muhammad a message telling him that we will not leave our homes and properties and that we refuse to comply with his orders. All we need to do is fortify our positions, fill up our granaries, barricade our streets, supply ourselves with stones for projectiles, and be ready. We have enough food to last a year, and our water supply is inexhaustible. Muhammad won't lay siege to us for a whole year." A message was also sent to Ibn Ubayy telling him that the Banu Nadir were counting on him to join the fight with his promised forces.

When his deadline expired, Muhammad ordered the Muslims to surround the Banu Nadir's neighborhood. For the next twenty days and nights, pitched battles raged throughout the southern quarter of the city as roving bands of Muslims and Jews clashed. There were no large melees, however, and casualties were light; the Jewish tactic was to engage the enemy and then quickly withdraw behind a rain of stones and arrows. The determined Muslims pressed on, capturing one house after another. The Jewish fighters took advantage of their strategic losses by taking positions on the roof of the next house and setting fire to the one they vacated, depriving the Muslims of momentum. In this way, they were able to hold out valiantly in the first few days and keep the Muslims off balance. They could not hold out forever, though. The Banu Nadir waited for any sign of the promised help from Ibn Ubayy, but Ibn Ubayy never came. He had no intention of helping the Banu Nadir. He only wanted to keep Muhammad distracted and create mischief for the Muslims, whom he hated.

With his focus undivided, Muhammad was able to come up with a novel strategy. Realizing that the Jews were fighting to hold on to their vast properties, Muhammad ordered his men to halt the advance and directed them to start destroying the orchards and date palms in the extensive plantations that surrounded the Banu Nadir's neighborhood. The Jews were furious. They sent a message to Muhammad that read, "How can you order such a thing, the destruction of our orchards, when you always forbade corruption and injustice?" Muhammad's tactic was indeed unusual; he had always ordered his men to refrain from harming the environment in their campaigns. However, in order to shorten the conflict, he took the drastic step, as men in war sometimes must, of choosing expediency over principle. The Banu Nadir, giving up all hope of preserving their lands and fearful of their fate if they held out any longer, sent a message to the Prophet asking for peace. They beseeched Muhammad to give them safe conduct to wherever they could go. The Prophet agreed and allowed each man to take three camel loads of goods with him.

The next day the Banu Nadir formally surrendered. They assembled a camel train of thousands of animals and left Medina forever. They headed northwards, except for those who had converted to Islam, who were of course allowed to remain in their homes. Most of the tribe settled in Syria, as their brethren the Banu Qaynuqa had done before them; a small remnant headed by Huyayy ibn Akhtab chose to reside in Khaybar. Soon this embittered chief would once again fight the Muslims. In the interim, the Qur'an extolled the victory as a sign of God's just punishment against wrongdoers and gave directions for the disposal of the considerable property that the Muslims gained (Qur'an 59:1–4):

> Everything in the heavens and the Earth glorifies God. He
> is the Mighty, the Wise. He drove away the rejecters of
> truth from among the followers of earlier revelation [the
> Jews of the Banu Nadir] even at their first gathering for
> battle. You never thought they would leave peacefully,
> even as they thought their fortresses could stand against
> God. But God came upon them from where they least
> expected. He cast fear into their hearts, causing them to
> destroy their own dwellings, even helping the believers to
> do it! You who have eyes to see, take heed.
>
> And if God had not ordered their exile, He would have
> certainly imposed on them far greater suffering in this
> world, though it may await them in the next. Indeed, they
> resisted God and His Messenger and whoever does that
> should know that God is severe in retribution. And
> whether you had cut the palm trees or let them stand, it
> was by the will of God, though He commanded them to
> be cut so that the corrupters would be disgraced.
>
> And the property that God removed from their control
> and bestowed on His Messenger required no expedition of
> cavalry or camelry, because God grants His Messengers
> victory over whomsoever He wills. He has power over all
> things.
>
> Whatever God restored to His Messenger from the
> people of the townships will be distributed to His Messenger,
> to relatives, to orphans, to the needy, and to the wayfarer
> so that the wealth doesn't remain circulating among the
> wealthy alone. Accept what the Messenger gives you and
> leave what he denies you. Stay conscious of God because
> He is severe in retribution.

The Prophet was an example to his community in all things related to the religion, including social and family life. Islam was a fairly egalitarian faith that sought to smooth distinctions between people based on race, color, and socioeconomic status. All believers were brothers and sisters, and the only cause for distinction between people was their piety, as much as it could be discerned by one's actions. This was the code the Prophet lived by, and his personal life is often examined to see how he put his ideals into practice. He was not an ostentatious man. Years of virtual asceticism high on the mountain overlooking Mecca had taught him that the goods men and women possess in this life are but "the glitter and baggage" of the world. In Medina, he built no palace or great reception hall. He neither amassed wealth for himself nor built grand monuments. By decree of the Qur'an, one fifth of all booty taken was to be turned over to the Prophet, though the Qur'an also stipulated what he was to do with it: Muhammad fed the poor, freed slaves, supported the war widows, sponsored orphans, and bought whatever necessities his community needed—so much so that he often had no food in his own house.

One day 'Umar came into Muhammad's dwelling and found him resting on a hard reed mat. He had shifted to his side, and the marks of the plant strands showed in his skin. 'Umar, who loved the Prophet more than his own life, began to weep and tearfully beseeched his friend, "Caesar of Byzantium and Chosroes of Persia sleep on soft feathers, while you, the Messenger of God, are sleeping on this hard mat. Can't you order us to make something for you or spread something out?" Muhammad replied, "Wouldn't you like them to have this world and us to have the next world that lasts forever?" "Of course," 'Umar answered. "Then let it be so," the Prophet said. "What have I got to do with this world? I am like a traveler who stops to rest under the shade of a tree, then I move on." Of his many famous sayings, or *hadiths*, one eloquently states what he stood for:

> My Lord has advised me to acquire nine traits which I, in turn, advise you to take on. He has commanded me to be sincere, openly and in secret, to be fair when calm or angry, to be thrifty in poverty or good fortune, to forgive someone who has wronged me, to give to the one who has taken from me, to build relations with whoever has severed them with me, to let silence be my meditation, to let speech be my prayer, and to let what I observe bring a lesson to me. (Hadith)

When the Prophet married Hafsah, whose husband had been killed in battle, he strengthened his bond with her father, 'Umar, and also helped to further change people's concepts of marriage and the rights of wives. 'Umar recalled,

> *Before Islam, we didn't attach any special importance to*
> *women. We changed course radically after God revealed*
> *all that he did about them and their numerous rights.*
> *Once my wife tried to change my mind about something.*
> *When I told her to stay out of my business, she chided*
> *me, "Son of Khattab! You forbid me to criticize you even*
> *though our daughter is allowed to do the same thing to the*
> *Prophet of God himself, may God bless him. She talks*
> *back to him so much sometimes that he spends the rest of*
> *the day angry."*

Muhammad set the tone in his family relations by allowing his wives to speak their mind without fear, and he never physically harmed any woman, each of his wives agreed in later years. He further expanded his family by marrying Zaynab bint Khuzaymah, a widow of Badr, and Zaynab bint Jahsh, who recently had divorced Zayd ibn Harithah because of his humble background. The former Zaynab, who was elderly and only lived for a year or two more, had the reputation of being extremely generous to the poor. Muhammad also married the widow of Abu Salamah, whose husband never recovered from a wound he received at Uhud. Previously, both Abu Bakr and 'Umar had asked for her hand in sympathy for her woeful condition, but she refused. Finally the Prophet asked her to marry him and she replied, "Messenger of God, I have three characteristics: I am a woman who is extremely jealous and I'm afraid that you'll see in me something that will anger you and cause God to punish me. Second, I am a woman who is already a bit old, and third, I am a woman who has a young family." The Prophet replied, "Regarding the jealousy you mentioned, I pray to God, the Almighty, to let it go away from you. Regarding the question of age, I am afflicted with the same problem as you. Regarding the dependent family you have mentioned, your family is like my family." Thus she accepted.

In the year 626, Abu Sufyan sent a message to Medina informing the Prophet that he was coming with an army even larger and
fiercer than the one at Uhud. The army would visit such pain, suffering, and humiliation on them, he threatened, that they would
never recover. He had promised the Muslims after Uhud that
Mecca would fight them again at Badr to settle the score on their
defeat there, and he had every intention of keeping his word. But
his vow this time was mostly bluster, for there had been a drought
in Mecca that season, and he was unsure whether mounting
another expensive campaign would be possible. He didn't want the
Muslims and the rest of the Arabs to think he had forgotten about
his challenge, but his real goal was to put the rematch off for
another year. Indeed, he hoped that Muhammad would shy away
from facing his forces again, possibly even beg for more time to prepare, which would play into the Meccans' favor.

When Mecca's challenge was publicly discussed in the mosque,
many of the companions were apprehensive about going into battle. They counseled that this time they should remain in the city,
as was proposed just before Uhud. Hadn't that debacle taught them
about the safety of fortifications? Muhammad scolded them for
their cowardice and warned them that he would go back to Badr if
he had to go by himself. Seeing the Prophet's resolve and determination made the assembled men and women ashamed. They clamored to go to Badr, and even a few hypocrites were swept away in
the bravado and asked to join.

'Abdullah ibn Ubayy, however, refrained once again. As the
anniversary of the Battle of Badr neared, Muhammad appointed the
son of 'Abdullah ibn Ubayy to be the governor of the city in his
absence. The son, also named 'Abdullah, was a staunch supporter of
Islam and often differed with his father over his anti-Muslim
remarks and secret machinations. At the head of nearly a thousand
men and some women, the Prophet marched his forces to the oasis
at Badr and made camp there on the day when, two years before,
the Muslims had achieved their first real victory. The Quraysh left
Mecca with an army of only two thousand fighters because of the
drought and a lack of interest among many for further fighting after
Uhud, which had satisfied most calls for revenge. After travelling

north for two days, Abu Sufyan called a halt and decided the expedition wasn't worth it. He turned his army around and returned to Mecca.

The Muslims waited for eight days, and when it looked as though the Quraysh weren't going to show, they began trading with passing merchants from Badr's small but well-trafficked bazaar. The eager Muslims took their handsome profits back to Medina rejoicing. A new revelation (Qur'an 3:173–175) came that stated the following:

> Even when they were told, "A great army masses against
> you," instead of wavering, they increased in their convic-
> tion proclaiming, "God is enough for us, the (only)
> Determiner of Events." And so, they returned with the
> grace and bounty of Allah, and no real harm overcame
> them. For they were striving for the acceptance of God,
> the Possessor of Endless Bounty. It is only Satan who
> instills the fear of his minions in you, so don't fear them,
> rather fear Me if you (really) have faith.

Thus the Muslims regained confidence in their martial abilities—and just in time. Disturbing news came into Medina of yet another tribal raid planned from the land of Najd to the east of Medina. The powerful Ghatafan tribe was assembling an army to attack. Muhammad quickly organized a strike force of four hundred men and rode at top speed to Dhat al-Riqa, an oasis where two armed groups of the Ghatafan had camped. Taking them completely by surprise, the Muslims drove off the Ghatafan warriors and seized their baggage train. This victory made the Muslims feel stronger and many began to shed the fears that had plagued them since Uhud.

After being in an almost constant state of war for three years, the Muslims were finally able to get back to building a stable and prosperous society. With the solid interdependence of the Auws, Khazraj, immigrants, and other converts, the Qur'an's ideal of a just and moderate society was beginning to come to fruition. The Prophet sought to reemphasize the true nature of Islam, which had thus far been overshadowed by their armed struggles. He told them, "We have left the smaller *jihad* [struggle] and are returning to the greater jihad." When his men asked him what the greater jihad was, he replied, "It is the jihad of man against his own self." The struggle against one's own greed, desires, lusts, and shortcomings was what made a person stronger, not winning honor on a battlefield.

Muhammad's Medina was not a tyrannical religious theocracy, nor was it a dictatorship. Any man or woman who desired to speak out on an issue felt free to do so. There were no armed religious police roving the streets looking for minor infractions of the dress code or for anyone who missed prayers in the mosque. It was a very open society for its time. Muhammad was the head of the city by majority consent, but he personally exerted little influence over day-to-day life. He only held firm to a position when he felt it was God's will, and in all other matters he let his decisions be challenged and gave much freedom to his companions to organize and run things. He also never engaged in nepotism. He chose people based on ability for the various offices, from collection of the annual tithe, called zakah, to leading security patrols and settling civil disputes.

To protect his expanding population of believers, for new converts from the countryside were always arriving, the Prophet also had to assemble a network of scouts and secret agents who could inform him of any movement among the tribes, whether in the east or west or from Mecca. Good intelligence was vital because Arabia was a patchwork of rival tribes with no central authority or governing body. The only thing that bound them together was an intricate system of tribal customs, intertribal rules, alliances, pacts, and traditions. Muhammad always had to be ready to respond to the myriad threats that existed all around his adopted home, but in the year 627 there came a day when his spy network proved ineffective.

A remnant of the Banu Nadir tribe still remained in Arabia, living in the Jewish fortress community of Khaybar, some days' ride to the north from Medina. These tribespeople never quite got over their eviction from their former homes and were as convinced as ever that Muhammad's teachings were an affront to their own religion. For a people who claimed that God spoke only to them, the success of Islam, propounded by a non-Jew, was a challenge to their religious and ethnic identity. Their erstwhile chief, Huyayy ibn

Akhtab, finally resolved to resume the fight against Muhammad, but he knew he couldn't do it alone. Hatching a grand scheme to unite all of Arabia in one irresistible force, he gathered two of his fellows and two local Arab chieftains and headed for Mecca. The delegation met with the leaders of the Quraysh and urged them to attack the Muslims in Medina, promising them numerous allies and the cooperation of the Banu Qurayza, the last Jewish tribe in the city. The Meccans listened intently. Abu Sufyan and the other leaders of the city were concerned that Muslim power and influence seemed to be growing again after the defeat of the Banu Nadir and the victory of the Muslims in minor battles with smaller Arab tribes. The Meccans resolved to join in this great undertaking and assail the Muslims again.

The idolatrous Quraysh were a little puzzled, however, that the Jews were coming to them and asking them to attack the followers of Muhammad. After all, the Jews claimed to believe in one God, just as the followers of Islam did. The Meccans asked the Jews if they thought that idolatry, as they practiced it, was better than Islam and its monotheism. The Jews answered that the idolatry of the Meccans was indeed better than what Muhammad brought. Satisfied that their cause was just, and affirmed by people who had a long history of religious knowledge and their own book from the Almighty, the Quraysh threw themselves into the enterprise with great enthusiasm.

After several more trips between Khaybar and Mecca, the plans were finalized: The Meccans would rally an army drawn from all the cities, towns, and territories near them while the Banu Nadir would secure the cooperation of the northern Arabs and the Banu Qurayza. After the date of the attack was set, Huyayy began sending messages to all the hostile Arab tribes in central and northern Arabia asking them to come and fight the Muslims as well. They even promised to the large tribe of Ghatafan a whole year's worth of produce from the orchards of Medina if they beat the Muslims. The leaders of almost every tribe contributed material and men in a spirit of cooperation rarely seen in the land. When the time to march came, the allies assembled an army of over ten thousand warriors who were fully equipped and armed for battle. This huge force set forth for Medina intending to end Islam forever.

When word of the huge mobilization reached Medina, the inhabitants of the city were struck with fear and panic. Never had there been an army that large in Arabia before. How could the Muslims hope to win? The Prophet called a council, and the Muslim leaders gravely pondered their coming fate. Leaving the city was out of the question this time. Barely three thousand Muslim warriors were available, and all were ill equipped.

Salman, the Persian who had been freed by Muhammad from slavery soon after he arrived in Medina, suggested a unique plan. He was from a well-settled land and knew how wars were fought between large armies. The Meccans were coming from the south, but impassable terrain would force them to travel in an arc and approach the city from the north. Salman proposed that the Muslims dig a deep trench around the exposed northern front of the city, which faced a fairly level plain. Other vulnerable areas could be fortified by connecting the walls of houses together into thick barriers. With mountains encircling a good portion of the city, the main defenses could be directed towards one side while the trench would prevent any cavalry assault. The only other weak spot would be the eastern border of the city where the Banu Qurayza lived. But they had fortresses that the enemy was unlikely to attack. They also had a treaty with the Muslims and were still honoring it, as far as people could tell.

The Prophet agreed with this plan and work began at once. The Muslims were divided into crews, and everyone participated in the construction. Some were given the job of building and joining walls together while others, including the Prophet himself, dug the enormous trench. The Prophet was out digging with the people and the Muslims sang songs while working to keep their spirits up. Muhammad also lifted his voice in verse: "By God, if not for Him, we'd never have been guided, nor gave nor prayed. So send down peace and make firm our stand. The others fought against us and when they wanted trouble, we refused, we refused." The men around him began chanting in response, "We are the ones who've pledged ourselves to Muhammad; that we will stay forever faithful in Islam." Then the Prophet sang in answer, "O God, there's no good but from the next life, so bless the immigrants and the Helpers."

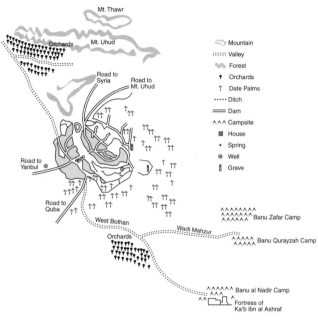

Medina and its environs.

Morale remained high, a testament to the Muslims' firm faith in their leader. During one day of digging, Muhammad struck a rock with his pickaxe and a flurry of sparks leapt up. Always looking for affirmation, the men nearest to him asked about it, and the Prophet replied that those sparks meant that one day Islam would encompass the lands of the Persians and the Byzantines. Both of those empires were the undisputed superpowers of the day, and Muhammad's confident assertion enlivened the workers. The Jews and hypocrites, of course, spread gossip about those remarks, which were seen as an impossibility. "Look at that! The Muslims are about to be wiped off the face of the earth, and Muhammad is telling them that one day the lands of Caesar and Chosroes will be theirs, and the fools believe him." Most Muslims were resolved to follow the Prophet without question and continued to trudge

ahead in their work. After six days of hard labor, the Muslims completed a trench five feet deep and nearly eight feet across. The
weary laborers were divided into defense units and stationed
around the perimeter of the city and trench to await the arrival of
the menacingly large army.

The huge Allied Army, as the Arab army was called, reached
Uhud hoping to meet the Muslims there, but seeing that they were
not to be found, the leaders directed their troops to Medina.
Imagine how the people of Medina must have felt seeing the huge
army advancing in the distance under a multitude of banners representing virtually every tribe of the Hijaz. Men, horses, and
camels seemed to fill the horizon and pour endlessly into the plain
beyond the city. The army assembled in a grand display and began
beating war drums and chanting battle cries. Muslim men and
women looked on from their posts and knew that if they lost, most
of them would be killed, and the survivors would be sold into slavery.
The Qur'an later recounted the emotions of the Muslims (Qur'an
33:10–11):

> When they came upon you from above and below, eyes
> glazed darkly, and hearts leapt up to the throats, and you
> imagined all sorts of bad thoughts about God. In this situ-
> ation were the believers tested and shaken tremendously.
> The hypocrites and the sick of heart said, "God and His
> Messenger promised us nothing but delusions."

The hypocrites were hard at work sowing fear and panic.
Muhammad and his closest companions knew that 'Abdullah ibn
Ubayy would betray them if the battle seemed to go against them.
Already he had succeeded in weakening the Muslim position by
encouraging his followers to desert their posts and protect their
exposed houses. With a determined foe at their gates and a knife
poised to strike them in the back, the Muslims shuddered in fear.

The Allied Army was about to begin an all-out assault on the
city when they noticed the huge trench around its walls.
The advance was halted; the soldiers were confused by this strategy, which had never been employed in the Arabian Peninsula
before. The trench was too wide for horses to get over and would
stop any charge, for archers would easily pick off any men who

were struggling out of a dry moat. They sent riders just near enough to shout, and they cursed at the Muslims and their cowardice, taunting them to come out. A few small groups of Arab fighters broke ranks and tried to rush the trench. After repeated assaults, however, each group was beaten back by the Muslim archers located in foxholes just inside the defensive area. Unsure about what to do next, the army made camp and prepared for a long siege.

It was winter, and cold winds howled across the desert at night. The Muslims were safe and warm in their homes, but the idolaters had only flimsy tents to keep out the chill. During the day the Allied Army tried to charge the trench, only to be met with a rain of arrows. Any who made it through the trench were met by the determined defenders and soon dispatched. Though they held the enemy at bay, food supplies soon ran low in Medina. Many Muslim soldiers tied rocks around their waists to press against their empty stomachs. But the defense of the city was holding, and the Allied Army began to lose its determination.

The Meccan leaders realized that the siege might have to be prolonged. The Banu Nadir also began to worry. They had worked hard to assemble the tribes of Arabia under the Meccans; such an accomplishment might never happen again. The leaders of the Banu Nadir sent messages to the Arab tribal leaders, begging them to stay and keep up the attack. Huyayy reiterated his promise to the tribal council to get the Banu Qurayza, his Jewish cousins, to attack the Muslims from behind.

Huyayy secretly slipped into the neighborhood of the Banu Qurayza and went to their chief, Ka'b ibn Asad. He tried to convince him to use his forces to attack the Muslims. Ka'b ibn Asad didn't want to join the cause or even listen to Huyayy, for he wished to honor his treaty with the Muslims. He also knew what happened to the two other Jewish clans who tried to fight the Muslims. But after Huyayy described the size of the Meccan army, the precarious position of the Muslims, and the need for Jewish solidarity, Ka'b ibn Asad agreed to consider the proposal. Huyayy laid out a plan for total war from without and ambush from within and promised to move his Banu Nadir warriors into the Banu Qurayza fortresses and defend Asad's people should the Muslims discover their plot and try to counterattack. Finally Ka'b agreed, convinced that the combined forces could wipe out the Muslims. The two leaders decided that the Banu Qurayza would attack the Muslims from behind on the same day that the Allied Army would make an all-out assault on the trench.

News of the betrayal of the Banu Qurayza reached the Prophet and his companions quickly. They were shocked and dismayed. They had held off the Allied Army thus far and depended on the Banu Qurayza to guard the rear of the city. Now that the Banu Qurayza had sealed their neighborhood and forbade any Muslim from entering, the situation looked bleak. A delegation of the chiefs of the Auws and Khazraj tribes went to the Jewish settlement to plead with them to honor the treaty and discovered that the situation was far worse than they expected. The Jews were preparing for war by gathering weapons and supplies. The two chiefs pointed out that the Banu Qurayza might suffer a worse fate than the two Jewish clans who were forced to leave Medina. But the Banu Qurayza began insulting the Prophet, and their elders declared the treaty null and void. The two Muslim chiefs hastily left the scene as the war fever began to rise, and informed the Prophet of the new situation. The Muslims now feared that the Allies might circle around to the other side of the city where the Jewish fortresses were and enter through the walls of the Banu Qurayza.

The Banu Qurayza then cut off all food supplies to the Muslims, and within days the Muslims began to feel the hunger. The leaders of the Allied Army were elated. Victory was in their grasp. The warriors began to dance and sing songs around their campfires in expectation of the day of the attack. The Meccans and their fellow tribal leaders planned a three-pronged attack, with Abu Sufyan leading the main body of men over the trench. The Banu Qurayza were to attack from the rear. It seemed flawless in its simplicity, and there were enough men to exert pressure on the Muslim defenders that they would simply be overwhelmed. The people of Medina became even more fearful as they watched the Allies preparing and moving their forces around. The hypocrites in the city tried to convince the Muslims to run away or flee, but the Prophet and the strongest companions remained firm, knowing that even if they died, they would win in the end by entering Paradise.

Some of the Arab horsemen were so encouraged by their new fortunes that they attempted an assault on the trench a few days before the main attack was to start. They found a spot where the trench was narrow and attacked fiercely until they gained a position on the other side. 'Ali ibn Abi Talib and the other Muslim defenders rushed to engage the enemy. Amr ibn Wudd, a fearsome Meccan warrior, challenged the Muslims to a hand-to-hand duel. 'Ali ibn Abi Talib came forward, pulled Amr off his horse, and dispatched him with one blow. The other invaders, seeing their champion dead, ran back across the trench to regroup while the Muslims cheered in amazement.

The front line was secure for the moment, but in the rear of the city, the Banu Qurayza's warriors were starting to descend from their fortresses and occupy the houses close to the Muslim area of the city. Many women and children were living in the walled houses there, and there were few Muslim soldiers to spare to protect them. Safiyah bint Abdel Muttalib saw a Jewish scout skulking through the alley inspecting the Muslim defenses. She asked an old man to go out and kill the spy. The old man refused out of fear. Safiyah then grabbed an iron rod and crept out in the street. She came upon the warrior from behind and killed him with one swift strike. Immediately she sounded the alarm, and other women took up a careful watch over the back alleys. Some Muslims stood on their rooftops and shouted, "God is great!" all night to frighten the Banu Qurayza and keep them from attacking.

Seeing that the Muslims were hemmed in on all sides, the Prophet had no other choice but to attempt to divide his enemies. He sent a secret message to the powerful Ghatafan tribe that if they withdrew, he would give them one third of the harvest of Medina for a year. The Ghatafan were there only to appease their friends among the Banu Nadir, and they were growing weary of the siege, which was now over three weeks old. They hesitated in their planning with the other tribes and the Meccans.

The Prophet also sent a man named Nu'aym to the Banu Qurayza. An old friend of the Jews, he pretended he was an unbeliever and convinced them that they shouldn't attack without a promise from the Meccans to help them if the tide of battle turned or if the Allies withdrew and left them to face Muhammad alone. Thus the Banu Qurayza began to hesitate and limit their activities to reconnaissance. Then Nu'aym went secretly to the Allied camp and told Abu Sufyan that the Banu Qurayza had broken the deal and gone back to the Muslim side. He went to the Ghatafan camp and told their leaders the same thing.

The next day, Abu Sufyan sent a messenger to the Banu Qurayza telling them that the attack was being rescheduled and would begin the very next day. The Jews replied that the next day was Saturday and that they wouldn't work or fight on their holy day. Abu Sufyan was incensed and replied that if they didn't attack on the morrow then the deal would be off and the Quraysh would attack them as well. The Jews refused again and said they would not attack on any day unless the Quraysh first promised to protect them from the Muslims should the tide of battle turn. Abu Sufyan was convinced now that the Banu Qurayza had gone back on their secret pact with him. When Abu Sufyan paid a visit to the leaders of the Ghatafan tribe, he found out they also wanted to postpone the attack. Abu Sufyan was apoplectic with rage.

That very night, as the confused and divided Allied Army slept uneasily in their drafty tents, a wind began blowing over the plain. Within an hour the army was in the middle of a raging winter storm. The exposed tents started to fall down, sand whipped in the faces of men, and horses grew terrified and bolted. Someone shouted that Muhammad was attacking, and bewildered men began striking out at their fellows blindly because no fire could burn in the buffeting winds. As the winds howled, the leaders met hastily and suggested a retreat. They saw in the storm evil signs and thought the Muslims might take advantage of the opportunity to attack. The undisciplined tribesmen were also tired of the siege and were looking for any excuse to leave. Abu Sufyan and Huyayy ibn Akhtab reluctantly agreed and gave the order to break camp just before dawn. By the time the morning had broken, the field of battle was empty. The Allied Army had gone home.

The Muslims rejoiced at this miracle, and shouts of "God is great!" rang through the streets. The Prophet and the grateful Muslims gathered in the mosque to give thanks to God. The ever-present Ibn Ubayy suggested that it was a ruse and that the army would return. It didn't, and scouts were sent to confirm its departure. One thing still had to be done. The Banu Qurayza had betrayed the Muslims in their greatest hour of need. They broke the treaty, cut off the Muslims' food supplies, and agreed to let the enemy enter the city. They made threatening moves against the ill-protected women and children and would have shown no mercy if they had won. They could no longer be trusted to remain a part of the city. The Prophet ordered Bilal to proclaim as part of the call to prayer, "No good Muslim will pray the afternoon prayer except in the neighborhood of the Banu Qurayza!"

The Muslims immediately mobilized and assaulted the Jewish fortresses. The Banu Qurayza held off the Muslim attacks, led principally by 'Ali, for twenty-five days and nights. But the Muslims pressed forward. During one assault, 'Ali picked up a huge door and used it as a shield while he led a charge of fighters. Finally, the Banu Qurayza realized that they could never win and asked for a negotiated settlement. The Prophet refused to negotiate and demanded their unconditional surrender. Although he likely would have allowed them to leave Medina despite their treacherous conduct, for he had done so in all other situations, the Banu Qurayza refused to submit to his judgment. They feared a harsh penalty and sent messages to the Auws asking them to help arrange an orderly exile rather than any stiffer punishment. Accordingly, some Auws men went to the Prophet and begged that he would treat the Banu Qurayza similarly to the Banu Qaynuqa. Muhammad, not wanting to antagonize them, replied, "Men of Auws, would you be happy if one of your own men decided the issue?" They replied in the affirmative, so Muhammad gave up his right to make a decision as an aggrieved party.

When this news was communicated to the Banu Qurayza, they immediately nominated Sa'd ibn Mu'adth, the chief of the Auws tribe, with whom they had been friendly in the past and who had pleaded with them not to break the treaty during the siege. Sa'd, who had himself been wounded in the fighting, made both sides sign an agreement promising to submit to his decision. Then he commanded that the Banu Qurayza surrender their weapons, leave their fortresses, and be taken into the custody of the Muslims. Next he gathered the leaders of the Banu Qurayza and asked them what the judgment was for a traitor according to their own religion. The clan leaders all bowed their heads. The punishment for betrayal in the Torah (the Jewish holy book) was death. Sa'd decreed that all the warriors should be executed and that the women and children be taken as captives of war and sold into servanthood.

Muhammad did not intervene because he had already given up his right to alter the judgment. He did stipulate that no family should be separated, equating it with injustice, and thus no mother was separated from her children as they were parceled out as servants to the various people who would have custody of them. Before the warriors were executed, they were offered a chance to convert to Islam. Four men did, and they were allowed to regain their properties and families. The rest chose death, saying that it was the will of their Lord. Thus the threat of the Banu Qurayza was eliminated. Although many Jews continued to live in Medina peacefully, no organized tribal group held their allegiance.

The Muslims rejoiced in their victory. Medina was safe from enemies inside as well as out. The time had now arrived for Muhammad to reach out to the rest of the world, to the lands of Caesar and of Chosroes of Persia. But first he had to decide what to do about Mecca.

Chapter 12

Going Home: The Conquest of Mecca

*God's good pleasure was on the believers when they swore
allegiance to you under the tree. He knew what was in
their hearts, and he sent tranquility down upon them. He
rewarded them with a swift victory, and there will be many
benefits for them out of this besides. God is indeed powerful
and wise.*

—Qur'an 48:18–19

After the siege of Medina was lifted, Muslim prestige rose considerably in the eyes of the surrounding tribes of the region. The Muslims had handed the Meccans a humiliating defeat; the grand coalition assembled by the great chief of the Banu Nadir collapsed; and Muhammad had withstood the greatest assault Arabia had ever known. At long last, peace seemed to be at hand, but one more tribe wanted to try its luck against the Muslims. When news reached Medina that the Banu Mustaliq was preparing for war, the Prophet organized yet another preemptive strike, and once again his men headed towards the lands of their latest foe.

The campaign went like others had. The enemy was taken unawares, and before it could mount an effective counterattack, the swift Muslims drove its forces into the hills and took the baggage and people that were left behind. This habit of seizing the goods and members of hostile tribes acted as both a punishment and a deterrent against future threats. (Captives were often freed upon the settling of a peace treaty with the offending party.)

But this latest military foray didn't end on an entirely peaceful note. While encamped for the night on the way back from the battle, two men in Muhammad's army, one an immigrant and the other a tribesman of the Khazraj, argued over whose turn it was to drink from the water supply. The latter called for help from his fellow tribe members, and the former called to the other immigrants. A few level-headed people nearby quickly mediated the quarrel, and all would have been forgotten, but one man standing in the crowd saw his chance to act. It was 'Abdullah ibn Ubayy. He had tried to regain his lost honor by agreeing to march on this expedition, but he was by no means reconciled to the expanding power of his rival, Muhammad. Speaking loudly to the gathered crowd, he said, "We let these immigrants into our city and homes, and now they want to take over and drive us out. Fatten your dog, and it will turn on you. By God, when we return to Medina, the respectable will drive out the beggars."

Rumors began to swirl around the camp that civil war was in the offing. Some of Ibn Ubayy's men tried to fan the flames by bringing up old feuds and past slights among the members of the diverse force. The rumors finally reached Muhammad's tent, where he was holding a small meeting, and when 'Umar heard the report he angrily insisted, "Tell Bilal to cut off his [Ibn Ubayy's] head!" The Prophet replied, "Would you have people say that Muhammad kills his own men?" He ordered that camp be struck, even though the weary soldiers had just finished constructing it. When the camels and horses were reloaded, the Prophet ordered a long march that lasted until the end of the next day. By then the men were too exhausted to pay any mind to Ibn Ubayy's machinations, and the matter was laid to rest for the moment.

The unexpected departure did have one unintended side effect that eventually proved disastrous. Whenever the Prophet went out to war, one of his wives always accompanied him. It was A'ishah's turn to go this time, and as the men were packing their baggage hastily, she suddenly realized that she had lost her necklace. Remembering where she had taken it off, she retraced her steps and searched until she located it. By the time she got back to camp, everyone was gone! Even her attendants failed to realize that she was not in her covered sedan chair. She sat down on the hard-packed earth and waited, not knowing what else to do. A short time later, a Muslim straggler, a young man named Safwan, happened by. He put her on his camel and walked beside it all the way back to Medina, arriving a day after the main contingent.

When the Muslim army reentered Medina, some of Ibn Ubayy's men started passing rumors to the crowds lining the streets. This time they said that their leader had been beheaded. A few hours of consternation followed, and when the truth was known, it was clear that Ibn Ubayy was determined to have a showdown with the Prophet. His conduct was deemed so dangerous and seditious that many felt he would have to be eliminated at some point. Muhammad, though, had already decided that he would not move against him and for more than just charitable reasons. If he ordered his death, then Ibn Ubayy's son, also named 'Abdullah, would be honor-bound to avenge his father. Although the Prophet feared no man, he desperately wanted to avoid putting the younger 'Abdullah in this emotional quandary.

Muhammad bided his time until the day it occurred to the young man that he would have to be the one who took action. He was a sincere Muslim who believed in all that Muhammad had brought. It pained him to see his own father working so vehemently against Islam. 'Abdullah went to the Prophet in grief and begged for permission to kill his own father because he was a danger to the community. If allowed to continue unchecked, his father might conspire with outside enemies or worse. Muhammad replied, "We will not kill him and instead will be good to him and remain his companion for as long as he lives with us."

The Prophet might have held his tongue had he known what new slander was busily circulating within the city. Many people had seen Safwan leading A'ishah in from the desert a full day after Muhammad had returned, and they wondered aloud about what the two young people were doing alone in the countryside away from the rest of the army. Ibn Ubayy, of course, was delighted and encouraged the hushed innuendoes to become full-blown accusations of infidelity. When the rumors reached the Prophet's ears, it was too late to stifle the suspicions with reason—people had begun to take sides, and a few vowed to fight to uphold A'ishah's honor. Muhammad was at a loss. He felt hurt when he considered whether the charges were true, but at the same time he expressed astonishment that A'ishah would ever commit adultery given how well he knew her after several years of marriage.

A'ishah noticed that her husband was avoiding her and treating her coldly when they did happen to meet. A'ishah, living a sheltered life, didn't know what was going on. She questioned her mother as to the possible reasons. Perhaps Muhammad's new marriage to Juwairiyah, a widowed captive from the Banu Mustaliq campaign, occupied his heart. Muhammad wedded her at the behest of his companions, who suggested that because her father was the chief of her tribe a new alliance could be formed, and indeed her tribe joined on the side of Medina and converted to Islam. But Juwairiyah wasn't the wife who distracted the Prophet. In anguish and despair at the loss of the Prophet's affection, A'ishah soon fell ill and became bedridden. Eventually, she moved back in with her parents to rest.

Muhammad received no words or guidance from Gabriel, and he began to doubt his own judgment in the matter of A'ishah. He stated in the mosque that the gossipmongers were ruining the reputations of two good people and hurting their families, and should desist. His request wasn't enough. One day a man from the Auws tribe told Muhammad in a public forum that if the authors of the gossip were from his tribe, then his own people would silence them. If they were from the Khazraj, then all Muhammad had to do was say the word and he and his people would cut off their heads. A man from the Khazraj interrupted him saying that the only reason he said what he did was because he knew the Khazraj were keeping the rumor alive. Men and women from both tribes began arguing in the mosque, and the argument would have escalated into a riot had Muhammad not called desperately for calm.

News of the real reason her husband was avoiding her finally reached A'ishah, and she reacted with revulsion and horror, weeping uncontrollably. She could not believe that her fidelity and honor should be so questioned, and in public! She said to her mother, "May God forgive you. You heard of such talk and didn't tell me?" In vain her mother tried to soothe her. A'ishah was heartbroken, realizing that her husband must have doubted her faithfulness. Just then Muhammad stopped by for a visit and found his wife with her parents trying their best to console her. He said, "A'ishah, fear God. If you did what people are saying, then turn to God in repentance for God accepts it with mercy."

Shocked to have her suspicions about her husband's doubts confirmed, she turned to her parents and asked them to answer for her. They didn't know what to say. She cried bitterly, realizing that her own parents would not rush to her defense. Then she paused, reigned in her tears, and angrily said, "No, I will not repent for something I did not do. God knows I am innocent. I will not say what has not been. When I deny it, though, you don't believe me. I can only say what the father of Joseph said, 'I have but to wait patiently against what you claim. Only God's help can be asked.'"

When she spoke these last words, a quotation from the Qur'an and an invocation of God's help to Jacob who was mourning the disappearance of his son, Muhammad began to tremble and break out in a cold sweat, which were signs that he was receiving a new passage of the Qur'an. Abu Bakr covered him with a blanket to keep him warm and rushed his family out of the room until Muhammad could revive. When he finally arose, he wiped the sweat from his brow and called the trio back in saying, "Be cheerful, A'ishah, for God has sent down proof of your innocence." He then went to the mosque and recited these words before an assembled crowd:

> *Those who fabricated the slander are a gang among you.*
> *Don't think, though, that it was a bad thing that the*
> *rumor was so aired, for it was good that it may be solved*
> *faster. For each of them there is a share of the sin and*
> *those who took the lead in this affair will have the worst*
> *penalty to pay. But when you first heard the rumor, why*
> *didn't the believing men and women think more positively*

and say, "This is an obvious lie"? Why didn't you bring
four witnesses to prove it? Without witnesses people will
stand before God as liars.

If it wasn't for the grace and mercy of God upon you
in both this life and the next, then a painful punishment
would have been sprung upon you as you rushed eagerly
into this affair. You accepted it on your tongues and said
from your own mouths things you didn't know anything
about. You thought it was a light matter while it was most
serious in the sight of God. And when you heard the
rumor, why didn't you say, "It's not right for us to speak
about this. Glory to God this is a terrible slander"? God
admonishes you to never behave this way again if you are
true believers. (Qur'an 24:11–17)

With her honor fully restored, A'ishah quickly recovered, and
the matter was forgotten. She returned to her own apartment, and
the Prophet regained his former fondness for her. The hypocrites
had been defeated once again. Thereafter, Islamic law dictated that
to slander a chaste woman was a crime punishable by a public lash-
ing. In addition, to accuse a woman of infidelity without being able
to produce four reliable witnesses carried the penalty of having
one's testimony ever afterwards rejected in any court of law.

Muhammad often listened to disputes among people and rendered judgment based on the principles of the Qur'an. In one famous case, an Arab
stole a piece of armor and hid it in the house of a Jew. When the owner
of the armor eventually learned of its location, he took the Jew before
Muhammad for redress. The Jew offered evidence that the thief had hidden the armor in a grain bag also stolen from his house. The plaintiff told
of how he followed a leak from that very bag right to the man's doorstep.
The thief, meanwhile, rallied his tribe to defend him against what he said
were false accusations. Muhammad received a revelation on the spot
telling him the truth of what had happened, and the Jew was found innocent of the crime.

The hypocrites were not completely cowed, however, and it
wasn't long before the aging Ibn Ubayy upped the ante by building
a small mosque of his own in his neighborhood. The bulk of the

meetings held there consisted of public challenges against various Islamic doctrines as well as assaults on the integrity of the companions and Muhammad himself. The Prophet ordered his men to dismantle the mosque, which had been labeled by the Qur'an as being built on hypocrisy. Ibn Ubayy, nearing the end of his life by now, continued his covert war and became so unrepentant and malicious that even his own family began chastising him. He soon fell ill, however, and on his deathbed, Muhammad came to visit him and asked God to forgive him, telling his stunned companions that he hoped God would.

One night late in the year 628, Muhammad had a dream in which he saw himself and a host of other Muslims clad only in white togas making a pilgrimage to Mecca. It had been six years since he had left the place of his birth in disgrace. Now he was the master of a religious community that stretched from central Arabia north almost to the borders of Syria. Written copies of chapters of the Qur'an were circulated widely; the rate of conversions increased daily; the danger of invasion had lessened. Muhammad now turned his thoughts back to Mecca and his dream of cleansing the ancient shrine of Abraham, the Ka'bah, of its hundreds of idols. But how could he march to Mecca at the head of an unarmed column while the Quraysh still held absolute power over the city?

Muhammad ardently believed that his dreams were from God, so the next morning he announced to the astonished community that he was organizing a *hajj* or pilgrimage to Mecca. This announcement came during the months of truce, so the Meccans would, as Arabian custom dictated, be honor-bound to observe a cessation of hostilities, even with their bitterest enemies. Hopeful in the justice of their cause, the Muslims immediately began to prepare for the trip. Though most Muslim men and women responded favorably, a number from the countryside demurred. The Prophet ultimately set out with fourteen hundred of his followers who were armed with nothing more than their small travelers' blades. This journey was to be the first pilgrimage in Islam and would reaffirm the Muslims' claim to the relics of Abraham. The winding column of pilgrims undertook the two-week journey toward Mecca, praising God and rejoicing in their new resolve.

"Here I am, O God, at your service, here I am. You have no partners. Here I am at your service," they chanted in unison throughout the days of walking and in their camp at night.

New verses from the Qur'an also came, declaring the Ka'bah to
be for all people of true faith and the duty of all believers to visit it
at least once in their lives, if they could afford it. In contrast to the
pagan Arabs who performed all manner of bizarre rituals at the
Ka'bah, Muhammad laid out clearly how and where religious devotions were to be carried out. Visiting the Ka'bah was a pious act to
praise God and renew one's devotion to him. It would be a rebirth,
of sorts, in which all people would reenact the rituals of the angels
who circled the throne of God and of Judgment Day where all would
stand shoulder to shoulder with nothing to hide. The Muslims who
accompanied the Prophet on this dangerous trek were as much filled
with fear as they were with excitement at the prospect of having all
their sins forgiven by God at the ritual's completion.

> *The* hajj *or pilgrimage falls during the first two weeks of the eleventh
> month of the Islamic lunar year. Any Muslim male making a pilgrimage
> is only allowed to wear simple white garments devoid of all ornamenta-
> tion or stitching, to emphasize the sameness of all men and impress upon
> the participants that ornaments and dress are intangible and hence status
> means nothing. (Women have wider latitude regarding what to wear.)
> The rituals consist of walking around the Ka'bah seven times and jour-
> neying into the countryside to say prayers. Stone pillars representing
> Satan are stoned, and a grand assembly is held on a hot desert plain to
> emulate Judgment Day. Fighting, cursing, and other immoral acts inval-
> idate the whole affair, and thus one's best behavior is required through-
> out. The* hajj *ends with a final circling of the Ka'bah, a ritual sacrificing
> of animals whose meat is given to the poor, and, for men, the shaving of
> the head to signify rebirth.*

The Prophet had no intention of forcing his way into Mecca.
He hoped to march peacefully right into the city with his followers, joining the throngs of idolaters also visiting during the truce
months. When the Meccans learned of Muhammad's pilgrimage,
however, they were thrown into panic. After reports from scouts
confirmed that the Muslims were coming in large numbers and

that it didn't appear to be an armed invasion, but rather a legitimate religious visit, they were doubly confused. If they didn't challenge the Muslims, how would such a humiliating imposition look to the rest of Arabia? At the same time, if they attacked their unarmed foes, all of Arabia would see that the custodians of the Ka'bah had violated the sacred months. Hadn't they castigated the Muslims for the same thing when one of their small caravans was ambushed before?

In the end, the clan leaders of the Quraysh decided to neither allow the Muslims to enter the city nor to engage them in battle. They sent out a combined infantry and cavalry regiment under Khalid ibn Walid and 'Ikrima, the son of Abu Jahl, to turn the Muslims back. Khalid was the same military commander who had surprised the Muslims from behind at Uhud when the archers left their posts, and 'Ikrima was still bitter over his father's death at Badr. They were given strict orders, however, not to attack. When the Prophet learned that Quraysh units were approaching, he asked his followers if any of them knew of another way to Mecca. One of them guided the group through some little-used passes in the mountains. When they arrived at a field called Hudaybiyah, just outside Mecca, the Prophet's camel stopped. Everyone thought the animal was exhausted, but Muhammad said, "No, the camel is not tired. It has stopped by the order of God. By the one who created me, I will accept any offers the Meccans make for peace."

The Meccan force failed to find the Muslims, searching in vain until they were many miles from home. Other scouts from the city soon discovered Muhammad's camp, however, and reported that they saw no preparations for war. The Quraysh then sent the head of the Abyssinian Guard, mercenaries hired to defend Mecca, to see what Muhammad was planning. When the Prophet learned of the commander's approach, he ordered all the animals brought for sacrifice to be arrayed in front of their tents. The commander saw the scene from afar and surmised that the Muslims really were on a peaceful foray. He returned and gave his report to the Meccan leaders, but he was soundly chastised for what they saw as his naiveté.

After much wrangling, the Quraysh decided to send a man named 'Urwa ibn Mas'ud to speak to the Prophet. He was an honest man and spoke plainly to Muhammad. "Mecca is an egg," he said, "placed in your hand." It was true—with the Meccan army off looking for Muhammad in the hinterland, nothing could prevent him from storming the city. Muhammad replied that he had come as a pilgrim and merely sought permission to enter the city peacefully to perform his religious rites. 'Urwa was impressed with his sincerity and returned to Mecca. "I have seen Chosroes of Persia in his kingdom, Caesar in his realm, and the Negus in his land," he told the Quraysh, "but never have I seen a people who love their leader more than these Muslims love Muhammad. Even the hair that falls from his head is cherished. They will never give him up, so consider carefully what you will do."

A few hours later Muhammad sent a swift rider into the city to meet the Quraysh and try to reason with them, but when the rider entered Mecca he was set upon by a mob and nearly killed. He barely escaped, thanks to the intervention of the Abyssinians, who thought it scandalous to attack an envoy. That night a group of over forty hooligans from Mecca crept to the edge of the Muslim camp and began pelting the tents with stones. Muhammad's sentries caught them but then let them go to emphasize that they were not there to fight or take prisoners.

In the morning, the Prophet decided to send a nobler delegate to the Quraysh, someone they respected and would more likely receive. The job fell to Uthman ibn Affan, who had once enjoyed access to the private councils of the clan elders. Upon entering Mecca, Uthman sought out a local man he had known for years for protection and then entered into a formal meeting with the city's leaders. The Meccans were pleased to see him and told him he could make a pilgrimage any time he liked, but when he replied that he was there to ask for Muhammad's participation, they flatly refused. They explained that they had all taken an oath to prevent Muhammad from coming anywhere near the Ka'bah. There were intense negotiations and arguments, and Uthman was long delayed in returning. A rumor spread through the Muslim camp that the Quraysh had killed their beloved compatriot, and many of the companions were filled with thoughts of revenge. The Prophet, too, was concerned for his friend and swore that if anything happened to Uthman, he would lead the Muslims to fight the Meccans, unarmed though they were. He moved under a nearby tall tree and took a pledge from all the people there that they would fight to the last man if the Meccans had killed Uthman and violated the holy months of pilgrimage. A short time later, Uthman returned from his fruitless discussions, and the issue passed, though the Qur'an later praised those who took the oath as being sincere in faith.

An official delegation from Mecca headed by the eloquent Suhayl ibn 'Amr arrived that night to discuss the situation with the Prophet. 'Amr's famed elocution, however, was laced with sarcasm as he addressed Muhammad in very disrespectful terms, laying out the points of a treaty that looked increasingly like a capitulation for the Muslim side. The Meccans insisted on these main concessions:

- The Muslims would not be allowed to complete their pilgrimage and would have to leave. They could return the following year for only a quick three-day visit.

- Neither side could make hostile moves against the other for several years. Both sides could enter into alliances with whatever tribes they wished.

- Any Meccan man who would leave and go to Medina henceforth without the permission of his family would be returned to Mecca while any man who would leave Medina for Mecca would not be returned.

Muhammad agreed to every one of these provisions, much to the surprise of his companions. He explained that he was instructed by God to make the deal in order to win breathing room for the Muslim community, no matter how unfair the treaty was. After Muhammad's secretary recorded the finalized treaty on parchment, Suhayl looked it over. When he noticed that it began by invoking God's name and asserted the prophetic nature of Muhammad, he objected. He would not sign a document that began with words he didn't believe in. Muhammad agreed to take out all such references and, with his own hand, crossed out the disputed terms. The final treaty became known as the Treaty of Hudaybiyah.

Privately, 'Umar took Abu Bakr aside and asked, "Aren't those people the idolaters?" Abu Bakr answered, "Most certainly, 'Umar, they are."

"Aren't we the ones who are surrendered to God's will?" 'Umar went on.

"We certainly are."

"So why are we making compromises in our religion?"

"Be silent, 'Umar, because I affirm that Muhammad is the Messenger of God."

"I affirm it as well."

After the Meccans left, satisfied that they had gotten the better of the Muslims, 'Umar ibn al-Khattab complained about the disadvantageous nature of the treaty to the Prophet. Muhammad listened and then replied confidently, "I am the servant of God, and his messenger. I always obey his commands, and he will never fail me." Many Muslims were not so sure God's favor was upon them, however. They had traveled hundreds of miles and were not going to be allowed to complete their pilgrimage after all. The Prophet declared that God would post the full reward of a pilgrimage to their account with him, and then Muhammad ordered the people present to complete their rituals right there, outside Mecca. When no one moved he went gloomily into his tent. Umm Salamah, the wife whose turn it was to accompany him this time, was waiting for him.

"Umm Salamah," he said, "the Muslims will surely be destroyed for they have refused to obey the command of the Messenger of God." His wife, whose age and wisdom served her well, replied, "No, Messenger of God, it's only because they are dejected. Go and start the rituals of the pilgrimage, and they will join you." After some initial reluctance, the crowds finally stood and performed the rites with their leader. Afterwards, they broke camp and began their return to Medina with the increasingly attractive prospect of several years' worth of peace. A chapter of the Qur'an was revealed along the way, emphasizing the hidden benefits of a treaty, no matter how flawed: "Truly, we have granted you a clear victory." (Qur'an 48:1)

The Muslims' patience was sorely tested, however, when a Meccan named Abu Jundal came running after their departing caravan. He had recently embraced Islam and wanted to go with the Muslims to Medina. Marks of torture were clearly evident on his body, and old memories of their own persecution welled up in the minds of many Muslims. When some Meccans came to retrieve him, the fugitive begged the Muslims to give him asylum saying, "Help me Muslims! Would you leave me to the idolaters?" Several of the companions put themselves between him and the Quraysh tribesmen with great determination, not wanting to give him up. The Prophet, who always honored his promises, sadly said that he had to return. Then he added, "Abu Jundal, be patient and control yourself. Surely God will make some way out for you and for the other Muslims in Mecca. We have bound ourselves to make peace, and we have exchanged the pact of God, and we will not break that."

A few weeks later, a woman who embraced Islam in Mecca escaped from her family and finally made it to Medina. Sure enough, her relatives showed up a short time later and demanded her return. But this time the Prophet refused to give up the refugee. The dismayed idolaters reminded him vociferously of their agreement calling for the return of any Meccans. The Prophet smiled and pointed out that the treaty said, in exact words, "any *man* from Mecca," and that this woman would not be returned. The Meccans could argue no further and left Medina. Thereafter, many women from Mecca who secretly embraced Islam escaped to Medina. A full chapter of the Qur'an soon came to Muhammad instructing him on the proper way to debrief the frequent female refugees and how to integrate them into Medinan society.

At about the same time another Muslim runaway from Mecca by the name of Abu Busir arrived in Medina. When two Meccan relatives arrived to take him back, the Prophet, as stipulated in the treaty, had to turn him over to them. Before his ignoble departure,

Muhammad encouraged him, "Abu Busir, we have promised them, and in our way of life to break a promise is a sin. Go and God will find some way to save you." Abu Busir reluctantly obeyed and was bound like a prisoner by the two men before they left for home. On the return journey Abu Busir managed to get free and escape into the surrounding hills. He didn't return to Medina, however, for he knew he would be turned over to the Meccans again. Instead, he took shelter in a cave near the route used by caravans going to Syria. Whenever he would see a caravan in the valley below, he would charge down and attack it, damage the goods, and disappear back into the hills.

The harried new converts to Islam of Mecca heard about Abu Busir and went to join him. Little by little, their number reached around seventy people. This good-sized band made it very difficult for the Meccans to send caravans northwards. Though they had a treaty with Muhammad, the bandits were not under his jurisdiction, and they became increasingly alarmed at their losses. Many merchants and guards ultimately paid with their lives in Abu Busir's raids. The Meccans suffered so many losses from these ambushes that they began to fear economic disaster. They did the only thing that would quickly save them. They sent a delegation to Medina and begged the Prophet to agree to cancel the part of the treaty that said Meccan men had to be returned to Mecca. The Prophet eagerly agreed, and Abu Busir's men were allowed to enter Medina. When the good news arrived at Abu Busir's camp, he was very sick. After he heard the news, he died smiling.

To firmly secure the peace Medina was now enjoying, the Muslims had to mount one more military campaign. The Jews of the Banu Nadir, who had instigated the siege of Medina, had taken up residence in Khaybar, a fortress town some days' ride northwards. Fearing that the same people might attempt to unite hostile Arabs once more against him, the Prophet mobilized an army to go on the offensive. Other considerations also propelled him to take action. Every Jewish tribe with whom he had an agreement had broken their covenant, and the Jews of Khaybar were more numerous and powerful than all three Jewish tribes that had lived in

Medina. If the Khaybari Jews took up arms against Islam, it would not bode well for Muslims anywhere in the region.

After assembling a force of fifteen hundred men and a few women, Muhammad began the three-day journey towards the city. Meanwhile, the Jews of Khaybar prepared for war and perhaps a long siege with great confidence in their ability to repel any invasion. They had four main fortresses: In two of them they lodged their families, in another their treasure, and their warriors remained in the larger, fourth fort. The Muslim army made camp on the fertile plain outside the mud-walled city. Offers of leniency in exchange for surrender were made and quickly rebuffed. When Muhammad learned that all the fighting men were in the fourth fort, he ordered it surrounded; he did not want to attack women and children.

On the first day of battle, the Muslims attempted a charge and succeeded in scaling a part of the wall, though fifty men died and the assault was eventually repelled by a hail of arrows and spears. The Khaybari Jews also lost many men that afternoon, even their leader, though he was quickly succeeded by another. The next day Abu Bakr led an attack on the main gate, but it also proved unsuccessful. 'Umar ibn al-Khattab was then tapped to take the gate, but his attempt was fruitless as well. Finally, on the third day, the Prophet chose 'Ali ibn Abi Talib to lead the fighters. He gave him a banner and told him not to stop advancing until God gave him the fort.

'Ali bravely led his men to the gate, and they made quick work of it. The defenders inside were too exhausted to protect it as before. Once inside, the Muslims forced the Jews to surrender and took them all into custody. Muhammad did not want to punish them, however, or force them to leave because they had broken no treaties with him. He merely wanted to prevent any untoward actions that would threaten his budding nation. Therefore, he made a treaty with his defeated foe that allowed them to stay in their homes and cultivate their land, though now they would have the status of tenants and have to turn over half of the yearly harvest to the Muslim government in perpetuity. To cement the peace, the Prophet married a Jewish widow named Safiyah who had been captured in the fighting. She was the daughter of the late chief of the Banu Nadir and her marriage to Muhammad would cement ties between Khaybar and Medina. She consented and converted to Islam of her own free will, remaining a firm and committed Muslim for the rest of her life. Soon other local Jewish settlements sent delegates to Medina and established treaties of peace, allowing them to remain unmolested as long as they never conspired with the enemies of Islam. None of them did.

A year had passed since the signing of the Treaty of Hudaybiyah, and the Muslims were able to enter Mecca on a pilgrimage. The Quraysh left them alone as agreed, preferring to watch the proceedings from the hillsides where they had set up temporary lodging. None of the Quraysh wanted to be known as pact-breakers, nor did they want to be influenced by the Muslims, who performed their rituals with dignity and comportment. But the treaty meant much more for Islam than merely opening up Mecca for pilgrimage. It provided the much-needed breathing space that would allow Muhammad to further consolidate his position and even to reach out to the leaders of the known world with his message.

> While observing his allotted three days of pilgrimage, Muhammad was approached by his uncle, 'Abbas, who proposed that he marry Maymuna, a lady from a noble Meccan family. She had secretly converted and had made it known to her relatives that she wished to be wed to the Prophet. 'Abbas suggested that the marriage would be a grand way to build a new relationship with the Quraysh and possibly open Mecca for Islam through marriage ties. Muhammad agreed, but the Meccans flatly refused to allow any marriage ceremony involving the Prophet in their city. On the return journey to Medina, Muhammad married Maymuna at a place called Sarif. She outlived him by fifty years. Near the end of her life, she requested to be buried in Sarif, where she had spent her honeymoon.

Muhammad had succeeded in transforming a large segment of Arabian society from being tribal partisans to being members of a brotherhood of faith whose relationships were built on mutual goals rather than status, lineage, or wealth. Along the way he outlawed such practices as female infanticide, the consumption of alcohol, gambling, adultery, blood revenge, and racism. Superstitions also fell before his relentless program, and soon his followers shunned fortune telling, astrology, soothsaying, magic amulets, and the veneration of sacred trees or landforms as works of the devil. New values were instituted that emphasized sincerity, honesty, charity, thoughtfulness, bravery, and good manners. Just as the message of Jesus had been irresistible to the Romans of Paul's time, Muhammad's message was about to appeal to others outside of northern and central Arabia.

Muhammad announced to his companions one day, "God has sent me to be a mercy for all people. Don't, therefore, dispute about me like the disciples of Jesus did."

"How did they dispute, Messenger of God?" one man asked.

Muhammad answered, "He called them to the same thing that I am calling you to, but whereas those who had shorter missions to perform for him accepted their charge, those who were sent on faraway missions begrudged the work and dawdled." He then told them of his plans to contact the known rulers of the world and invite them to Islam. His followers eagerly accepted, and the next day Muhammad dictated a series of letters calling upon those who read them to submit to God and to remember that the welfare of their people was their responsibility. He then sent couriers instructed to deliver these letters and return with news about how they were received. Two letters were reserved for the rulers of the empires of Persia and Byzantium; the rest went to Egypt, Yemen, Abyssinia, and a small kingdom in southern Syria.

The Egyptian patriarch received Muhammad's letter and sent several camels laden with gifts to Muhammad as a sign of respect. He also sent two female slaves, Maria and Serene. The Christian sisters were quite fearful for their safety in these unknown regions of Arabia, but the Muslim courier making the journey with them spoke convincingly of Islam and of the Prophet's kindly demeanor. When the small caravan arrived in Medina, Muhammad gave Serene to one of his companions as a wife while Maria lodged in her own apartment and had the initial status of a concubine. It was an ill-defined position because Islam had little to say on this subject. Eventually, Maria converted to Islam and was elevated to the status of a wife of the Prophet.

Chosroes, the king of Persia, reacted quite differently to Muhammad's message. His armies had recently suffered a humiliating defeat at the hands of the Byzantines, and his mood was foul. After the letter was translated for him, he tore it up in anger and ordered his viceroy in Yemen to bring him the head of Muhammad. When the Prophet heard this, he remarked, "What Chosroes did to our letter, God will do to his empire." The emperor died a few weeks later, and a bitter battle of succession to the throne so weakened the Persian Empire that it eventually fell to Muslim forces during the rule of 'Umar, the second caliph of Islam after the Prophet passed away.

The Negus of Abyssinia replied warmly to the letter he received. He even acted as the Prophet's representative in a marriage arrangement between Muhammad and Umm Habibah, the daughter of Abu Sufyan, who fled to that land with the other Muslim refugees years before and became widowed. She eventually returned with the last remaining Meccan exiles to Arabia and settled in Medina in her own apartment, as all the wives of the Prophet had.

Heraclius, the Byzantine Roman emperor, also received a letter during his visit to the Holy Land. It read as follows:

> In the Name of God, the Compassionate Source of All
> Mercy. From Muhammad, the son of 'Abdullah, to
> Heraclius, the Emperor of Byzantium. Peace be upon the
> followers of righteous guidance. I call you to the way of
> self-surrender. If you accept it, you will be saved, and
> God will double your reward. If you don't accept it, the
> responsibility for the salvation of your subjects will be
> upon you. O People of the Book, come to a fair principle,
> common to us both, that we serve only God, that we
> make no partners with Him, and that we don't take others
> as lords besides God. But if they refuse, take note that we
> are surrendered [to God's will].

After the emperor read it, he wanted to know more about the man who sent it. He asked his servants to find someone in

Palestine who knew Muhammad and bring him in for an interview. As fate would have it, Abu Sufyan was in the city on a trading mission. He was brought to Heraclius and questioned about Muhammad's background, teachings, status, and reputation. Abu Sufyan answered all the questions truthfully, and when the interview was finished, Heraclius remarked, "If all of what you say is true, I'm sure his kingdom will reach the place here where I walk. I was certain that a prophet was coming, but I didn't think he would be born in Arabia." Some controversy exists about whether he entertained the idea of converting to Islam, but in the end he took no action and affirmed his allegiance to Christianity when his nobles threatened mutiny if he hearkened to the Prophet's invitation.

Nearly two years passed after the signing of the Treaty of Hudaybiyah, and a relative peace remained between Mecca and Medina. During this time, the tribe of Banu Khuza'a became allies of the Muslims, and the tribe of Banu Bakr became allies of the Quraysh in Mecca. One night the Banu Bakr, supplied with fresh weapons by the Quraysh, attacked the camp of the Banu Khuza'a and caused much slaughter and destruction. The warriors of the Banu Bakr then carried off all their loot to Mecca where they took shelter. The chief of the Banu Khuza'a went to Medina some days later and loudly complained about the injustice done against his people. The Prophet came out of the mosque and was told what happened. Angered by the senseless attack by the Meccan allies, he sent a message to Mecca: The Banu Bakr must pay compensation for the victims they killed. Also, the Meccans must break their alliance with the Banu Bakr or declare the entire Treaty of Hudaybiyah null and void.

The Quraysh, who perhaps saw the victory of the Banu Bakr as a sign of good fortune in their interrupted war against the Muslims, replied that the treaty was already canceled in their eyes. The Prophet held several meetings with his most senior companions. They decided that the time had come to march on Mecca. Preparations began to amass an army as large as the one that had laid siege to Medina three years before. After a few days of sober thought, the Meccans realized that they had miscalculated their strength against that of Medina's and Muslim power to their north. When the extent of the Prophet's resources dawned on them, they began to panic. Abu Sufyan went straight to Medina and begged for the treaty to be reinstated. The Prophet refused to see him or meet with him. Then Abu Sufyan went to Abu Bakr, 'Umar, 'Ali, Fatimah, and even his own daughter, Umm Habibah, and begged for their help. They all refused to talk to him. Abu Sufyan returned to Mecca bitter and frightened.

The Prophet called in all of the tribes that had converted and joined them with his contingent from Medina, creating an army of over ten thousand men and women. During the month of Ramadan in the year 630, he set out for Mecca and the greatest triumph of his life. He took great care to keep his army's departure as secret as possible. After two weeks' travel, the huge force entered the hills just outside of Mecca. There the Prophet ordered them to make camp. He asked each band of fighters to build several cooking fires to give the illusion of many more men than he had. The ruse worked; when evening fell and the Meccans looked upon the sea of campfires on the surrounding hillsides, they saw no hope of fighting such an army. Few fighters were left in the city, and nearly all the famous warriors of Arabia had already gone over to the Muslim side, even Muhammad's uncle, 'Abbas, and also Khalid ibn Walid, the famed Meccan horseman. Abu Sufyan had no choice but to go to the Muslim camp and see the Prophet. 'Abbas led the nervous Meccan into the camp after nightfall and the Prophet sent word that he should stay the night in the camp and see him in the morning. Before a large gathering the next day, Abu Sufyan declared that although he had always believed in the idols before, he saw now that they were of no use. He then announced his acceptance of Islam and agreed to surrender Mecca peacefully. 'Abbas privately asked the Prophet for a personal favor. "Abu Sufyan," he began, "doesn't like to lose face, so give him something he can be proud of." Muhammad thought for a moment and then announced to the gathering, "Whoever enters Abu Sufyan's house is safe, whoever is in his own house behind closed doors is safe and whoever enters the courtyard of the Ka'bah is safe." Abu Sufyan then returned to Mecca and informed the people that he was giving up the city and that there was no hope of opposing the huge Muslim forces. He told them about Muhammad's promise of safety and that everyone should go home.

Later that morning, the Prophet divided his army into three massive columns and instructed each to enter Mecca from a different direction. Ten thousand Muslims dressed in white victoriously entered the city from which Muhammad had been forced to flee for his life only eight years earlier. The transfer of power was peaceful save for one incident in which a party of vengeful Qurayshi youth, following 'Ikrimah, son of Abu Jahl, attacked a group of Muslim soldiers in an alley. Khalid ibn Walid's swift horsemen quickly subdued them.

The first thing the Prophet wanted to do was to clear the Ka'bah of idols. When he approached the sacred shrine, with all the Muslims and Meccans looking on, he gave thanks to God for the victory. The keeper of the key to the Ka'bah door, still an idolater, was brought forward. When asked for the key, he refused to give it. 'Ali snatched it away and brought it to the Prophet. The Prophet, however, ordered it returned to the keeper, who was so amazed that he declared himself a Muslim and gave the key to the Prophet himself. With jubilation and celebration, the Muslims set upon the idols posted all around the Ka'bah and threw them down. Cries of "God is great!" echoed through the square as Muhammad entered the Ka'bah and tossed out the first idol inside. As the work of cleansing Abraham's ancient shrine continued, Muhammad recited the following Qur'anic verse: "Declare: The Truth is now clear. Falsehood is broken as it should be." (Qur'an 17:81)

When that task was done, the Prophet addressed the crowd of Meccans who had come to watch:

> There is no god but God. No one shares in His power.
> He has fulfilled His promise. He helped His servant,
> Muhammad. O People of Quraysh! God has done away
> with the evils of ignorance. Blind loyalty to tribe is gone
> forever. All human beings are brothers to each other.
> They are the children of Adam, and Adam was made
> from dust. From now on, no one should take revenge.
> People must learn to live in peace.

Then he recited this verse from the Qur'an, "O Humanity! We have created you from a male and female and made you into nations and ethnic groups so you can come to know each other. The best among you is the one who has the most piety." (Qur'an 49:13)

Then he asked the assembled Meccans, "People of Mecca! What do you think I am going to do with you?" They answered, "Noble Brother, and son of a noble brother, only goodness." Then they held their breath to hear what their punishment would be. After all, these people had murdered, tortured, and persecuted Muhammad's religion and followers. It would be well within his rights to revenge himself upon them. The Prophet replied in words that are famous to this day for their clemency and nobility. "There is no blame on you this day. Go to your homes, for you are all free." Within days nearly the whole of the population of Mecca converted to Islam in response to Muhammad's magnanimity.

As the final act on the day Mecca was captured, the Prophet asked Bilal to climb to the top of the Ka'bah and give the call to prayer. No one before or since has had that honor. The Muslims performed their afternoon prayer filled with emotion. For the rest of the day, the immigrants reunited with their families, and the Muslims from the north performed religious devotions in and around the city. This day of victory would live on in the hearts and minds of Muslims. For Muhammad, it was the vindication of all that he had stood for.

Part Four

Tomorrow the World

Chapter 13

Arabia's Last Stand

*Do they feel secure against the plan of God? No one can
feel secure against the plan of God except those who are
about to be ruined.*

—Qur'an 7:99

For some of Muhammad's companions the victory in Mecca was
bittersweet. Certainly it was a great triumph for Islam that
Muhammad conquered Mecca without a battle. But the Prophet
neither took revenge nor allowed anyone else to do so. Abu Sufyan
and his wife Hind, who mutilated the Prophet's uncle at Uhud, and
all the other prominent Meccans freely moved about the city in
wonder that they were unharmed when any other conqueror might
have wrought vengeance upon his captured foes. The Quraysh were
subdued, and many converted to Islam during the two weeks that
followed Muhammad's triumphant entry into the city.

The helpers of Medina, however, had a different perspective.
Many of them were in Mecca for the first time and looked in awe
at the many religious sites in and around the city. There were the
sacred hills of Safa and Marwa, where centuries before Hagar ran
frantically back and forth to look for water for her son, Ishmael.
The well of Zamzam, an unfailing spring whose taste was unlike
any other fountain in Arabia, continued to bubble and provide the
Quraysh with liquid wealth in an otherwise parched land. The

land itself, with its rocky crags and sun-dappled valleys, was both inspiring and beautiful. At the center of the city stood the ancient shrine of Abraham, the Ka'bah, the center of God's veneration, now freshly cleansed of all traces of idolatry. Many of Muhammad's followers from Medina became worried that he might choose to stay in his hometown.

Many of the helpers from Medina began to discuss this matter amongst themselves. One of them said, "Mecca has the sacred shrine, the holy hills, the place of Abraham, and it is Muhammad's first home. Surely he is not going to leave all of this and return to Medina with us." They were fearful because of their great love for the Prophet, who had lived among them for almost ten years. He had become an indispensable part of their lives, and they had gone through numerous trials and tribulations for his sake, always surviving against all odds and emerging stronger than before. A good portion of the Qur'an's revelations were directly related to events that had transpired in their city. Muhammad was their Prophet and their neighbor. They could not imagine their lives without the Prophet among them.

Muhammad became aware of their concerns after several of them approached him privately. He addressed them one day after congregational prayers. "God forbid that I would leave you," he said. "I made a promise with you that my life and my death will be among you. I will remain true to my promise." He thus affirmed his loyalty to the people who, when he was most desperate, had given him refuge, sworn allegiance to him, and accepted him as one of their own. The helpers breathed easier and were more confident and eager to play their role in the reorganization of the city.

The Meccans watched as their city was transformed into a thriving Islamic metropolis peopled by men and women from every corner of Arabia. The surrounding hills were filled with the tents of Muhammad's army. The Prophet took up residence in his old house and held many meetings there or in the courtyard of the Ka'bah. The returning immigrants also rejoined their families and eagerly visited places they had not seen for many years. What must have seemed most unusual of all to the Quraysh, however, was their ancient shrine's new appearance. Gone were the statues and even the paintings inside which depicted Abraham, the angels, the gods of nature, and even Mary, the mother of Jesus. The latter Muhammad ordered to be respectfully plastered over and of the former he joked that Abraham was grossly misrepresented by the unknown artist's hands. Those images were washed off the walls.

An announcer was sent throughout the city in the first few days after the Muslim victory to declare, "Whoever believes in God and the Day of Judgment will destroy this very day every idol and remnant of idolatry in his home." Most of the Meccans soon realized that their religion had not saved their city and that their idols were quite powerless. The proof was overwhelming that Muhammad must have had the one true God on his side. In two decades, he had gone from persecuted religious rebel to the head of a state that now spanned a good portion of northern and central Arabia. His unprecedented magnanimity in pardoning the thousands of Qurayshi tribesmen impressed the Meccans even further. The conversions came in great numbers until nearly the entire population swore its allegiance to Muhammad.

An aerial view of Mecca and its surrounding countryside as it appears today.

A number of Meccans, however, were not covered in the general amnesty and were ordered arrested. Seventeen in all were given sentences of death for crimes committed before the fall of the city. When the names were announced, many of the condemned fled, and the rest went into hiding. Around this time Muhammad publicly declared amnesty for many of his worst enemies, so the families of the fugitives approached Muhammad hoping to win clemency for them as well. Thirteen had their sentences commuted, including Ikrimah, who had led the pointless attack in a back alley after the city had been formally surrendered to the Muslims. Only four people were eventually executed. One was a man who had previously assaulted Muhammad's daughter, Zaynab; two were people from Medina who had committed murder and sought refuge with the Quraysh; the last was a propagandist who had incited the idolaters to war with Muhammad.

Only one unfortunate incident of violence occurred in those first few days of occupation. A group of Bedouin tribesmen of the Banu Khuza'a killed an idolater from a rival tribe they found within the city. News of this unprovoked attack angered the Prophet so much that he gave an impromptu speech in the public square:

> All you people, God made Mecca a holy place on the day
> when the heavens and the earth were created. Mecca is
> holy, holy, holy until the end of time. No one who be-
> lieves in God and the Day of Judgment is allowed to shed
> any blood or destroy any tree in its city limits. Mecca has
> never been despoiled by anyone before me, and it will
> never be despoiled by anyone after me. Only for the brief
> hour of conquest, and because God's wrath was upon its
> people, did He permit me to enter it at the head of an
> armed force. Now Mecca is restored fully to its previous
> holiness. Whoever is here let him inform those who are
> absent. Whoever argues with you that the Prophet of God
> fought in Mecca, say to him that God temporarily sus-
> pended its sanctity for His Prophet but not for anyone
> else, and surely not for you, men of Khuza'a. All killing
> must stop, for it is an evil crime that brings no advantage
> when employed. You have killed a man, and now I have

to pay his blood money to his people. From this day for-
ward, the relatives of a murder victim will have the choice
between executing the murderer or receiving compensation
from him.

Muhammad now turned his attention to completing his campaign against idolatry in the immediate region, hoping to obliter-
ate any vestige of its practice. He sent organized groups to every
hamlet, encampment, and town to offer Islam to its people and
also, destroy any idols they encountered. They were given strict
orders not to fight or forcibly convert anyone they met. Many local
tribes and clans in the countryside converted peacefully.

Khalid ibn Walid commanded a contingent of men and successfully destroyed the large idol of 'Uzza, which was venerated by
the Banu Shayban tribe. He then proceeded to the camp of the
Banu Jadhimah and was surprised to find them ready for battle. He
ordered them to lay down their arms, but some tribesmen were
afraid to stand down, fearing Khalid's reputation as a merciless
man. Many in the tribe wanted to resolve the standoff peacefully,
however, because they had recently accepted Islam, and they succeeded in convincing the holdouts to surrender. Khalid decided
against mercy and ordered those who were belligerent to be bound;
he even executed a few of them. When word reached Medina,
Muhammad raised his arms and beseeched God loudly, "O God! I
condemn what Khalid ibn Walid has done." He sent 'Ali with a
large sum of money to the Banu Jadhimah and settled all blood
money claims and property losses.

Many enemies of Islam, as well as men who had a personal
hatred against Muhammad, still lived in Arabia. One of these was
Malik ibn 'Awf al-Nadri, the youthful leader of the Thaqif tribe of
Ta'if. His tribe had driven Muhammad away with rocks when he
desperately asked to be taken in, and the tribe considered the
Quraysh of Mecca their archrivals. Too young to have been
involved in those past actions and disputes, Malik ibn 'Awf nevertheless felt it his duty to uphold the position of his tribe. That
Muhammad, whom he now despised, should have the Quraysh on
his side was too much to take. Even worse, the fate of their great
idol also looked grim.

With the Prophet and the bulk of his followers concentrated in one location, Malik ibn 'Awf decided the time for decisive action was at hand. His plan was to organize a large army and take the Muslims unawares, crushing them completely as they continued to revel in their victory over Mecca. He counted on the Quraysh to rebel against their new masters in the confusion. After a few days of careful coalition building, he formed a grand alliance between his tribe and the local Nasr and Jusham tribes. He also swayed most of the great Hawazin tribe of the east, though two minor clans of that tribe who had accepted Islam demurred. Malik then sent to the clan leaders of each of the four tribes the unusual order that every warrior should bring his wives, children, and wealth along with him to the staging area in the valley of Awtas, a day's journey to the north of Ta'if. His feeling was that the presence of every-thing they valued would make the men fight harder and discourage them from any thought of retreating. After some discussion in which many expressed their reservations at such a tactic, the chiefs reluctantly agreed. The huge force of men, women, children, fully laden camels, herds of cows and sheep, and carts filled with the wealth of four tribes began its slow journey westward towards Mecca where they hoped to find good ground that would favor them in battle.

They eventually took up positions on some hills above a well-traveled canyon named Hunayn that had a narrow pass leading into it. The Muslims would have to make their way through it on their search for the enemy; news of Malik's hostile moves had surely reached Mecca, and it would only be a matter of days before the Muslims would come. The bold war chief placed his four thou-sand warriors under cover among the rocks near the top of the ridge. This great tactical advantage would enable his forces to avoid a headlong assault on massed infantry or cavalry. He com-manded his fighters not to emerge from their hidden posts until the signal was given; the element of surprise was essential to gain the upper hand. Malik hoped to force a Muslim withdrawal back to Medina, bringing to his tribe the honor of reversing the occupa-tion of Mecca and possibly killing Muhammad in the process.

Back in Mecca, the Prophet had indeed received the alarming news of the march of the new alliance against his people. He mustered the ten thousand who had accompanied him from Medina and added two thousand volunteers from the Quraysh. The Muslim army headed east towards Ta'if, confident that no enemy could withstand their great numbers. With dozens of tribes, each of whose clans marched under a bold banner, the Muslims were celebrating their victory even before it had arrived. One man was heard saying, "Our numerical strength has made us unbeatable." Little did they realize that numbers would be inconsequential.

The Muslims arrived at the entrance to the pass of Hunayn without meeting any resistance. As evening was fast approaching, the decision was made to set up camp before resuming the march in the morning. Sentries were posted, and the soldiers slept easily. Long before sunrise the next day, the Muslims, clad in their white robes and turbans, broke camp and reformed their columns. They were soon ready to enter the pass. Khalid ibn Walid was at the head of the vanguard, and the Prophet was riding a white mule near the rear. The soldiers entered the trail at the bottom of the narrow canyon and thus were strung out in a long line. While darkness still enshrouded the valley, Malik ibn 'Awf ordered his men to attack.

A rain of arrows fell upon the Muslim ranks from all directions. Hundreds fell dead or wounded. Immediately after the initial volley, the darkly clad attackers arose from their hiding places and charged down the sides of the canyon wall shouting war cries and cutting down all whom they came upon. The fearsome sight of Malik ibn 'Awf riding a red war camel and lofting a black banner on a deadly accurate lance provoked sheer terror in the Muslims, who immediately broke ranks and ran in a rabble back out of the canyon. Abu Sufyan, who witnessed the onslaught and retreat from farther back, commented to some of his friends, "The Muslims won't be fully defeated until they are drowned in the sea." Another Meccan, whose father had been killed at Uhud, said, "This is my day of revenge against Muhammad." Clearly, many of the Quraysh were secretly elated by Muhammad's rout.

The Prophet, however, stood his ground and refused to run away as the enemy rushed towards him and the few men who stood resolutely beside him. He called out to the fighters fleeing all around him, "Where are you going? Where are you going?" He was about to lead a charge, trusting in God's will though he was nearly alone, when Abu Sufyan came and for inexplicable reasons held the reins of Muhammad's mule and would not let him move forward. Perhaps Abu Sufyan recalled the words of one of his fellows who said, "By God, it is better to be ruled by a man from the Quraysh than a man of the Hawazin."

The Prophet's uncle, 'Abbas, who had a loud voice, shouted to the panic-stricken Muslims, "Men of the helpers! Men who opened their homes to aid Muhammad! Men of the immigrants! Men who pledged their allegiance under the tree! Muhammad is alive! Charge forward with him!" The sound of his powerful voice echoed off the upper reaches of the sheer canyon walls, and a stunning reversal occurred. Many heard the call and came to their senses. Ashamed at their cowardice, they began to swell back into the valley toward the Prophet and the few dozen men who had remained with him. Six hundred fighters rushed to where the Prophet was mounting a desperate defense. They joined in the battle fiercely as their numbers swelled behind them.

The entire force of the Hawazin and Thaqif were out of their hiding places and engaging the Muslims all over the valley, and the battle raged loudly in the crisp morning light. The returning Muslims cried out, "At your service, God! At your service!" The Muslim clans and units that had already fled reorganized themselves and marched forward shoulder to shoulder. The Prophet saw his men pouring in behind him and cried out, "Now the battle has begun! God will not fail the Prophet and will fulfill the promise He gave him." He asked 'Abbas to scoop up a handful of stones. The Prophet took them and flung them in the faces of the enemy soldiers in front of him and declared, "Ruin to the enemies of God!" Men fell on all sides as the Muslims surged forward. The shouts of "God is great" began to erode the confidence of the Thaqif and their allies, and soon they started to fall back.

Before noon the leaders of the alliance realized that their cause was hopeless. Many of their warriors were killed, wounded, or captured, and they were in danger of total annihilation. They ordered a general retreat, and the remnants of their fighters fled from the rear of the canyon to their camps in the valley of Awtas. They attempted one more stand, but they were so pressured by the superior numbers of Muslims that they fled again in terror, leaving their stunned wives and children behind. The advancing Muslim columns took custody of these civilians as well as all their herds and wealth. The prisoners and baggage were taken under guard to a nearby valley while the pursuit of the fleeing enemy continued. The Muslim soldiers continued hot on the heels of the fleeing tribesmen who eventually made it back to their fortress city of Ta'if. There they barricaded the gates and prepared for their last stand. The Muslims hurriedly made camp nearby and began the long siege of the city. They also destroyed a small isolated fort that belonged to Malik ibn 'Awf, though it had no defenders.

The Day of Hunayn, as the battle came to be known, was very costly for the Muslims. Many had died. Two tribes lost so many members that they were practically extinct. The Prophet led a mass funeral prayer for them and begged God to enter them all into Paradise. Their sorrow was mitigated by the fact that their victory permanently vanquished any remaining threat to Muslim supremacy in all of the Hijaz. The last of their enemies lay hidden behind the fortress in front of them, with no hope of escape.

The Muslim camp had to be moved further from the city due to the constant arrows from Ta'if. They built a makeshift mosque in their camp and erected two red tents for the Prophet. Later that day he held a war council to discuss their next move. An all-out assault would be too costly; the walls and towers were very high and manned by determined defenders. Given that the Muslims were in possession of the enemy's families and wealth, the besieged might fight with fierce desperation. It would be a bitter fight, and too many Muslims had been lost already. As the Muslims debated their options, some new verses of the Qur'an (Qur'an 9:25–27) encouraged them and also explained the reasons for their initial setback:

> Assuredly God has helped you on many battlefields and
> also on the Day of Hunayn. Your great numbers elated
> you at first, but they availed you naught for the tide

*overwhelmed you and you ran away in the face of the
enemy. But God poured His calm on the Messenger and
on the believers and sent down forces which you couldn't
see. He punished the unbelievers and that is a recompense
they deserve. God still accepts repentance, however, from
whomsoever He pleases for He is the Forgiving, the
Source of All Mercy.*

Tufayl, one of the Muslim soldiers, happened to be from a tribe
in southern Arabia with experience in siege warfare. He quickly
suggested that the walls might be breached. The Prophet asked
him to bring experts from his tribe with their war machinery to
help end the siege. Four days later, men of the Banu Daws arrived
with catapults and wooden canopies that could be moved by men
hiding inside, much like a crude tank, protecting the soldiers from
the arrows that the Thaqif were raining down. After several days,
however, the Muslims were still unable to penetrate the massive
fortress. The crafty Thaqif threw hot pieces of iron down upon the
tanks, causing them to burn. Those who escaped the flames had to
dodge arrows all the way back to safety. The catapults were also
ineffective against the city's thick walls.

The Prophet, realizing that the wealth of Ta'if was in its cultivation, ordered his men to destroy the orchards and vineyards
within view of the city. When the defenders saw their fertile fields
in danger of being decimated, their remaining clan chiefs sent a
message to the Prophet begging that their orchards be spared. They
would rather have someone else own them than see their labor
obliterated. At about the same time, the Prophet learned from some
Thaqif members who had joined the Muslim side that the city was
well prepared for a siege and could hold out for a long time. Because
the holy months of pilgrimage were arriving, the Prophet lifted the
siege and began the long march of his victorious army back to
Mecca. He vowed to resume the siege the following year.

Along the way, the Muslims stopped back at the valley where the
wealth and prisoners of the defeated alliance were held. The division of the booty began, and the Prophet took his customary one
fifth with which to support the objectives of the Islamic state. The
rest of the captives and goods were doled out to his companions.

A delegation from the Muslim clans of the Hawazin, who had not joined their brethren in the alliance, arrived and begged the Prophet to release their captured tribesmen and their families. Their arguments were compelling because Muhammad was distantly related to some branches of their people and had been raised by a wet nurse, Halimah, who was of the Banu Sa'd, a Hawazin subclan. Muhammad listened to their appeal, and their chief spokesmen, Zuhayr, pressed his case further. "Messenger of God, those held captive by your army are your relatives. Among them are your aunts and your nurse-mothers who held you in their arms as a baby …. You are supremely merciful and don't need to be reminded of your obligations." He then recited a poem that said, "Have pity on us, Messenger of God, in kindness for you are the man we beg and beseech. Have pity on a tribe ruined by fate, divided and whose fortune is adversely changed so that we now cry out in sorrow; a people in whose hearts there is gloom and tragedy …."

Muhammad was moved, and a chance encounter sealed his decision. He saw an old woman among the captives who had been treated roughly by the soldiers. She swore at them loudly, "You're ruined! Know that I am the sister of your leader by virtue of having had the same wet nurse as he!" When she was brought before the Prophet, he immediately recognized her as his foster sister, Shayma, the daughter of Halimah. He had grown up with her among the Banu Sa'd and still cherished fond memories of all she had taught him about life in the desert. He quickly spread his cloak on the ground for her to sit on and told her she could go where she wished. She desired to return home, and the Prophet sent her with gifts and a mount.

Turning to the leaders of the Muslim Hawazin clans, the Prophet asked, "Which is dearer to you, your women and children or your wealth?" They called out loudly that their families were the most important to them. Muhammad announced that he was freeing every captive in his share and the share of his own clan. He told them to appeal for the freedom of their people to the rest of the men in the army after the noon prayer, and he would announce publicly what he had promised them privately. The gathered soldiers all agreed to let their captives go free. Six thousand captives walked away, and Muhammad gave them nearly half a million dirhams' worth of goods as well. The entire Hawazin tribe converted to Islam in gratitude. To his own men the Prophet promised a six-fold reward in any future campaign to compensate them for their generosity that day.

As for Malik ibn 'Awf, Muhammad learned that he was holed up in Ta'if with the rest of his disillusioned men. Muhammad sent a message promising him that if he surrendered and converted to Islam, his family and property would be returned to him, and he would get a gift of one hundred camels. Without hesitation, the fugitive rode out of Ta'if under the cover of darkness and entered the Muslim camp to speak with Muhammad. He swore allegiance to Islam, took his family and gifts, and went home to rebuild his wrecked fort. Thus Ta'if lost its leader and ceased to be an immediate threat to the Muslims.

Before the army moved on from the valley, some of the men began to grumble at Muhammad's seemingly endless generosity. He was giving freedom to their captives, bestowing gifts on their enemies, and even awarding the choicest booty to members of the Quraysh who had only recently converted and until a few weeks ago had been the bitterest enemies of Islam. Several men began picking through the piles of goods, thinking that they had better get their fair share while there was still something left. Suddenly hundreds rushed at the bales and bags, not wanting to be left out. Even the Prophet's cloak, still lying on the ground, was taken. Muhammad angrily ordered the goods returned for proper distribution and promised a fair and equitable grant to all.

The next day some of the Muslims from Medina began to whisper among themselves that it looked as though the men of the Quraysh were receiving the lion's share of the booty while they received little. Muhammad passionately reminded them that he had united them when they were weak, preferred them when they had no guidance, and loved them more than any other people:

> *Helpers, are you angry because I have given away some goods to those whom I want to reconcile to Islam? I felt their faith would be strengthened by material possessions while I felt yours was built upon solid conviction that would never swerve. Aren't you satisfied, helpers, that*

> those people will return from this campaign with camels
> and goats whereas you will return with the Messenger of
> God? By the One who controls my soul, except for the
> fact of my birth, there is no people that I love associating
> with more than that of the helpers. If all of humanity went
> in one direction and the helpers went in another, I would
> choose the way of the helpers.

The helpers felt ashamed and answered, "We are pleased and
content to have the Messenger of God as our share and our destiny."

With that crisis quelled, Muhammad led his troops back to
Mecca accompanied by thousands of his companions. A short
time later, he appointed a governor for the city as well as a chief
religious instructor to educate the Quraysh in the ways of Islam
and the Qur'an. With the central Hijaz completely under his control, Muhammad set out for Medina at the head of a long line of
helpers and tribesmen from the north. He was both jubilant and
expectant—his Egyptian wife, Maria, was due to give birth to a
baby. She was the only one of his wives after Khadijah who ever
became pregnant, and the prospect of a new child brought a visi-
ble light to Muhammad's face. Maria gave birth to a boy a short
time later, and his name was Ibrahim, the Arabic form of the
name Abraham. Muhammad was completely devoted to Ibrahim,
spending most of his free time holding and playing with the baby.

Muhammad's personal and family life were not always smooth. His
wives sometimes bickered amongst themselves and even once engaged in
a petty plot against him. A'ishah, for example, disliked her Jewish co-
wife, Safiyah, and insulted her periodically. Muhammad had to defend
her status and honor a number of times and scold the youthful A'ishah.
Hafsah became jealous of her co-wife, Maria, when she found her and
Muhammad resting in her apartment one day. Sawdah gave up her allotted day with the Prophet when she realized that he was not really attracted
to her. As for the conspiracy, A'ishah agreed with two other co-wives
to convince the Prophet that eating honey made him unpleasant to be
around. When Muhammad vowed to never eat honey again, she privately repented to her co-conspirators. Though these incidents were not
the norm, they demonstrate that the women in Muhammad's life were as
human as the rest of us.

This joyful turn of events consoled him as his eldest living daughter, Zaynab, succumbed to an illness from which she had suffered since fleeing Mecca many years before. The Quraysh didn't want to let a member of Muhammad's own family slip away so brazenly, and thus assaulted her. When she had set out for the long journey northwards, an idolater had attacked her and struck her in the stomach, knowing she was pregnant. She suffered a miscarriage after arriving in Medina and never fully recovered. (The man who hit her who was one of the four executed when Muhammad took Mecca.) His daughter's death saddened the Prophet greatly, and he led her funeral prayer in sorrow. Fatimah was his only surviving child from his first wife.

Muhammad taught that he was the last prophet sent by God to the world. His message, as enshrined in the Qur'an, would remain unaltered until the end of time and would be sufficient for every challenge that humanity would face. Between his time and the time of Jesus, Muhammad explained, there had been no prophets, and after him there would be no more authentic messengers from God. The Qur'an went so far as to label him the Seal of Prophethood.

This clear pronouncement did not deter others from seeing an opportunity to exploit the religious currents sweeping over Arabia. After the conquest of Mecca, three men claimed revelation from God and his commission as prophets. One of these men was Tulayhah, a leader of the Banu Asad tribe. He had found a well in the deep desert while traveling with his people and had thus saved them from death. He became convinced he had supernatural abilities and told his people that his premonition about the oasis was proof of his prophethood. Some in his tribe rallied to him and only reluctantly signed treaties with Medina. He was too afraid to publicly rebel while Muhammad was alive, however. Khalid ibn Walid was sent with a force to put down this rebellion, and thereafter the vanquished Tulayhah lived the rest of his life as an orthodox Muslim.

Another false prophet was a man named Musaylimah ibn Habib of the tribe of Banu Hanifah. When a delegation from his tribe entered Medina to declare their allegiance to the Prophet,

Musaylimah was left to watch their horses. When Muhammad learned that one man remained behind, he ordered that he be given gifts as his fellows had in the audience chamber. Musaylimah became puffed up with pride. Upon returning to his people, he began to compose poetry and claimed it was revelations from God. Though few listened to him in his tribe, he did succeed in attracting a few followers. Eventually he sent a letter to Muhammad saying, "I, too, am a prophet like you. To us belongs half the world, and to the Quraysh belongs the other half, if only the Quraysh would be fair about it." His thinly veiled call to partition Arabia demanded a curt reply; Muhammad replied with a note that said, "The world belongs to no one but God, and God grants it to whomsoever He wills among His worthy and righteous servants. Peace belongs to the rightly guided." A new verse of the Qur'an was received as well, saying, "Who can be more wicked than one who invents a lie against God, or who says, 'I have received revelation' when he hasn't received any at all?" (Qur'an 6:93)

Musaylimah, who became known as "the liar," was later able to form a coalition of several southern tribes and succeeded in making the Prophet's reach in the south shaky. He allowed his followers to drink wine, abolished daily prayer, and made adultery legal. He also continued to stir up enmity against the Muslims and promised to bring war to the lands of Islam when they least expected it. He was eventually killed in a desperate battle against the outnumbered forces of the first Muslim Caliph, Abu Bakr, though not before inflicting grievous casualties on the military prowess of the fledgling Islamic state.

A third and more dangerous challenge came in the form of a deranged man named al-Aswad al-Ansi. At first a loyal governor in Yemen who succeeded the man the Prophet originally appointed, he began to practice bizarre rituals and claim that he was in contact with God. Many people flocked to his banner because Islam had very thin roots in that distant corner of Arabia, and he finally declared himself independent of Medina's authority. He mustered a large army and invaded Najran directly to his north and just south of Mecca. He killed the Muslim governor there, and to further legitimize his position he forced the governor's widow to marry him.

Soon his raiding parties were attacking Muslim tribes all over southern Arabia and moving steadily northward. Muhammad knew that this villain's treachery could divide the peninsula, weaken Islam, and give a green light to others to claim prophethood as well. Unable to march an army so far south himself, Muhammad sent a secret message to faithful followers in Yemen, directing them to stop al-Ansi by any means necessary. A Muslim named Fayruz al-Daylami succeeded in convincing al-Ansi's top general to join Muhammad's side because al-Ansi's erratic behavior frightened even the general. A third conspirator was al-Ansi's unwilling bride, who desired to avenge her husband's murder. The trio crept into the main fortress in the city of Sana after dark, surprised al-Ansi, and killed him. The next morning Fayruz climbed to the highest wall of the fort and gave the Islamic call to prayer, adding an extra line that went, "I declare that al-Aswad al-Ansi is a liar!" That was the signal for the rest of the Muslims, waiting in the alleys, to attack the castle and dispatch al-Ansi's remaining men.

A few others sought to rival Muhammad and declared themselves his temporal or religious equals, but none got as far as these three. With their demise, all challenge to the supremacy of Muhammad as the legitimate spokesman of God in the land was ended. It was vitally important for Arabia to finally unite under a single leadership structure, for with the last conversions of rulers in the far corners of the peninsula, new challenges from longstanding and powerful empires to the north tested the mettle and strength of Muhammad's followers on a scale never imagined before. The Byzantines and the Persians were the next to attack the Muslims, and Muhammad's followers faced desperate odds in these battles for their very survival.

Chapter 14

Looking Northward

*People of Faith, fight the unbelievers who surround you
and show them your resolve. Know that Allah is with
those who fear Him.*

—Qur'an 9:123

Through a skillful blend of diplomacy and tactical prowess,
Muhammad had been able to establish his nation of believers
on a solid footing. With the Quraysh subdued in the south, and
central and western Arabs rapidly coming within his sphere of
influence, he was now able to turn his attention to the lands
beyond Arabia: Palestine, Syria, Persia, and beyond. Beginning in
the year 629, Muhammad sent letters to the rulers of the surrounding areas, hoping to gain permission from various rulers for
his missionaries to begin preaching in their lands. The Qur'an
plainly called for its message to be conveyed to the rest of the
world so that peoples other than Arabs would have the chance to
accept the teachings of God's last prophet. Those who refused to
accept Islam would be allowed to follow their conscience and live
freely within Muslim society, though the Qur'an announced that
eternal torment in an afterlife would await them.

There is no evidence that the Prophet intended to fight per se
against the great Byzantine or Persian empires, nor did he call his
followers to do so unless hostile moves were made against them

first. Both massive empires did indeed make attempts against Muhammad's Medina, which set the tone of future relations. Having worked for a decade to enjoy a measure of safety, Muhammad wasn't going to wait for these new enemies to come to him; he would go to them first no matter how desperate the odds were against such an enterprise.

The Byzantine Roman Empire, which lay to the northwest of Medina, was heir to the glory of Rome. Situated astride a swath of territory that stretched from southern France to Syria, the Byzantines commanded nearly two thirds of the territory that had been held by Julius Caesar during the height of his reign seven centuries earlier. The empire's magnificent capital city of Constantinople, on the western tip of the Anatolian Peninsula, rivaled the splendor of its forbear in Italy. The head of the empire was also the protector of the traditional Catholic Church, and the Byzantines held fast to the creed formulated in Nicea. Byzantine policy toward Christians with different dogmas, such as the Syrian churches and Christian Copts of Egypt, was brutal and merciless; many a Christian died at the hands of fellow Christians. As a result, the territories where nontraditional Christian groups lived did not fully support the Byzantines.

The highly civilized Byzantine Empire's greatest rival was the dynamic Persian Empire, whose forces controlled an equally large domain from the borders of India in the east through central Asia and into Mesopotamia. Its people were either followers of an ancient seer named Zoroaster who envisioned dual gods of light and darkness, or they were animists and pagans. The government followed the path of the enigmatic Zoroaster, however, and thus, wherever the Persians settled, they established fire temples in which the flame representing the light god was never allowed to go out.

The behemoth empires most often battled over Syria and its environs, much to the detriment of the people who dwelled there. The lands changed hands every few years, and most towns and cities bore the scars of war. The population lived in constant fear of marauding armies and the inevitable looting that would take place. To support their soldiers, whichever empire held sway would also impose high taxes on the population. Decades of intermittent warfare exhausted the people and sapped their morale. The Muslim state eventually capitalized on this situation.

When Muhammad was still a persecuted, threatened man living in Mecca, the Persians delivered a crushing blow to the Byzantines, driving them almost completely out of the Middle East. The Quraysh, whose affinity for the idolatrous Persians contrasted with the Muslims' identification with the Christian Byzantines, taunted the followers of Muhammad that Persia's victory was a sign that monotheism was doomed. An early verse of the Qur'an predicted that the Romans would counterattack within nine years. By the time Muhammad was consolidating his position in Medina, Heraclius, the Byzantine emperor, was on his way to join celebrations marking his army's recapture of Jerusalem, and Muhammad's envoy brought him the invitation to join Islam.

Heraclius was at first well disposed towards Islam (as described in Chapter 12, "Going Home: Conquest of Mecca"), or at least neutral about it, but he soon changed. When Muhammad's letter was first read to Heraclius, his hesitation and musings on Muhammad's legitimacy outraged his nobles and officers. He was, after all, the titular upholder of Christianity! His people threatened mutiny if he entertained the idea of accepting or even accomodating Muhammad's religion. Fearful of losing his crown and loathing the potential for a new rival in the region, Heraclius gradually hardened towards the Muslim state and even stationed troops in southern Syria to prevent Muslim expansion. Heraclius had just wrested Palestine and Syria from the Persians; he didn't want to lose those choice territories to the Arabs.

As the Byzantines became more hostile, their tribal allies in southern Syria also began to act more boldly against the Muslims. Tribesmen ambushed one of Muhammad's delegations and killed every man among them save one. The powerful Ghassan tribe killed another courier on his way to the city of Bostra with a new letter for Heraclius. The king of the Ghassanids sent a message to the Byzantine emperor asking permission to invade Arabia, but Heraclius commanded him to attend his victory ceremonies in Jerusalem instead. Meanwhile Muhammad decided that these affronts could not go unpunished. A year before the fall of Mecca, he raised an army of three thousand men to march northward with all speed to confront the tribes that had murdered his envoys.

Zayd ibn Harith was placed in command of the force, and the Prophet handed him a white banner to use as the standard for his army. The enemies would greatly outnumber the Muslims, so Muhammad outlined an order of succession should Zayd fall. If the two successors he named, Ja'far and 'Abdullah, were killed, then the remaining soldiers could choose their own leader. On camel and horseback, the long column of soldiers left the city. The Prophet and others watched from a nearby hill. This attack would be the Muslims' first war outside of Arabia and certainly one of the most dangerous. Muhammad's parting words outlined the rules of war according to Islam: The soldiers were not to kill women, children, the elderly, or civilians, nor were they to cut any green trees or disturb religious buildings of any type.

> Islam has no official flags, though the Prophet did seem to prefer white or black banners. White symbolized God's purity while black stood for God's vengeance and justice. The crescent and star, a symbol often associated with Islam and Muslims, actually was a Byzantine imperial symbol that the Turks adopted after conquering parts of Anatolia in the fourteenth century. Due to the Ottoman Turks' long ascendancy through the early twentieth century, many Muslim countries also took that symbol for their emblems. Today many purist movements shun the crescent and star in favor of green flags with the shahadah, or testimony of faith, written on it. The Prophet was reported to have liked the colors green, white, and red.

When the Muslim army finally arrived at the borders of Syria, reports from forward scouts informed Zayd that a huge coalition of local tribes was forming to meet them. In addition, there were indications that Byzantine imperial troops were in the vicinity. In all, the Muslims could be facing odds upwards of twenty to one. The senior officers of the Muslim army held a council of war to discuss their options. Some believed that their situation was hopeless and that they should immediately send a message to Medina asking to be either recalled or reinforced. Others, filled with bottomless zeal and the desire to win martyrdom, protested that they should go forward as the Prophet commanded. One man stated flatly, "In front of us is one of two outcomes, either victory or martyrdom that would send us to join our brethren in the garden of Paradise. Let us go to the attack then!" Another added, "We don't fight by weapons or numbers alone but by the great religion that God has given us." After further debate, the decision was made to move deeper into Byzantine territory.

The Muslims continued into the district of Mu'tah near the southern end of the Dead Sea. They expected to find the tribal camps of their enemies and take them by surprise, a tactic that had worked in the Muslims' favor so many times before. As they crested one of the many dry hills, however, they saw the entire imperial army on a high plateau ahead of them, joined by all of its tribal allies. The sprawling force was larger than the Muslims could have imagined. Worse still, the Byzantines had been warned of the Muslims' arrival, and their armored legions were fully drawn up for battle: crack troops wearing expensive shields, sparkling metal helmets, and breastplates and reinforced with a well-equipped cavalry. Zayd's men had never seen such military might before. All of their previous experience had been against Arabian tribesmen, whose lack of discipline and equipment were legendary. Three thousand against nearly one hundred thousand was stiff odds indeed, even suicidal. Zayd considered this great disparity between forces, as well as the fact that the enemy held the high ground. A full charge uphill into a prepared foe would be out of the question, no matter how much some within his ranks desired to die in God's cause. Zayd decided to withdraw to ground of his own choosing.

Stopping on a high slope near a village called Masharif, Zayd positioned his men in a defensive formation and waited for the arrival of the massive enemy force. It was close behind; clouds of dust rose from the hills before them. When the first of the endless columns of soldiers came into view, Zayd ordered a general charge before the enemy could bring its full force to bear. The Muslim warriors raced forward on their camels and horses, clad in white robes and crying, "God is great!" It is said that Muhammad was given a vision of the battle as it unfolded and that he narrated what he saw to his gathered companions in the mosque. He described the mad rush of the Muslims as they plunged at the

Byzantines' lead regiment, fighting so fiercely that the enemy was forced to halt. Zayd, he said sadly, fell immediately under the swords of multiple attackers, and Ja'far and 'Abdullah were killed soon after. Finally, the "Sword of God," as Khalid ibn Walid was known, was given the white banner. Khalid had enough presence of mind to take advantage of a pause in the enemy advance to order a hasty rearguard action. He kept his men together as they retreated further and further back into the hinterland until night fell and the two armies disengaged.

That night Khalid made a series of strategic decisions in hopes of throwing the enemy off-guard. He ordered his flanking regiments to change positions with each other, and then he sent a long line of men behind some hills with orders to make such a noise and display that it would seem as if a great number of reinforcements were coming to aid the Muslims. The next morning, the Byzantine Romans began moving toward the Muslim lines. The soldiers on either wing of the imperial army saw new banners and faces before them and thought for sure that fresh troops had arrived. Behind the hills in the distance the Byzantines also heard loud marching drums and saw the tips of hundreds of banners held high on spears coming towards them. Surely each banner represented thousands of warriors. What they didn't know then was that the banners were held by a single column of men walking in a loop and lowering their banners and running to the rear to loft them again. The Byzantines, who hadn't been able to defeat a puny force of three thousand the day before, began to fear what a larger force of Muslims would do to them. Their commanders ordered a hasty retreat, and the imperial army withdrew. Khalid then ordered a retreat, and the Muslims began their long ride back to Medina.

Meanwhile, Muhammad visited and consoled the families of each of the leaders who had fallen in the first day's battle. He went first to his uncle Ja'far's home, where his wife, Asma' had just finished preparing a meal. He asked her to bring out her children, and placing them on his knee, he began to weep. Asma' asked, "Messenger of Allah, has anything happened to Ja'far and the others?" Muhammad replied, "Yes, he was killed today." Asma' collapsed in sorrow, and Muhammad asked his companions to look after and cook for the family. On his way to Zayd's house, he was met by the man's little daughter, and he scooped her up in his arms and hugged her, tears streaming down his face. After telling her mother the sad news, he returned to the mosque to inform the congregation that the army was riding back to rejoin them.

When the army finally arrived home, Muhammad rode out to greet the advancing column with the eldest son of Ja'far. Others, too, had come out to meet the returnees, but many began throwing dust at the soldiers, accusing them of fleeing from battle. Perhaps they were surprised at the light casualties and assumed the men failed to exert themselves with vigor and bravery. "Did you run away from fighting in God's cause?" they cried. Muhammad called out loudly to the spectators, "No! They are not cowards, but people who have returned again to fight once more, if God wills."

Muhammad soon had to dispatch another force, this time of five hundred men, to deter two isolated southern Syrian tribes from going on the offensive. After a forced march of ten days, the Muslims entered the tribes' territory and so surprised them that they fled with only a brief exchange of arrows. The Muslim commander signed peace treaties with several friendly tribes in the area and returned home with the promise that the Syrian border would be quiet, at least for a time. Soon thereafter, the Muslims made their triumphant entry into Mecca after the dissolution of the Treaty of Hudaybiyah.

For a few months after the Day of Hunayn (when the Muslims defeated the Arab alliance led by Malik ibn 'Awf), things began looking extremely bright for Muhammad and his followers. No Arab tribe could threaten them, and Mecca had been reclaimed as the eternal legacy of Abraham's unswerving faith in the one true God. Muslim missionaries were sent far and wide, and the many tribes that had converted were sending regular alms to support the Islamic state. Muhammad had personal reasons to celebrate as well. He was delighted with his new son, Ibrahim, and had a new lightness in his step and strength in his voice despite his advanced years. Even his well-groomed beard remained black with not a single gray hair. His two beautiful grandsons, the children of 'Ali and Fatimah, also filled his days with laughter and exuberance. The pair of toddlers, known as Hassan and Husayn, would climb all over their grandfather's back while he was in prayer, and he would patiently pause to ensure that they didn't get hurt.

But happiness, the Qur'an taught, was not for this world, but for the hereafter. Ibrahim, who had been growing stronger each day, continued to bring delight to Muhammad's life; that is until one day when Maria informed her husband that their child had suddenly fallen ill. Muhammad rushed to be at Ibrahim's side, but along the way he felt weak in the knees and could hardly stand, so great was the shock to him. A companion named 'Abdul Rahman ibn 'Awf had to help him walk to where Ibrahim lay. Muhammad cradled the babe in his lap, watching helplessly as he slowly slipped away. As the little boy's movements ebbed, Muhammad cried profusely and said, "Ibrahim, against the judgment of God, we can do nothing." When the babe breathed his last, the Prophet closed his eyes and whispered, "The eyes rain tears, the heart is somber, but we can only say what pleases the Lord. Ibrahim, I mourn for you and to God we belong and to Him we return."

The Prophet led the funeral procession, and when his son was buried, he smoothed over the gravesite with his own hands. Suddenly, an eclipse of the sun occurred, blotting out all light for a few moments. Some exclaimed that it was a sign of the grief of heaven itself for the death of the baby. Muhammad, ever cognizant of the dangers of superstition, spoke loudly, "The sun and the moon are two of God's signs," he said. "They don't eclipse for the birth or death of anyone. When you see that sign, hasten to remember God through prayer."

In the middle of September in the year 630, the Prophet received unsettling news that a large force of Byzantine soldiers had gathered again in Syria. The Roman emperor, Heraclius, was thinking seriously of invading Arabia and occupying Medina. In addition, he was giving arms and money to his vassal tribes in southern Syria to raid isolated Muslim settlements. Muhammad reasoned that swift action was needed to stave off further attacks. He couldn't afford to send someone in his stead this time; the stakes were too high. Although a severe drought was affecting the region, the Prophet, at over sixty years of age, announced he was going on campaign. The call to arms was raised, and every Bedouin tribe was asked to contribute as many warriors as they could spare.

The funds required to equip the army properly were more than the treasury could provide, and the true generosity of the Muslims became evident. Uthman donated one thousand gold coins and three hundred camels. 'Umar donated half of everything he owned. Abu Bakr donated all his worldly wealth except the clothes he had on his back, stating that God and His Messenger were all he needed. Muslim women came forward to donate money and jewelry. In one instance, Bilal walked by a line of them with a large sack, and they threw in all the bangles they were wearing. Many poor people despaired that they were unable to share in the reward of giving God a "beautiful loan that He would repay many times over." The Prophet informed them that the amount was unimportant; the intention behind the donations was what mattered to God. One poor man eagerly worked all night watering someone's garden so that he could donate his salary of a handful of dates to the war effort. The Prophet was so pleased with that gift that he ordered the dates to be placed on top of the pile of donated money and goods in the treasury.

As all this goodwill was being displayed, a few hypocrites made excuses about why they should stay behind. They were greatly dismayed at the prospect of facing the heir to Caesar and his minions, and tried everything to convince their friends and relatives not to go. They even designated a meeting place in one man's house to plan their strategy to try to prevent the expedition. A Qur'anic verse (Qur'an 9:81–82) was revealed in response:

> They advise against venturing out in the desert heat. Tell
> them, "The fire of hell is hotter, if they only knew." They
> laugh now, but their pleasure is short lived. They shall cry
> much more, and they will deserve every bit of it.

When the Muslim army finally left for Syria and set out for the burning rocks and waterless desert, the force numbered an unprecedented thirty thousand men mounted on either camel or horseback. A contingent of women also accompanied the army to act as doctors and support. The grand sight of so many people bravely marching off in the heat of late summer to fight a superior foe hundreds of miles away swayed some of the hypocrites into reconsidering their position. One man, who had gone back to his house to find his lunch prepared for him, had a quick change of heart saying, "The Messenger of God is in the noonday heat buffeted by hot winds, and I am in the cool shade with food, drink, and two comely women. Never! Gather supplies for me so I can catch up with the Messenger of God!"

After many days of hard travel, the Muslims made camp at a place called al-Hijr, which was near the ruins of the famed Thamud people, mentioned in the Qur'an as an ancient nation that God destroyed for its wickedness. Muhammad forbade them to drink from the wells nearby, explaining that they had been made foul when God chastised the errant tribe that held those lands. Water, therefore, was scarce, and the desert winds were fierce. The Prophet ordered that no one should go out alone into the countryside, but two men disobeyed. One of them disappeared, and the other was found dead, buried in the sand. One night, while the Muslims were encamped a little farther north, a violent sandstorm descended and filled the only available well with debris. In the morning some soldiers began to panic because the nearest water sources were now miles away, but a passing rain cloud came a few hours later and filled some dry pools with water for the army. Many proclaimed it a miracle.

The Muslim army finally entered Syria and took up positions near a small town called Tabuk. There the Prophet was reported to have performed another miracle by coaxing a torrent of water from a formerly dry well. The Byzantines were aware of the Muslim advance and decided to withdraw rather than engage their enemy in battle. Apparently they didn't want to face thirty thousand Muslims when only three thousand had given them so much trouble at Mu'tah. There would be no battle after all.

The Prophet took this opportunity to make alliances with the tribal leaders of the area. One after another, the local governors and chieftains came to the Prophet's camp and declared their submission to the government of Medina. Those tribes that chose not to convert to Islam, such as one Jewish clan that lived near the

Gulf of Aqaba, were given the option to pay a defense tax known as the *jizya*, which entitled them to the protection of the Islamic state but exempted them from conscription.

One such formal agreement between Muhammad and a prominent Christian bishop read as follows:

> *In the Name of God, the Merciful and the Compassionate. This is a secure pact from God and Muhammad, the Messenger of God, to Yuhanna the son of Ruba and the people of Iliya. Their ships and transport vessels whether on sea or land are under the protection of God and Muhammad, as are those who travel with them of Syria or Yemen or of lands over the seas. Any of them who suffers loss due to aggression shall not try to regain their property from the usurpers, but will go to Muhammad who will get it back for them. They shall not be prevented from enjoying any oasis they wish to visit nor road they wish to travel whether upon land or sea.*

One local ruler named Ukaydir refused to meet with the Muslims, so the Prophet sent Khalid ibn Walid with five hundred mounted warriors to his strategically situated city of Dumat al-Jandal. Khalid found the gates of the fortress-like town barricaded and seemingly impregnable, but he learned that its prince was out in the countryside on a hunting trip. Khalid's men tracked him down, captured him, and forced him to open the city to them. The Muslims were then given an enormous tribute, including thousands of animals, coats of armor, and loads of grain. Ukaydir eventually accepted Islam after a formal meeting with the Prophet in Medina, and a small Muslim presence was established in his kingdom, which bordered the territory of Persian-ruled Iraq.

With only treaties to occupy them, the Muslim army enjoyed the temperate countryside of Syria and the many amenities of its well-established towns. After several uneventful weeks, the Muslims packed up for their long journey home. Muhammad had proven that he could successfully engage in international as well as local relations. The buffer zone he effortlessly created would ensure security from outside aggressors for the entire Arabian Peninsula.

A view inside the Prophet's mosque in Medina as it appears today.

When the Muslim army reentered Medina to the cheers of all its citizens, the hypocrites who had been predicting gloom and doom were chastened and humiliated. They felt sure that Muhammad and his followers were bound to perish, either from the drought-ridden journey or the might of the Romans. When neither came to pass, they regretted terribly their miscalculation and their influence finally waned to negligible levels. The Qur'an said of them:

> *People of Faith, have fear of God and associate only with those who are sincere. It wasn't right that some of the people of Medina and some of the nearby Bedouins refused to*

follow God's Messenger. Nor was it right that they pre-
ferred their own lives to his. There were no hardships they
could have suffered, whether from thirst, fatigue or hunger
except that it would have been counted as a righteous act
in God's cause. That they might have traveled widely to
confront the unbelievers or been injured in their pursuit
would have been rewarded likewise. God doesn't let the
reward for goodness become lost. (Qur'an 9:120)

Several events occurred rapidly towards the beginning of the
year 631. The men of Ta'if, still hostile to Islam, were approached
by one of their own nobles who had accepted Islam. He had
received reluctant permission from the Prophet to try to reason
with his people, but he was killed the morning after his first meeting with them. Shock waves from his murder reverberated among
the surrounding tribes, most of whom had already converted to
Islam. Soon Ta'if found itself isolated and cut off from its traditional allies. The remnant of the once powerful Thaqif tribe that
controlled the city could no longer conduct business or even social
visits outside the city's walls; any who ventured out were kidnapped or killed. Ta'if would have to come to terms with Muhammad or risk extinction.

A delegation consisting of six men, each representing a different clan, went to Medina to speak with the Prophet. The lead
negotiator proposed first that his people would accept Islam if they
could keep their great idol al-Lat and if they also were exempted
from performing daily prayers. The Prophet refused, saying, "There
is no good in a faith that has no prayer." Further proposals were to
no avail.

Realizing that Muhammad would not compromise the practices
or principles of his faith, and that the people of Ta'if had no
options left to them, the ambassador of Ta'if reluctantly agreed to
the Prophet's provisions, with the caveat that someone else would
have to break their idol because they didn't have the heart to do it
themselves. Muhammad agreed and sent Abu Sufyan and another
man, each respected in Ta'if, to do the job. As the women of the
city wailed in mourning, the pair toppled the great statue from its
sanctuary and broke it to pieces. A bag of treasure that was kept as

an offering to the idol was requisitioned to pay for an old debt that the murdered noble of Ta'if had left unpaid. Meanwhile, the six men of the embassy remained in Medina for the entire holy month of Ramadan, spending their days in fasting and their nights in prayer. They went back to their people and taught them to follow Islamic religious practices. The last enemy of Islam in Arabia had acquiesced.

The rest of the year was filled with activity for the Prophet. There were embassies to establish, letters to write, disputes to settle, taxes to collect, and a government to run. When the month of hajj arrived, so many delegations were pouring into Medina that Muhammad decided that he could not perform the rite that year (thus the nickname for that year, the Year of Deputations). Although Islam only required one pilgrimage in a person's lifetime, Muhammad had always assumed he should lead the throngs of pilgrims to teach them and inspire them with his presence. Reluctantly he tapped Abu Bakr to lead the ritual.

As the Prophet's longtime friend led the winding line of pilgrims southward, new verses of the Qur'an came that forbade the entry of any non-Muslims to the holy precincts of Mecca. Forever more, Mecca would be the sanctified shrine of Islam, hearkening back to the days of Abraham, who prayed,

> Accept this from us, Our Lord, because You are the
> Receptive and Knowing. Help us to surrender to Your will
> and guide our descendants. Teach us to serve only You
> and forgive us our sins, because You are the Forgiving,
> the Source of All Mercy. Bless our descendants with
> Messengers of their own to guide them. Teach them
> the Scripture, give them wisdom, and correct their
> faults, because You are indeed Mighty and Wise."
> (Qur'an 2:127–129)

Chapter 15

The Passing of a Prophet

Faith isn't turning towards east nor west. Faith is believing in God, the Last Day, the Angels, the Scriptures, and the Prophets. Faith is conquering your greed and giving generously to relatives, orphans, travelers, and those in need. It's freeing slaves, establishing prayer, giving in charity, fulfilling your promises, and being patient in danger, hardship, and adversity. Such people affirm the truth and are the truly pious.

—Qur'an 2:177

The pilgrimage led by Abu Bakr in the year 631 had wide ramifications beyond the great honor Muhammad bestowed upon his friend. While the pilgrims were in Mecca, a courier arrived with the proclamation from the Prophet that after that year's four truce months, no idolater would ever be allowed to enter Mecca again, and that the longstanding practice of walking around the Ka'bah naked (a peculiar custom followed by generations of idolaters, which Muhammad had always opposed) would be banned. After so many sweeping changes in so short a time, it is understandable how awkward it would have been for two diametrically opposed ways of life to share the same holy place. Monotheism and idolatry have rarely coexisted in any society; the history of Judaism and Christianity is a testament to this fact.

Twenty-three years after receiving Muhammad's first revelation in a cave outside of Mecca, his teachings had grown into a well-defined religion with practices and dogmas that distinguished it from other spiritual traditions. The main rituals that appeared over the years coalesced into the famous Five Pillars of Islam.

The Five Pillars of Islam were duties laid by God upon every believer; the faithful performance of these duties would be examined on the Day of Judgment. The first pillar consisted of the *shahadah*, a two-part statement of one's creed that every Muslim was taught to say every day: "I testify that there is no god but God, and I testify that Muhammad is the Messenger of God." Next came the five daily prayers, which combined physical movements of reverent bowing and prostration with the recitation of prayer formulas not unlike an extended Lord's Prayer. Following this daily exercise in spiritual renewal were two annual rites: the month-long, dawn-to-dusk fast of Ramadan and the payment of a charity tithe of two and a half percent of one's yearly savings. Lastly, the once-in-a-lifetime pilgrimage to Mecca to affirm one's faith rounded out a well-ordered program intended to bring God's good graces to the believer.

The seven cardinal beliefs of Islam were equally organized and clear, laying the theological groundwork that defined the faith of a Muslim. These beliefs consisted of the following doctrines:

- **Monotheism**   Absolute faith in a single God who was all-powerful and without need of partners or sons. He was neither male nor female nor anything resembling creation at all. His Arabic name, *Allah*, literally meant "the God before whom there are no others."

- **Angels**   These beings made of light energy took on various physical shapes and performed certain tasks at the direction of God. They would never disobey or rebel against their master.

- **Revealed scriptures**   These writings were revelations from God to chosen prophets, such as the Torah of Moses, the Psalms of David, and the Gospel of Christ. Their inevitable alteration by later generations necessitated the final revelation of a perfect and unchanging book, the Qur'an.

- **Messengers and prophets** These people were raised by God to guide their nations to his way of life. They were sent to the various peoples of earth from one corner of the globe to the other. Adam was the first prophet, and Muhammad was the last. Many prophets common to Judaism and Christianity were acknowledged in Islam as well, such as Abraham, Moses, David, and Jesus.

- **The Last Day heralding the Day of Judgment** Earth would be destroyed one distant day, and the entire population of humanity and jinn, elemental creatures made from fire who continually tempt people to do wrong, would be made to stand before God for judgment. Salvation would hinge on one's belief in God and the application of that faith through good deeds.

- **Destiny** Islam's version of destiny and fate emphasized each individual's ability to act within the larger framework of God's plan.

- **Life after death** Eternal life in heaven or hell was based on one's faith, virtuous deeds, and adherence to God's laws.

The Qur'an and the *hadith,* or sayings of Muhammad, which were a kind of supplemental commentary on the Qur'an and Islam, formed the basis for all these practices and beliefs. Islam was codified and solidified within Muhammad's lifetime, and unlike many other religious systems, it never underwent centuries of revision and addition to its core principles. Nearly every act of devotion, word of supplication, and ideological belief practiced among Muslims today was initiated and established by Muhammad himself.

On February 23, 632, the Prophet prepared to make what would be his last and most memorable journey. He set out on a pilgrimage to Mecca with tens of thousands of his followers who had converged on Medina at his invitation. Muhammad had a strong desire to personally lead this journey because he had never performed a full pilgrimage in the way he envisioned. He had only been able to visit Mecca for brief periods, and the rituals he had performed had been abbreviated versions of a proper hajj. He would now show his followers the complete ritual, so it could be performed uniformly thereafter. The Prophet asked every one of his wives to accompany him.

After nearly two weeks on the road, the endless line of almost a hundred thousand men and women walking or riding horses and camels finally reached the outskirts of Mecca, where the pilgrims made camp. The encampment extended for over a mile. The following morning, Muhammad instructed the men to change into their pilgrim's garb: two white sheets wound upon the body like a toga. Women were not required to wear such spartan attire and could dress more comfortably. For the remainder of the hajj, no one was allowed to engage in intercourse, argument, or violence toward any living thing. As the pilgrims began marching into the city, the chant arose in unison among them, "Here I am God, at your service. Here I am."

For the next several days, Muhammad led his followers along the stations of devotion. They began with a solemn procession seven times around the Ka'bah, followed by a climb to the top of the sacred hill of Safa. From there they reenacted Hagar's desperate search for water by walking briskly back and forth between that hill and the far hill of Marwa. After a day of rest, the throng proceeded to a location outside the city of Mina, where they spent the remainder of the day and night in prayer. The next morning they moved to a large, rocky hill called Arafat. After a few hours of observing his thousands of companions praying and beseeching God's forgiveness for their sins, Muhammad mounted his camel and led them to a small valley whose shape was reminiscent of a large amphitheater. There he gave a speech that is still revered among Muslims to this day. It is known as the "Farewell Sermon" of the Prophet. Here is part of what he said:

> O People, listen to my words, because I don't know if I
> will ever be with you here again after this year. Therefore,
> listen to what I'm saying carefully and take these words to
> those who could not be here today. O People, your lives,
> property, and honor are sacred for you until you appear
> before your Lord, just as you consider this month, this

day, and this city sacred. Return the things that are entrusted to you to their rightful owners. You will meet your Lord, and He will hold you answerable for your actions.

Know that every Muslim is a brother to every other Muslim and that Muslims are one brotherhood. Nothing is allowed for a Muslim if it belongs to another unless it was given freely and willingly, so do not oppress each other. All practices of idolatry and ignorance are now under my feet. Every right of revenge coming from unjust murder in pre-Islamic times is rescinded .... Charging interest is forbidden; therefore, all interest obligations are also canceled. Your original money is yours to keep. Do no wrong and you will not be wronged.

O People, be aware of God concerning women. Indeed, you've taken them on the security of God and made them lawful to you with God's words. Indeed, it is true you have certain rights with your women, but they also have rights over you. It is their duty to honor their intimate obligations and not to do improper actions. If they do, then you will have the right to reprimand them, though not harshly. If they respect your rights, then to them belongs the right to be fed and clothed in kindness. Treat your women well and be kind to them for they are your partners and committed helpers. It is also your right that they not make friends with anyone you don't approve of and never be unfaithful.

Beware of Satan for the safety of your way of life. He has lost all hope in leading you astray in this land, but he will be happy if you follow him in small things. Therefore, abstain from obedience to Satan. Indeed, I'm leaving behind me two things, the Book of God and my example, and if you follow these two you will never go astray. If you were asked about me, what would you say?

At that the pilgrims replied from all quarters, "We declare that you have conveyed the message and fulfilled your mission!" Although the throngs of people listening and responding to the Prophet were highly enthused, some of the elder companions began to understand that the Prophet was intimating that his mission was accomplished. Muhammad continued:

> O People, listen to me closely. Serve God, say your five
> daily prayers, fast during the month of Ramadan, and
> give of your wealth in charity. Perform the hajj if you can
> afford it and obey whatever I command you, for that is
> the only way you will get into Paradise. O People, indeed
> your Lord is One and your ancestor is one. All of you
> belong to the line of Adam, and Adam was created from
> dust. An Arab is not better than a non-Arab nor is a
> white better than a black or a black better than a white
> except in piety. The noblest among you all is the one who
> is the most pious.
>
> O People, no prophet will come after me, and no new
> way of life will be born. Reason well and absorb the
> words that I am telling you. All those who listen to me
> shall pass on my words to others and those to others
> again; and may the last ones understand my words better
> than the first. Be my witness, O God, that I have con-
> veyed Your Message to Your people.

When he finished, he looked above his assembly and called out loudly, "My Lord, have I delivered the message?" Thousands of his followers replied, "Yes, you have." After breaking for congregational prayers, Muhammad reconvened the gathering a little ways outside the valley and recited the following new revelation, "Today, I have completed for you your way of life, and granted you the last of my blessings. I have chosen peaceful surrender (Islam) as your way of life." (Qur'an 5:3) When Abu Bakr heard these thinly veiled words of parting his suspicions were confirmed, and he burst into tears.

The Prophet's mosque as it appears today in Medina, Saudi Arabia.

Indeed, the Prophet's longtime friend was among the first to realize that he was saying good-bye to the world. He had struggled to establish Islam for nearly twenty-three years, undergoing intense hardships and trials. Now that Islam was established, there was no further need for the Prophet. Abu Bakr and the handful of others who deduced the real reason for the lengthy speech kept their speculations to themselves for the time being. The pilgrims completed the last rites of the hajj and celebrated the Festival of the Sacrifice, one of the two holidays of Islam, the other being the conclusion of Ramadan. Muhammad's prediction came true: He would never see his place of birth again.

The Islamic holidays are called 'Eids, or festivals. One falls at the end of the pilgrimage to Mecca and the other marks the end of the fasting month of Ramadan. Celebrated over three days, these holidays are the most joyous days on the Islamic calendar. Gift-giving is commonly practiced, especially for children. In Medina, the Muslims used to engage in public shows, songs, and processions after their morning 'Eid prayers. Muhammad sat with his wife A'ishah during one such celebration and watched a group of Abyssinians performing a public dance with their spears.

The Prophet returned to Medina at the conclusion of his pilgrimage to Mecca. He should have been able to congratulate himself on an exceptional career. The Qur'an, an oral book consisting of over six thousand verses, was complete. An entire population was transformed from wine-drinking, raiding idolaters into thoughtful, disciplined men and women of manners, prayer, and intellectual discourse. Medina, the capital of his state, was safe from all enemies both internal and external, and even the borders in the far north were secured. Or were they?

The threat posed by the Byzantine Empire had not receded after Tabuk, and a massive invasion could occur at any time. In addition, the Arab tribes of Syria that had signed treaties with Muhammad were under constant pressure from their rivals and begged for any assistance that Medina could send. Persia also loomed large; its constant civil wars kept it from mounting an attack, though conflict with it seemed inevitable as well. Seeing the strategic disadvantage his nation suffered in the north, the Prophet ordered that another large army be mobilized to drive the Byzantines back even farther into their territory.

The Prophet chose Usamah, a young man barely twenty years old, to be the commanding officer. Usamah was the son of Zayd, who was the commander martyred at Mu'tah, and Barakah, Muhammad's nurse from his youth. This new army would consist of many of the most experienced companions and would be better equipped than any before. Though many in the army were unsettled about the choice for their leader, the opposition was muted for the moment. Muhammad didn't place Usamah in command in ignorance of his inexperience. He wanted to honor the sacrifice of the young man's father and began giving Usamah lessons in military tactics. He counseled him to strike early in the mornings, to continuously rain down fire-tipped arrows on the enemy, and to maintain secrecy of movement at all costs. After his tutoring in battlefield operations, the new general organized his men for the expedition. The sprawling military camp that sprang up outside Medina was filled with the noise of preparation, but its departure would be delayed—not by fear of the enemy or a lack of provisions, but by something far worse: Muhammad suddenly fell gravely ill.

The ailment was unexpected and shocking to those around Muhammad because he had never been seriously ill before. There had been one incident three years before when a vengeful Jewess almost succeeded in poisoning him with tainted lamb, but although one of his companions died, Muhammad took only one bite of the sabotaged meal, was under the weather for only a few days, and then suffered no other aftereffects. Now at sixty-three, though he still seemed fit and healthy, his illness continued to worsen, and the Muslims feared for his recovery. The scheduled march of the army northwards was postponed by unspoken, unanimous consent. A strange somberness descended over the city as people went about their business with one ear cocked for any news of the Prophet's condition.

Muhammad led his followers in special night prayers during the fasting month of Ramadan. He would recite part of the Qur'an each night so that in thirty days the entire book had been read. New verses were revealed frequently, so the text increased each year. In the last year of his life, Muhammad read the Qur'an publicly two times; the last verses had been revealed and the book was complete. He had a complete, unbound written copy, copied by his secretaries. The number of people who had memorized the entire text was in the hundreds, and thousands more had mastered significant chapters. After Muhammad's death, a bound book was produced and kept in the custody of Hafsah, one of his widows. In the time of the third caliph, Usman ibn Affan, the Prophet's former secretaries prepared copies for the major population centers of the Islamic world, to quell any controversies about the text. New non-Arabic converts had begun to write what they memorized in broken Arabic, differing in the correct pronunciation.

Muhammad was functional in the first days of his infirmity and tried his best to maintain his regular habits. One night, however, he suffered from such acute insomnia that he decided to take a walk in the midnight air to clear his head. Accompanied by his attendant, a young man named Abu Muwayhibah, he headed for the graveyard and stared at the silent tombstones. He said, "Peace be upon you, people of the graves. You are blessed in your present state, which is different from the state of people who still live on earth. Attacks are falling one after another like waves of darkness, each worse than the previous one." After praying for the souls of the dead, Muhammad said, "Abu Muwayhibah! I have been given the keys of this world and eternity in it. And now I am being offered Paradise and meeting with God. I am asked to choose between them." The alarmed young man, understanding the choice Muhammad spoke of, replied, "I would give everything for your sake, Sir! Isn't it possible to have both? Please take the keys of this world, eternity in it, as well as Paradise." Muhammad's answered quickly, "No, by God, Abu Muwayhibah. I have chosen Paradise and meeting with my Lord."

When people learned the next day what the Prophet had said, their apprehension grew. That afternoon, Muhammad went to stay with A'ishah, as all his wives agreed he should remain in one place for the sake of rest. When he entered her apartment, he found her complaining about a severe headache. The Prophet, now gravely ill, replied, "But rather, A'ishah, what of my own aching head?" His fever came and went at irregular intervals. When he was feeling better, he would meet with delegations and lead the congregational prayers in the mosque. When he felt too weak, he would send Abu Bakr to lead the prayers and entertain the ambassadors.

In the meantime, dissatisfaction with the youthful Usamah's leadership of the army created a serious public controversy. When Muhammad heard that elder Muslims were grumbling, even suggesting that the Prophet had been affected by his illness and made an error in judgment, he asked his wife Hafsa to pour some cold water over his head to reduce his fever so he could get up and address the people in the mosque. When the Prophet entered, the startled gathering fell silent. He began by telling them that he had chosen Usamah and that no one had the right to second-guess his decision because they also used to complain about his father, Zayd, who proved them wrong with his bravery at Mu'tah. After a lengthy review of the basic teachings of Islam and exhortations that the Muslims had to be good to each other, the Prophet concluded, "Didn't he make the best choice who, when given the option of taking this world, the other world, or in submitting to whatever is with God, chose the last alternative?"

Some of the Muslims realized that the Prophet was referring to himself and were filled with remorse. Abu Bakr began weeping, and the crowd fell silent. The Prophet had chosen Usamah, and no one would question it further. The Prophet's condition worsened over the next few days, and he asked Abu Bakr to take charge of leading the prayers. This request was later interpreted by many Muslims to mean that the Prophet had tapped his faithful friend to lead after him. Even when Muhammad felt strong enough to come to the mosque for prayer, he asked Abu Bakr to continue leading while he prayed behind him in the rows.

Muhammad's daughter Fatimah visited him every day while he was sick. One day when he was feeling particularly bad, the Prophet called her close and whispered something in her ear that made her cry. Then he whispered something else that made her laugh. A'ishah asked her what he had said, but Fatimah refused to tell her secret. The next morning her father's fever abated, and he felt strong enough to walk. He went to the mosque to attend the dawn prayers, and when he entered, the people standing reverently in their rows began to shift, and a few actually jumped for joy, so great was their relief that the Prophet seemed to be improving. Abu Bakr, leading the congregation, was about to step back to allow the Prophet to take the position of honor when Muhammad laid his hand on his shoulder and nudged him back to where he was standing. Muhammad prayed behind him with all the other supplicants. After the prayers, the Prophet addressed the assembly. "The fire is stoked, and temptation comes like the dark folds of night. I have not made permissible anything unless the Qur'an permitted it, and I have not made forbidden anything unless the Qur'an forbade it. After me you will have many differences.

Anything that complies with the Qur'an is from me, and anything that differs from the Qur'an is not from me." Looking past the import of his words, the Muslims were elated that their guide should be so much improved and acting like his former self. Usamah asked for formal permission to lead his army out, and many of the companions went back to their homes satisfied that the Prophet's condition had taken a turn for the better.

That same day Muhammad asked A'ishah to dispose of his last worldly goods—only seven coins. When he asked her later if she had done so, she replied that she had forgotten. He exclaimed, "How would it be if Muhammad met his Lord with those still in his possession?" When he left her house, he met many of his companions in the street and greeted them warmly, but by afternoon he began feeling weak again. He walked with the aid of a few close companions to Fatimah's home and lay down, much to the consternation of his family and followers. His fever continued to worsen, and soon his body shivered with chills. Muhammad could hear Fatimah lamenting, "Oh, the terrible pain my father is suffering!" He opened his eyes and said, "Your father will suffer no more pain after this day." The anxious Muslims filed in and out throughout the rest of the afternoon, some offering medicines and others praying. The entire community was confused and saddened, heartsick for their beloved Prophet.

In his last hour, his head resting on A'ishah's lap, the Prophet dipped his hand into a bowl of water and wiped it on his head saying, "My Lord, help me bear the pangs of death." What happened next is told in A'ishah's own words:

> The Prophet's head was getting heavier in my lap. I looked at his face and found that his eyes were still. I heard him murmur, "Rather, God on High and Paradise." I said to him, "By the one who sent you as a prophet to teach the truth, you have been given the choice and you chose well." The Prophet of God passed away while his head was on my side between my chest and my heart. It was my youth and inexperience that made me let him die in my lap. I then placed his head on the pillow and got up to bemoan my fate and to join the other women in our sadness and sorrow.

It was June 8, 632. The wailing and weeping of Muhammad's wives alerted the people outside. Many stood in stunned disbelief. Only a few hours earlier Muhammad had been walking among them. A crowd gathered, and the sorrowful cries of thousands erupted as news of the Prophet's death reached every corner of the city. The army, making final preparations for its march, postponed its mission indefinitely. With the Prophet alive and with them, there were no doubts or uncertainties. Now he was gone, and the community had to make sense of what his life meant and how they were going to get along without him.

A view of the gate that marks the Prophet's tomb inside the main mosque of Medina.

When 'Umar heard of the Prophet's demise, he ran to the mosque and drew his sword in anger. He declared that he didn't believe it and that he'd fight anyone who said otherwise, so overcome was he at the thought of losing his beloved friend and mentor. Abu Bakr arrived from his home on the outskirts of the city, and when he saw the distraught 'Umar, he went to his friend, lowered his sword arm, and announced in a loud voice, "If anyone worships Muhammad, know that Muhammad has died. But if anyone worships God, then know that He is alive and cannot die." Then he recited an appropriate verse from the Qur'an (Qur'an 3:144) to drive the point home:

> *Muhammad is no more than a Messenger. There were*
> *many Messengers who passed away before him. If he dies*
> *or is killed, would you then turn around and run? If any-*
> *one ran away, it wouldn't do any harm to God. But God*
> *will reward quickly those who serve Him thankfully.*

'Umar accepted the wisdom of those words and fainted in the arms of Abu Bakr, who continued to recite Qur'anic verses to remind the community of their obligation to serve God in any circumstance. A few hours later, when the time came for the next congregational devotions, Bilal began giving the call to prayer. When he came to the name "Muhammad," he broke down in tears. People in the streets heard him pause and saw him weeping. Everyone else began weeping as well. After a few moments, Bilal resumed his duty and finished the *adhan*. Then, in his sorrow, he vowed to never say it again. A few days later Fatimah told A'ishah what the Prophet had whispered to her. She said, "The first time he told me that he would not recover from his sickness, I cried. The second time he told me I would be the first from his family to join him in Paradise, I smiled." Fatimah passed away six months later.

'Ali ibn Abi Talib was placed in charge of the funeral arrangements for the Prophet. It was agreed that the Prophet would be buried exactly where he died. The community mournfully performed the task of laying the Prophet to rest. Tens of thousands attended the funeral ceremony. Barakah, his nursemaid from childhood, who was now well over seventy years old, took to visiting his grave every day, crying softly. Once a person asked her why she came so frequently, and she replied, "By God, I knew that the Messenger of God would die someday, but I cry now because the revelation from on high has come to an end for us."

After the burial, the Muslim community had to choose a leader. There was no argument about whether they should do this; the Prophet had made it clear that someone should lead the community after him and had even given instructions about the qualities of leadership and how Muslims should obey those in authority. Everyone understood that revelation from God was ended with the Prophet, for he said it would. The job of the leader, then, would be to lead the state, strengthen it, implement the laws of Islam in society, promote Islamic teachings, defend Muslims, and make justice among all people.

The senior members of the Muslim community gathered and, after some discussion, they elected Abu Bakr to be the first caliph, or steward of the nation. Abu Bakr, one of the first to believe in the Message of Islam, had been the Prophet's best friend and had earned the title "truth-affirmer" for declaring the truth of the Prophet's teachings. Abu Bakr addressed the crowds as they gathered in the mosque after his election. In his acceptance speech, he spoke of his duties as a leader and the rights of the people under his rule. He spoke with the words of one who recognized the huge responsibility that now rested on his shoulders:

> O people, I have been elected your leader, even though I
> am no better than any of you. If I do right, help me. If I
> do wrong, correct me. Listen well, truth is a trust and lies
> are treason. The weak among you shall be strong with me
> until I secure their rights. The powerful among you shall
> be weak with me until, if God wills, I have taken what is
> due from them. Listen well, if people give up striving in
> the Cause of God, He will send disgrace upon them. If a
> people become wrongdoers, God will send disasters upon
> them. Obey me as long as I obey God and His Messenger.
> If I disobey God and His Messenger, then you are free to
> disobey me.

Thus began the next chapter in the story of Islam. Muhammad had put everything into building a community based on monotheism and justice and had succeeded against all odds in only two decades. An entire nation now followed a religion that had not existed a short time before and was poised to take on the two greatest empires of the day. After Abu Bakr, 'Umar, Uthman, and then 'Ali would each succeed to the office of caliph. Under their tireless efforts, the area under Muslim control would steadily expand to encompass an area stretching from the borders of Spain to India. Islam would become a world phenomenon, a civilization, and the preserver of the knowledge of the Greeks and the Romans, which was lost to Europe for over a thousand years during the Dark Ages. Although the Islamic Empire would later fragment and fall into competing principalities, the religion of Islam continues to grow and be practiced to this very day. Muhammad's legacy is his religion, and his teachings continue to provide solace and guidance for people in many diverse cultures all throughout the world.

Muhammad in Western Literature

R ecent events in our world have made it painfully obvious that the West has a serious gap in its knowledge of the world of Islam and its progenitor, Muhammad. Hithertofore, schools in both Europe and North America have taken it for granted that Western civilization has risen to the peak of ascendancy in our global society and that its rise is independent of any debt of gratitude to other cultures, save for the Greco-Roman phenomenon.

The truth is that Islam was the single largest influence on the rise of Europe, the Renaissance, and the Enlightenment, although this fact has been carefully buried under centuries of inward-looking polemics. Consider that in the West we write in *Arabic* numerals, we study *algebra,* and we rely on *chemistry* to sustain both our industry and technology. When we earn money, we place it safely in a *bank* from which we write *checks.* When we eat, we enjoy *lemons, sherbet,* and *sugar,* and when we watch the sun descend past the *horizon* in the evening, we eagerly await the *zenith* of the moon in the night sky. Our clothes are made of *cotton,* we measure diamonds in *carats,* our children enjoy *candy,* and we like to sit on the *sofa* to read our *magazines.* All of these terms represent elements of civilization imported to Europe from the realm of Islam during the twelfth through the seventeenth centuries.

When Europe was sunk in its Dark Ages, Islam was carrying the torch of science, culture, and free thought. Muslim colleges in Spain and North Africa enrolled thousands of Christian European students whose own lands lacked educational services. These people in turn coaxed their slumbering nations to awaken with their newly acquired tools of scientific method and deductive reasoning. Many of the great colleges of Europe owe their existence to the desire of local rulers to emulate the schools found in Spain and Baghdad. One modern author (P. Dreiker in *Dispute Between Science and Religion*) describes this phenomenon in this way: "Moslem universities were opened to all European students who came seeking further knowledge, and European kings and princes went to Moslem countries for medical treatment."

The religions that lie at the heart of Europe and Arabia were both founded by prophets who resided in nearly the same geographic location in the Middle East, and the teachings of each were essentially similar on many issues such as monotheism, responsibility for one's conduct, and an afterlife. Jesus arrived a full six centuries before Muhammad, and his message permeated more than half of the old Greco-Roman world. By Muhammad's time, north Africa, Syria, Palestine, southern Europe, and a large swath of central Europe were already Christianized, and the Gospel was beginning to spread to northern Europe, east Africa, and beyond.

When Muhammad started Islam in seventh-century Arabia, he brought a new scripture that proclaimed its superiority over all others that had gone before it. While accepting the Jewish and Christian prophets of old, the Qur'an declared itself to be the final and unalterable revelation from God that would supercede all others. The posture of Islam, then, was clear from the onset: It must prevail over all other religions. But Islam was not a coercive faith, and the Qur'an vigorously banned forced conversions. A non-Muslim residing in Muslim-controlled territory could either accept Islam or live in peace with his or her Muslim neighbors upon the payment of a special yearly tax that exempted him or her from the draft. Islamic law did not apply to such people, called *dhimmis*, or protected citizens, who would instead be largely governed by local religious authorities from their own community.

Muhammad's first enemies were the idolaters of the Hijaz who opposed his monotheistic teachings. They waged three major wars against him and his followers and nearly succeeded in wiping out

Islam in two of them. After finally subduing the idolaters in the end, Muhammad could claim the allegiance of most of his fellow countrymen. Three Jewish-Arabian tribes defied Muhammad as well, and in each case a war was fought against them. They declined to accept the notion that an Arab could be a prophet, and thus they broke the treaties they had signed with the Muslim polity, preferring to ally with the idolaters. Although the Muslims won each of the three resulting campaigns and forced the exile or capitulation of those particular Jews, several other Jewish communities lived under the protection of the Islamic state for many generations.

Islam initially encountered Christianity in Arabia. Muhammad had excellent relations with the Christians of the peninsula and across the Red Sea in Abyssinia. The Qur'an praised the followers of Christ as "nearest in love" and "humble in their devotions." Muhammad fought no wars against any Christian tribe in Arabia, nor did any Christians attack his community, which was centered in Medina. The hostility between the two religions occurred with the expansion of Islam into northern Arabia. The Byzantine Empire opposed the introduction of the new religion in its southern reaches as vigorously as it fought against Persian fire worship from the east.

Turkish Muslim armies would eventually conquer the entire Byzantine Empire east of Italy. Europe, in its stead, would eventually seek to wrest a portion of its former territories in Palestine back during the Crusades. During those times, Europe began to write in earnest about Islam and Muhammad, and what its authors said was greatly influenced by the historical circumstances of the time. Muslims and Christians fought over land much more so than religion, though the temporal fight was often cloaked in ideological terms and slogans.

The earliest European writers to tackle the subject of Islam were working from woefully inadequate sources. The Byzantine polemists portrayed Islam as a barbaric religion of cannibals, heathens, and drunkenness whose founder was a camel rustler, sorcerer, and liar. Giving him the derogatory name Mahomet, they went on to accuse Islam of being a religion devoted to the worship of Muhammad and the devil. One Christian intellectual, St. John of Damascus, stood out in this period in his more even-handed approach to the subject. Perhaps due to his upbringing in the Muslim territory of Syria, he had a greater appreciation for the similarities of his religion and that of Muhammad.

During the era of the Crusades (1095–1270) the general tradition of negative propaganda expanded exponentially (vilification of the enemy is often a by-product of war). The troubadours of Europe recited such epics as the *Song of Roland* in which Charlemagne's troops were described as toppling the many idols of the Muslims. Islam was also said to promote the worship of a trinity composed of Mahomet, Apollo, and Termagant. Muhammad, too, suffered a scathing review with elaborate works penned by the likes of Guibert de Norgent and Rudolph de Ludheim, who described him as a drunk, a sensualist, and a wizard. In his book, *The Life of Mohammed*, Emile Deir Mongem says,

> *When the war blazed up between Islam and Christianity*
> *... each side misunderstood the other one. It should be*
> *admitted, however, that the basic misunderstanding was*
> *more on the part of westerners than the easterners.*
> *... argumentative debaters overloaded Islam with vices,*
> *degradation, and abasement without taking the trouble*
> *to study it ...*

By the Middle Ages, the image was firmly set in Europe that Muhammad was a minion of the devil whose religion preached human sacrifice, barbarity, and occultism. Pope Innocent III once labeled the Prophet as the Antichrist. In the twelfth century, the first Latin translation of the Qur'an was made under papal authority. This work was carried out by a Catholic priest whose knowledge of Arabic was extremely limited, and thus the words in the translation appeared disjointed, chaotic, and bizarre. It was the first in a long line of many faulty translations by European scholars, culminating with the awkward and offensive works of Lane, Sales, and Palmer.

The Muslim-influenced Enlightenment saw a new generation of European scholars who took a more thorough approach to the subject of Muhammad and Islam. This new breed of researchers made it a point to master Arabic. The term *Orientalist* was eventually coined to describe these scholars in recognition of their desire to uncover the secrets of the Orient that had seemed to elude Europe for so long. As a result of the work of these scholars, many works of classical Arabic literature were translated into Latin, German, and French in the eighteenth and nineteenth centuries.

Though many of the old stereotypes existed, many authors were willing to take a fresh look at the meaning of Muhammad's mission. Rousseau, Arnold, Toynbee, Watt, and even the unlikely author Napolean Bonaparte recognized the noble nature of Muhammad and his message and were more apt to present their findings respectfully and thoughtfully. Indeed, many Orientalists were genuinely interested in their subject and sought to paint a more accurate picture of the faith of Islam.

However, a few writers, Zwemer and Sales, for example, were motivated more by their Christian religious convictions than by their sense of objectivity. These writers intentionally engaged in slander or misinterpretation to make Islam appear illogical or sinful as opposed to Christianity, which was portrayed as civilizing and noble. The fact that European armies gobbled up territory after territory in the Muslim world during the era of colonialism added to the sense that European military triumphs were directly related to Europe's allegiance to Christianity, whereas the Muslims' subjugation was a result of their backward and fatalistic religion. Rudyard Kipling described the mission of Christian Europe to civilize the Muslims as the "white man's burden." What he failed to mention was that Europe had invaded and conquered its restive subjects using raw power and maintained its precarious rule through fear and reprisal, dismantling traditional political and religious institutions along the way.

This sense of being at odds with Islam carried on into the twentieth century and is best highlighted by the words of Field Marshall Allenby who stood on the steps of the Dome of the Rock in Jerusalem after World War I and proclaimed, "Today the Crusades have come to an end." The aftereffects of foreign military rule have plagued the world of Islam to this day, resulting in the seemingly endless conflicts and chaos from that part of the globe.

Appendix B

An Outline of the Major Events of Muhammad's Life

Year	Muhammad's Age	Event
570	0	Mecca repels an invading army from Yemen in what is called the Year of the Elephant. Muhammad's father, 'Abdullah, dies in Yathrib. Muhammad is born.
570–575	0–5	Muhammad is raised by the Bedouin tribe of Banu Sa'd.
576	6	Muhammad's mother, Aminah, dies near Medina.
578	8	Muhammad's grandfather, 'Abdel Muttalib, dies in Mecca. Muhammad joins his Uncle Abu Talib's household.
582	12	Muhammad accompanies a caravan to Syria.
594	24	Muhammad leads Khadijah's caravan to Syria.

Year	Muhammad's Age	Event
595	25	Muhammad marries Khadijah in Mecca. They eventually have six children: two boys and four girls. The boys pass away in infancy.
610	40	Muhammad receives his first revelation on Mount Hira' just outside Mecca.
613	43	Muhammad preaches in public and is persecuted by the Quraysh tribe.
615	45	Some of Muhammad's followers migrate to Abyssinia.
617–619	47–49	Muhammad and the other Muslims are forced to leave Mecca and live in the surrounding desert. This time becomes known as the Boycott.
619	49	Abu Talib and Khadijah die. Muhammad goes on his Night Journey and Ascension to Heaven.
620	50	Muhammad marries a widow named Sawdah and is engaged to A'ishah. Muhammad meets the first delegation of six people from Yathrib.
621	51	Twelve citizens of Yathrib make the First Pledge of 'Aqaba.

Year	Muhammad's Age	Event
622	52	Seventy-five citizens of Yathrib take the Second Pledge of 'Aqaba. Muhammad and the other Muslims leave Mecca on the Hijrah, or migration to Yathrib.
623	53	Yathrib is renamed Medina. The Muslims sign treaties with the three Jewish tribes of the city. Muhammad marries A'ishah.
624	54	The Muslims defeat the Quraysh in the Battle of Badr. The Banu Qaynuqa are exiled from Medina. The Ka'bah becomes the direction of prayer, supplanting Jerusalem. Muhammad's daughter Fatimah marries 'Ali, the son of Abu Talib. Muhammad's other daughter, Ruqqayah, dies a few days after Badr.
625	55	The Quraysh defeat the Muslims on the Day of Uhud. The Banu Nadir are exiled from Medina. Muhammad marries Hafsa, the daughter of 'Umar.
626	56	Muhammad marries Zaynab bint Khuzaima, Umm Salamah, and Juwairiyah.

Year	Muhammad's Age	Event
627	57	After laying siege to Medina, an army of Arab tribes is forced to retreat. The Banu Qurayza are subdued. Muhammad marries Zaynab bint Jahsh.
628	58	The Muslims and the Quraysh sign the Treaty of Hudaybiyah. The Muslims defeat the Jews at Khaybar. Muhammad marries Safiyah, Umm Habibah, and Maria. Maria gives birth to a boy named Ibrahim, but he dies in infancy.
629	59	Muhammad leads a lesser pilgrimage to Mecca. A famed Meccan general, Khalid ibn Walid, as well as Muhammad's uncle, 'Abbas, convert to Islam. Muhammad marries Maymunah and sends letters to world rulers to tell them about Islam. The Muslims hold off the Byzantines at the Battle of Mu'tah.
630	60	The Quraysh of Mecca surrender peacefully to Muhammad's army. Abu Sufyan, the last idolatrous leader of Mecca, converts to Islam. The Muslims defeat the Arab alliance led by Malik ibn 'Awf on

Year	Muhammad's Age	Event
		the Day of Hunayn and during the siege of Ta'if. Muhammad leads an army to Tabuk to fight the Byzantines and winds up making alliances with Syrian tribes instead.
631	61	Ta'if surrenders. Abu Bakr takes on more duties. The Year of Deputations begins.
632	63	Muhammad leads the Farewell Pilgrimage to Mecca. Muhammad dies, and Abu Bakr is elected the first Caliph of Islam.

Appendix C

Islam's First Twenty Years

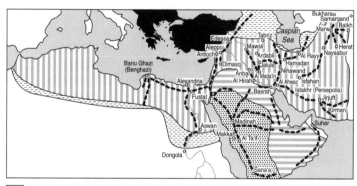

Islamic state at the death of the Prophet, 632

Lands of apostates brought under control by
Abu Bakr al Siddiq, 632-634

Lands conquered under Umar ibn al Khattab, 632-634

Conquests under Uthman ibn Affan, 644-656

Byzantium

Appendix D

Resources and References

In recent years, interest in learning about Muhammad and what he stood for has greatly increased. Learning about Muhammad and his message is all the more important given that in the Muslim world his message is understood in vastly different ways by various sects, movements, and cultures. These differences in interpretation have caused the rest of the world to search for the elusive truth wherein Muhammad's true greatness lies. This appendix outlines a variety of resources encompassing both ancient and modern works that present a good overview of the literature on the subject. (Note that I have listed only those works that are widely available.) Each of these sources has proved useful in the compilation of this book as well.

Ancient Biographical Materials

Ibn Ishaq, Muhammad. *The Life of Muhammad.* Translated by A. Guillaume. Oxford University Press: Karachi, 1996.

> This book is one of the earliest attempts at presenting a complete biography of Muhammad using a wide variety of sources. The work was completed in the eighth century under the title, *Sirat Rasulullah,* or *History of the Messenger of Allah.*

Ibn Kathir, Imad al-Deen Isma'il. *The Life of the Prophet Muhammad.* Translated by Dr. Trevor Le Gassick. Garnet Publishing LTD: Reading, 1998.

This book is an excellent summation of the literature on Muhammad as it was understood in the fourteenth century. It was originally published under the title *Al-Sirah al-Nabawiyya, or The History of Prophethood.*

Ibn Sa'd, Muhammad. *The Women of Medina.* Translated by Aisha Bewley. Ta-Ha Publishers Ltd: London, 1997.

This book provides good source material on Muhammad's relations with his followers in Medina, particularly women and how they viewed their society as it shifted from one cultural context to another. This book is one of a number of sections from a larger work released in the ninth century entitled *Kitab Tabaqat al-Kabir, or The Book of the Greatest Levels.*

al-Bukhari, Muhammad ibn Isma'il. *Imam Bukhari's Book of Muslim Morals and Manners.* Translated by Yusuf Talal DeLorenzo. Al-Saadawi Publications: Herndon, 1997.

This compilation of anecdotes from the life of Muhammad center on his personal habits, his moral exhortations, and his relations with a variety of different people in many social contexts. It was completed in the ninth century under the title, *Al-Adab al-Mufrad, or The Required Manners.*

Recent Biographical Materials

Haykal, Muhammad Husayn. *The Life of Muhammad.* Translated by Isma'il R. al-Faruqi. North American Trust Publications: Chicago, 1976.

This book is one of the most respected contemporary books on Muhammad's life and is written from a sociopolitical perspective.

Lings, Martin. *Muhammad: His Life Based on the Earliest Sources.* Inner Traditions International, Ltd: Rochester, 1983.

This dramatic presentation of the Prophet's life is told in a lively style with voluminous background material.

al-Ismail, Tahia. *The Life of Muhammad.* Ta-Ha Publishers Ltd: London, 1988.

Although this book takes a narrower view of the subject matter, it gives a good summation of the major events of Muhammad's career without burying the reader in a sea of arcane knowledge.

Sradar, Ziauddin & Malik, Zafar Abbas. *Introducing Muhammad.* Totem Books: New York, 1994.

A whimsical presentation of Muhammad's life and its meaning in cartoon format with loads of valuable snippets and tidbits in an attractive format.

Screen Adaptations of Muhammad's Life

Only one movie has been made to date that has sought to dramatize Muhammad's life. Due to the prohibition in Islam of showing a prophet's face or of making God a character in a play, the movie tells the story through the eyes of Muhammad's companions as a sort of story within many stories. The production of *The Message,* which was released in the 1970s, was initially met by protests from the Muslim community, but it has since gained wide acceptance. Due to Hollywood's habit of embellishment, the film is inaccurate in some aspects.

Muhammad on the Internet

Many good websites provide information about Muhammad's life. Here are three of the best:

- The www.prophetmuhammed.org/ site contains complete biographies on the life of Muhammad covering everything related to his culture and political environment as well as wide-reaching ancillary materials.

- The www.usc.edu/dept/MSA/fundamentals/prophet/ site looks at Muhammad from a number of angles and also gives a comprehensive understanding of his personal life and relations.

- The www.muhammad.net/ site provides a comprehensive look into the meaning of Muhammad's message by providing a wide variety of source materials.

Appendix E

The Lineage of Muhammad

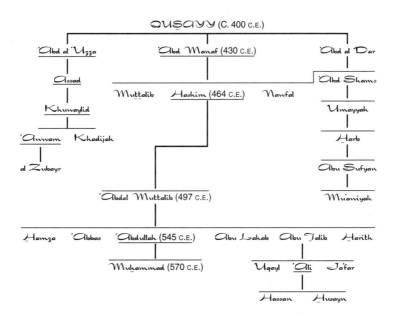

Index

H

haddiths, 212, 283

Hafsa (wife of Muhammad), 186, 213, 290
  jealousy of Maria (a wife of Muhammad), 263

Hagar (wife of Abraham), 10-12

hajj, 233-239, 242
  Muhammad's final pilgrimage, 283-287
  Year of Deputations, 280

Halah (wife of 'Abdel Muttalib), 21

Halimah (foster mother of Muhammad), 30-31, 261
  Shayma (daughter), 31, 261

Hamza (son of 'Abdel Muttalib and uncle of Muhammad), 21, 32, 68, 126
  Battle of Badr, 169
  confrontation with Meccans at Red Sea, 153
  death, 195
  defeat of al-Aswad al-Makhzumi, 168

Hani (son of Fakhitah and Hubayrah), 40

hanifs, 28, 49

Harith, 205

Hashim (son of Abd Manaf and grandson of Qusayy), 13, 16

Hashim clan, Abu Lahab's leadership, 94

Hassan (grandson of Muhammad), 274

Hassan ibn Thabit (poet), 206

Hawazin clan, 261
  war with Quraysh, 35-36

health problems, Muhammad, 74

heaven, 68

hell, 68

helpers (Ansar), 129

helpers of Medina, 251-252, 263

Heraclius (emperor)
  plan to invade Medina, 274
  reaction to Muhammad's letter, 244-245, 269

Hijaz, 6, 56, 71

al-Hijr, 276

Hijrah, 122-128

Hind (wife of Abu Sufyan), 181, 194, 251
  Battle of Uhud, 197

Hisham ibn 'Amr, 89

al-Hubab, 166

Hubal idol, 19

Hubayrah (husband of Fakhitah), 40

Hudaybiyah, 235

Hunayn battle, 256-259

Husayn (grandson of Muhammad), 274

Huyayy ibn Akhtab, 224
  refusal to allow Banu Nadir tribe to leave Medina, 209
  scheme to unite Arabia against Muslims, 216-218

hypocrites, 138-139
  'Abdullah ibn Ubayy, 229, 232
    A'ishah scandal, 230
    encouragement of civil war, 228
  attempt to prevent expedition to Syria, 275
  Banu Nadir tribe, 207
  dissent after Uhud battle, 202-203
  Qur'an, 202

I

Ibn Ubayy, 190-191

Ibrahim (son of Muhammad), 263
  death, 274

idolatry, 9-11
  destruction of after Meccan defeat, 253, 255
  Hubal, 19
  al-Lat, 279
  Quraysh tribe, 61
  removal of idols from Ka'bah after Meccan defeat, 248
  Waraqah ibn Nawfal's protests against, 50

Ikrimah (son of Abu Jahl), 191, 254

immigrants (Muhajirun), 129-130

India, 3, 6

infancy, 29-30

infanticide, 56

Ishmael (son of Abraham and Hagar), 10-12